FEA

D0271899

WITHDRAWN

The
Romanov Conspiracies

By the same author

ARMOUR AGAINST FATE: BRITISH MILITARY INTELLIGENCE IN
THE FIRST WORLD WAR

The —— Romanov Conspiracies

Michael Occleshaw

CHAPMANS

Chapmans Publishers
A division of The Orion Publishing Group Ltd
Orion House
5 Upper St Martin's Lane
London WC2H 9EA

947.083

BRITISH LIBRARY CATALOGUING IN PUBLICATION DATA
Occleshaw, Michael
Romanov Conspiracies
I. Title
947.046
ISBN 1-85592-518-4
1855 925 184 1302
First published by Chapmans 1993

© Michael Occleshaw 1993

The right of Michael Occleshaw to be identified as the
author of this work has been asserted by him in
accordance with the Copyright, Designs and Patents Act,
1988

Photoset in Times Roman by Create Publishing Services Ltd, Bath, Avon
Printed and bound in Great Britain by
The Bath Press Ltd, Bath, Avon

ACKNOWLEDGEMENTS

One of the greatest pleasures upon completing a book is to be able to pay tribute to the often generous assistance of both individuals and institutions whose time, efforts and facilities made the road so much easier. I owe most of all to my wife Elizabeth, who has always willingly acted in roles as diverse as chauffeuse, research assistant and translator. Her continuous support and encouragement have been invaluable and, while never taken for granted, are gratefully acknowledged here.

The assistance given by Mr Anthony Summers in the shape of leads, ideas and access to his impressive collection of documents on the Romanov case deserves a special thank you. While I may disagree with the findings of *The File on the Tsar*, its effect on the study of the Romanov case has been profound, encapsulating very neatly the valid criticisms that have been levelled over the years against Sokolov's version of events.

For the Lydd connection, I am indebted to Mrs Eva Bowler and Mrs June Daniels, without whose tireless work and thoughtful minds three chapters of this book would never have been written. In this respect, too, I am deeply indebted to Mrs Hilary Swinburne, who helped with her memories, ideas and criticism. I ought also to record my thanks to Colonel Nigel

Watson for sharing his views with me in both his letters and conversation.

It would have been impossible to have written this book without the patience and effort of the staff of the following institutions: the British Museum and British Library; the Public Record Office, crown copyright material from there being reproduced by the permission of the Controller of Her Majesty's Stationery Office. They merit and are offered my warmest thanks.

On a rather smaller scale, the help provided by the staff at the Imperial War Museum, the Immigration and Nationality Department of the Home Office, the Hussars' Museum at Warwick and the Royal Tank Corps Museum at Bovington should not pass without notice or thanks.

The contributions of the following people covered a wide area and their contributions were of varying significance. All of them were important in one field or another and no weight should be attached to the order in which their names are printed (alphabetical order seems to be the most equitable arrangement here): Mr Alexander Anderson; Mr Frederick Batt; Mr William Booth; Mrs Alice Clayphon; Mr A. B. T. Davey; Mrs Patricia Eykyn; the Lord Fanshawe; Edith Gilchrist, Hon. Archivist at the Royal Free Hospital, Hampstead; the Earl Haig, OBE; Mr Russ Karel; Mr Ian Lilburn, FSA (Scot); Mr R. R. Meinertzhagen and the Trustees of the estate of the late Colonel Richard Meinertzhagen, CBE, DSO; Mr H. Prebble; Sir Ronald Preston, Bt.; Mr Steve Seidenberg of the BBC; Mrs E. Terry; Mr R. G. Thomas, the son of Sir Thomas Preston's colleague at Ekaterinburg; Mrs K. Winkfield.

Special thanks are also due to Mr Peter Hofschröer, whose assistance in translating the German records was most valuable.

Overseas I particularly wish to record my grateful thanks for the help provided by the staff of the then Central State Archive of the October Revolution in Moscow, and also to Msgr Marcello Camisassa of the Segretaria Di Stato, Sezione II, Rapporti con gli Stati in the Vatican City.

CONTENTS

ILLUSTRATIONS

Between pages 110 and 111

The four daughters of Tsar Nicholas II

Chaya Goloschekin, Alexander Beloborodov,
Yakob Yurovksy and Georgi Biron
(*Public Record Office*)

Colonel Richard Meinertzhagen
(*Nicholas Meinertzhagen*)

Major Stephen Alley
(*Summers Collection*)

Arthur Thomas, Consul Preston's Deputy
(*Robert Thomas*)

A photograph from the *Harrogate Herald*
(*Ackrill Newspapers Ltd*)

The Grand Duchess Tatiana?
(*Ackrill Newspapers Ltd*)

Owen Tudor
(*Mrs Hilary Swinburne*)

The grave of 'Larissa Feodorovna'

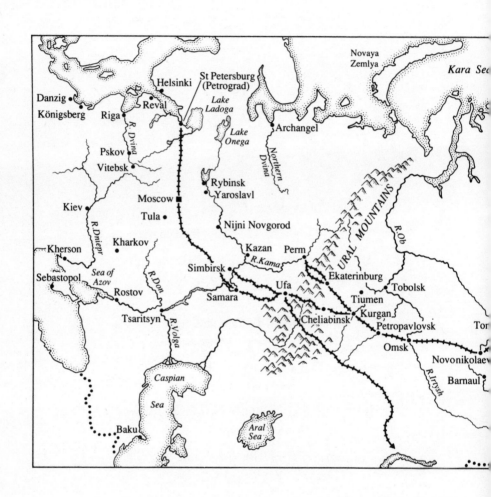

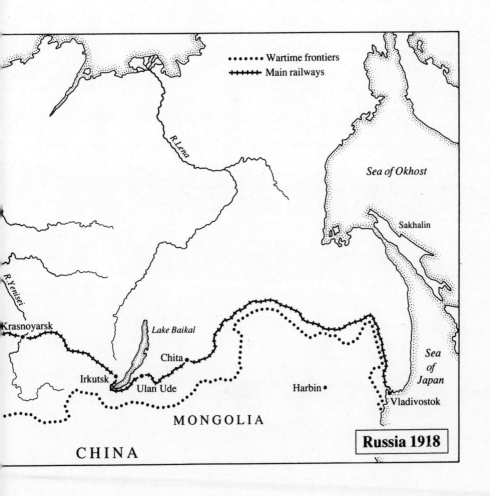

Wartime frontiers
Main railways

R.Lena

Sea of Okhost

Sakhalin

R.Yenisei

Krasnoyarsk

Lake Baikal

Chita

Irkutsk

Ulan Ude

Harbin

Sea
of
Japan

Vladivostok

MONGOLIA

CHINA

Russia 1918

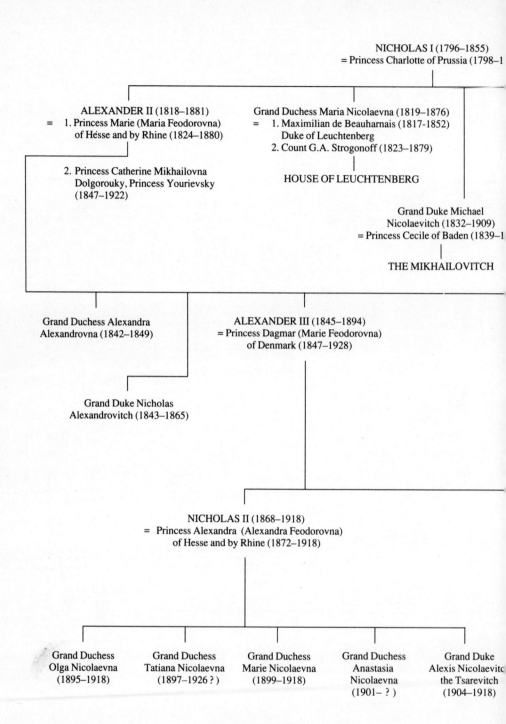

NICHOLAS I (1796–1855)
= Princess Charlotte of Prussia (1798–1

ALEXANDER II (1818–1881)
= 1. Princess Marie (Maria Feodorovna)
of Hésse and by Rhine (1824–1880)

2. Princess Catherine Mikhailovna
Dolgorouky, Princess Yourievsky
(1847–1922)

Grand Duchess Maria Nicolaevna (1819–1876)
= 1. Maximilian de Beauharnais (1817-1852)
Duke of Leuchtenberg
2. Count G.A. Strogonoff (1823–1879)

HOUSE OF LEUCHTENBERG

Grand Duke Michael
Nicolaevitch (1832–1909)
= Princess Cecile of Baden (1839–1

THE MIKHAILOVITCH

Grand Duchess Alexandra
Alexandrovna (1842–1849)

ALEXANDER III (1845–1894)
= Princess Dagmar (Marie Feodorovna)
of Denmark (1847–1928)

Grand Duke Nicholas
Alexandrovitch (1843–1865)

NICHOLAS II (1868–1918)
= Princess Alexandra (Alexandra Feodorovna)
of Hesse and by Rhine (1872–1918)

Grand Duchess
Olga Nicolaevna
(1895–1918)

Grand Duchess
Tatiana Nicolaevna
(1897–1926 ?)

Grand Duchess
Marie Nicolaevna
(1899–1918)

Grand Duchess
Anastasia
Nicolaevna
(1901– ?)

Grand Duke
Alexis Nicolaevitc
the Tsarevitch
(1904–1918)

The Family History of Tsar Nicholas II

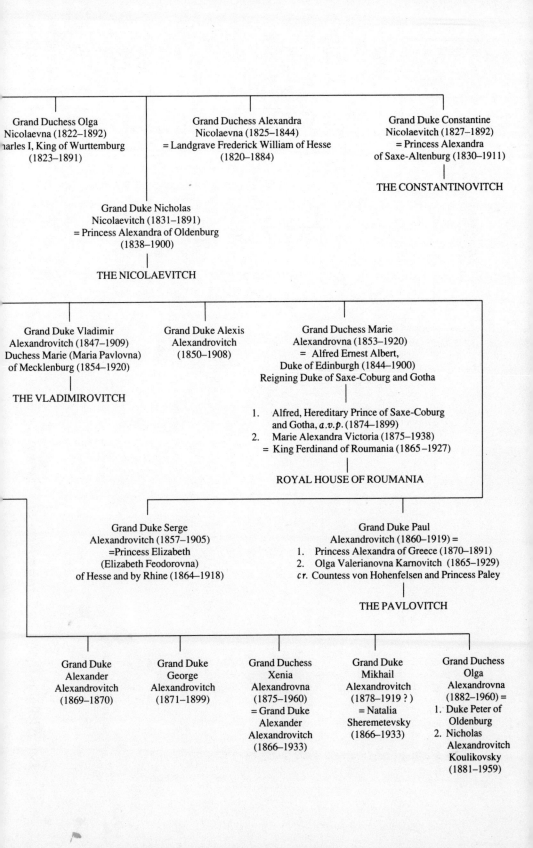

Grand Duchess Olga
Nicolaevna (1822–1892)
harles I, King of Wurttemburg
(1823–1891)

Grand Duchess Alexandra
Nicolaevna (1825–1844)
= Landgrave Frederick William of Hesse
(1820–1884)

Grand Duke Constantine
Nicolaevitch (1827–1892)
= Princess Alexandra
of Saxe-Altenburg (1830–1911)

THE CONSTANTINOVITCH

Grand Duke Nicholas
Nicolaevitch (1831–1891)
= Princess Alexandra of Oldenburg
(1838–1900)

THE NICOLAEVITCH

Grand Duke Vladimir
Alexandrovitch (1847–1909)
Duchess Marie (Maria Pavlovna)
of Mecklenburg (1854–1920)

THE VLADIMIROVITCH

Grand Duke Alexis
Alexandrovitch
(1850–1908)

Grand Duchess Marie
Alexandrovna (1853–1920)
= Alfred Ernest Albert,
Duke of Edinburgh (1844–1900)
Reigning Duke of Saxe-Coburg and Gotha

1. Alfred, Hereditary Prince of Saxe-Coburg
   and Gotha, *a.v.p.* (1874–1899)
2. Marie Alexandra Victoria (1875–1938)
   = King Ferdinand of Roumania (1865–1927)

ROYAL HOUSE OF ROUMANIA

Grand Duke Serge
Alexandrovitch (1857–1905)
=Princess Elizabeth
(Elizabeth Feodorovna)
of Hesse and by Rhine (1864–1918)

Grand Duke Paul
Alexandrovitch (1860–1919) =
1. Princess Alexandra of Greece (1870–1891)
2. Olga Valerianovna Karnovitch (1865–1929)
cr. Countess von Hohenfelsen and Princess Paley

THE PAVLOVITCH

Grand Duke
Alexander
Alexandrovitch
(1869–1870)

Grand Duke
George
Alexandrovitch
(1871–1899)

Grand Duchess
Xenia
Alexandrovna
(1875–1960)
= Grand Duke
Alexander
Alexandrovitch
(1866–1933)

Grand Duke
Mikhail
Alexandrovitch
(1878–1919 ?)
= Natalia
Sheremetevsky
(1866–1933)

Grand Duchess
Olga
Alexandrovna
(1882–1960) =
1. Duke Peter of
   Oldenburg
2. Nicholas
   Alexandrovitch
   Koulikovsky
   (1881–1959)

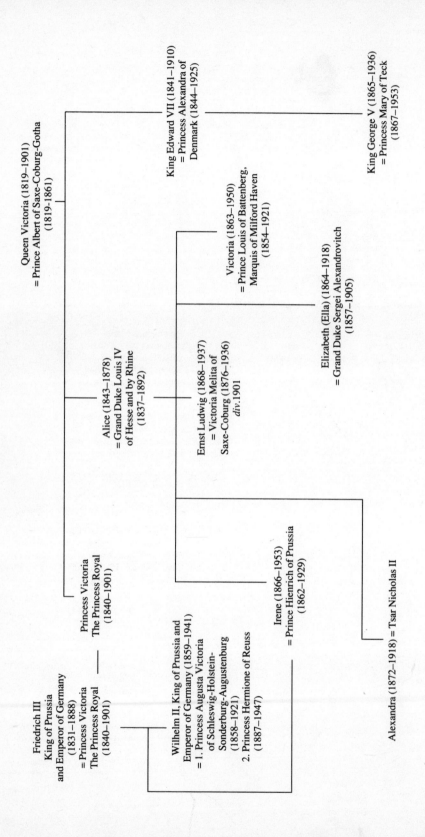

Tsar Nicholas II and the Crown Heads of Europe

FOREWORD

This book is not offered as the last word on the last days of the Russian royal family. It is an attempt to shed light on the reality of the position adopted by the British over the fate of that family. It is by no means so simple and neat a picture as the unhappy and misleading one the publicly available official documents would have us believe. The material I have uncovered shows that the Tsar's brother, the Grand Duke Mikhail Alexandrovitch, certainly survived and that attempts to rescue the Tsar's family were at least planned and that one of those plans was probably put into action. The evidence suggests that the real reason for the continuing secrecy surrounding the events of 1918 in Siberia, so far as they concern the Romanovs, is acute embarrassment.

The recent discovery of the remains of nine people in the forest outside Ekaterinburg has not really helped matters very much. These may indeed be the remains of the Romanovs and their servants, but there are solid grounds for caution. The burial pit was located by following the account of the murder written two years after the event by Yakob Yurovsky, the commander of the execution squad. As will be seen, there are a number of serious discrepancies in this protocol which may be explained by the tricks played by memory after a lapse of two years, but are more probably the result of an effort to hide the full truth.

These remains were originally discovered in July 1991. They were taken to Sverdlov, now renamed Ekaterinburg, for forensic tests, yet a year later the best that can be offered to identify these remains is a computer reconstruction from the skulls. In itself that is hardly the most convincing evidence and it looks weaker when we remind ourselves that the computer reconstruction was not based upon work done on the skulls alone, but was founded upon the use of photographs of the Tsar and Tsarina which were used to give the reconstruction its direction, indicating that perhaps the decision had already been taken that these were the remains of the Romanovs irrespective of what the forensic evidence might disclose. Computers do not operate independently, but are dependent upon the information fed into them.

Much speculation has been inspired by expectations that DNA tests being carried out at Aldermaston in England will finally prove that these are indeed the remains of the Tsar's family. These expectations are probably pitched too high. DNA fingerprinting ultimately relies on a statistical probability that forensic samples stem from a particular source. They can be expected to prove that such samples do *not* originate from a suspect, but the probability that they do originate from a suspect is much less certain. Errors have been known to have been made in DNA tests, but the biggest single disadvantage with tests of this sort is that there is no reliable data on how frequently a particular pattern of DNA recurs in any given population. The typical procedures for calculating the frequency of distribution of such patterns do not take this into account – indeed, I understand that it is this aspect which is responsible for the lengthy delay in announcing the results of the Aldermaston tests.

Scepticism is reinforced by the fact that the American FBI, a supporter of DNA fingerprinting, carried out a series of tests in 1989–90 which showed that DNA samples became badly degraded after being buried in raw soil for more than five days; these bones have lain in the earth for over seventy years. Similarly, no reliable chain of custody – a prerequisite when DNA samples are used in the courts – has been established for these remains. Some Russians have claimed that bones from the Tsar's brother, George, or other members of the family might have been substituted for the original bones. Such is the distrust this discovery has raised in Russia that Archbishop Ioann of St Petersburg has stated that he will refuse to bury the remains with those of other members of the imperial family. Such problems have led the English scientist who pioneered DNA fingerprinting, Dr Alec Jeffreys, to voice doubts about the practicability of the exercise.

I have been deliberately inconsistent with the transliteration of Russian words, choosing to use versions familiar to English-speaking readers; thus Ekaterinburg remains Ekaterinburg instead of Yekaterinburg. The use of the Germanic Dietrichs instead of Diterikhs is purely my own preference – and I make no apology for it.

I

A DECLARATION OF INTEREST

The Russian royal family disappeared in the early hours of 17 July 1918. Exactly what happened to them remains one of the most persistent riddles of the twentieth century, and one which continues to arouse passions as well as theories. This inhibits serious historical discussion of the subject, as does a marked reluctance to open relevant historical archives. It is still a subject which strikes surprisingly raw nerves.

Officially, eleven defenceless people were slaughtered in a ground floor room of a house in the Siberian city of Ekaterinburg, to the east of the Ural mountains. The victims were reputedly Nicholas Romanov, the fifty-year-old former Tsar who, a mere sixteen months before, had been considered the most powerful man in the world; his German wife, the Tsarina, Alexandra; and their five children – the sick, fourteen-year-old Alexei, the Tsarevich and the one-time heir to the Russian throne, and his sisters, Olga, aged twenty-three, Tatiana, aged twenty-one, Marie, aged nineteen, and Anastasia, aged seventeen. With them perished their retainers: the family doctor, Eugene Botkin; the footman, Alexis Yegorovitch Trupp; the cook, Ivan Mikhailovitch Kharitonov; and the chambermaid, Anna Stepanova Demidova. Only two facts can be stated with absolute certainty: none of the victims' bodies was found and none of these people was ever seen, or at least officially recognized, alive again.

I had always regarded this official version as the most probable version of events, the more so since there had been so many claims of survival by one improbable means or another, and just as many improbable claimants – the most famous and the most plausible of whom was Anna Anderson, who maintained throughout a long and contentious lifetime that she was, in fact, the Tsar's daughter Anastasia. These survival stories could, of course, never be checked conclusively, but too many of them were so obviously spurious that in the end they engendered feelings of boredom and contempt for the whole issue.

Admittedly, there were flaws in the official version which meant that it had to be treated with a degree of caution. Not least was the fact that the three states most closely connected with the Romanovs – Britain, Germany and the Soviet Union – showed an inexplicable reluctance to release files which would, surely, settle the question once and for all. Why was such a degree of secrecy necessary, in what was to all appearances an open and shut case? Nevertheless, these were minor, niggling doubts and did not affect the broad acceptance of what I understood to be the truth.

It was while I was working on British Military Intelligence during the First World War that I began seriously to question the official story.

In the Public Record Office at Kew I discovered that document No. 461, entitled *Irkutsk Prisoners-of-War and Ex-Czar* had been removed from the file *Siberia 4*, which covered events in Siberia in May and the greater part of June 1918.[1] It had also been deleted from the contents list by a stroke of green ink, a colour then used by C, the head of the British Secret Intelligence Service.

There was nothing secret about the fact that former Austrian and German prisoners-of-war were massing for repatriation in Siberia at this time, or that they posed a serious threat to Allied interests. The only conceivable reason for the suppression of this document was that it contained something about the Tsar, by then a prisoner with his family in Ekaterinburg. Yet according to the official account, based on such documents as have been released, Nicholas and his family had been abandoned by the British in 1917. What did this deletion mean? What did the document reveal about the Romanovs in the late spring or early summer of 1918 that needed to be kept from public view?

In 1976 a book called *The File on the Tsar* had been published, reviving the whole debate about the fate of the Romanovs. Written by two BBC investigative journalists, Anthony Summers and Tom Mangold, it had not produced conclusive evidence about their fate, but it did provide incontrovertible evidence that the official inquiry conducted after the family's disappearance had reached its conclusion that they had been murdered only by dint of deliberately suppressing and distorting the available evidence. Summers and Mangold had also uncovered traces of covert British efforts to help the family. Could this deletion be connected with these efforts?

Alongside the deletion, in the same green ink, had been written in the margin 'RM8480'. What did that mean? Did RM stand for somebody's initials, as was so often the case with British records? If so, whose were they? The puzzle was made all the more intriguing and even more suspicious because the whole of the next file in the Siberia series, *Siberia 5*, covering the end of June to August 1918, had disappeared as completely as the victims' bodies. There was no explanation for its absence. Years later I learnt that this file exists, and has been deliberately withheld.

Later that same year, 1981, my research into Military Intelligence led me to the private diary of one of Britain's most remarkable and successful Intelligence Officers, Colonel Richard Meinertzhagen, CBE, DSO. The diary is held under restricted access in the Rhodes House Library, Oxford, and covers the life and times of its creator in 70 bound volumes. I was entirely unprepared for what I was to find: an entry, dated 18 August 1918, which spoke of a desperate mission to rescue Nicholas and his family the previous month. There was an uncanny degree of coincidence between this diary and the deletions in the official files; they could not have been contrived, as both were written

3

entirely independently of each other. The coincidences ranged from the initials in the margin of the contents list of *Siberia 4* to the fact that in 1918 Meinertzhagen was responsible for organizing a Military Intelligence network in Russia. These coincidences argued against the idea of dismissing the diary out of hand. The scenario presented was so startling that it cried out for investigation; and in my book on British Military Intelligence in the First World War, *Armour Against Fate*, which was published in 1989, I included a chapter on the subject which, despite its brevity, offered an entirely new interpretation of events in the summer of 1918. I not only drew on the evidence of Meinertzhagen's diary, but went on to reveal how the Tsar's second daughter, Tatiana, was rescued and brought across Siberia and the Pacific Ocean to Canada and thence to Britain.[2] There were still, however, so many gaps in the story, so many fascinating trails and by-ways, that I was determined to pursue the matter further and with luck to a definite conclusion.

Meinertzhagen was not always the most reliable of sources, I knew, but I was inclined to accept his account because so much of the normal documentary source material which I discovered to have been withheld related directly to the trail stemming from the diary entry. That in itself seemed to indicate a consistent thread, which was difficult to explain except in terms of the attempted concealment of a rescue operation.

There was also the fact that the scenario clashed sharply with the familiar Anastasia story. According to Meinertzhagen, the rest of the family were murdered after the rescue operation, but there was considerable evidence which supported the Anastasia story. How were these to be reconciled? Indeed, was it possible, or even desirable, to reconcile them? One answer might lie in Meinertzhagen and Military Intelligence having lost touch with the Romanov case after the attempted rescue had proved to be only partially successful. Yet there is as much doubt about the validity of the Anastasia claim as there is support. The whole issue has never been settled satisfactorily, though it seems very probable that the well-known and highly publicized Anastasia affair has completely overshadowed all other inquiries.

2

THE END OF TSARDOM

In 1912 Russia celebrated 300 years of Romanov rule. Huge, cheering crowds greeted members of Russia's royal family wherever they appeared. Amid scenes of such popular enthusiasm, how could it be doubted that the Romanovs were perfectly secure in their tenure of the throne of all the Russias? Yet beneath the jubilation there was cause for unease. The Tsar was an autocrat and here lay at once tsardom's greatest strength and weakness. The government of the mighty Russian empire lay in the hands of one man, who held the power of life and death over all his subjects. No major decision of state could be taken without his agreement; there were no democratic rights, and no form of representative government. Not only was the Tsar head of the secular state: he was a figure as near to God as many of his subjects could conceive, his position as head of the Russian Orthodox Church reinforcing his quasi-religious status.

Society was changing rapidly. Russia was going through the painful toils of industrializing a relatively backward agricultural society. Most of Western Europe was already a long way down the same road, but there the journey had been accompanied by political and social reform which ameliorated the hardship of life by subjecting governments to some form of popular control and by improvements in working conditions.

Pressures for change existed in Russia, but change was dependent upon the will of the Tsar. Alexander II, Nicholas's grandfather, had abolished serfdom but was assassinated for his pains: his young grandson was present when his body, shattered by a bomb, was carried into the Winter Palace. The next Tsar, Alexander III, had reinforced autocracy, suppressing both reformers and revolutionaries with the same heavy hand; those who opposed the Tsar risked death, exile, or internal exile to the wastes of Siberia. Nicholas II adopted the same stance, perhaps for want of an alternative example. In the first year of his reign he rebuffed one tentative suggestion for reform with the haughty retort, 'I shall defend the principles of autocracy as unswervingly as my deceased father.' The sorry chapter of exile and executions ran on, as did the oppression of Jews, Poles and Circassians. In Western Europe Russia was viewed as a country ruled by the knout and the Cossacks.

Given the Tsar's opposition to reform, and the absence of a parliament, some Russians turned to rebellion and then to terrorism. In the 1870s, the *narodniki* (populists) tried to incite revolt among the peasants who made up the bulk of Russia's population: the most the *narodniki* could achieve were a few isolated and easily crushed uprisings, for such was the state of the peasantry that they greeted these approaches with bewilderment, hostility or apathy. This failure caused a split in the ranks of the *narodniki*. Some formed a small terrorist organization called The People's Will, responsible for the murder of Alexander II in 1881. Others went on to codify their agrarian socialism and formed the Social Revolutionary Party in 1901. Although there was an element of socialism among the SRs, their main goal was reform of land ownership by distributing the land among the peasants.

Other parties were gradually formed too, notably the Social Democratic Labour Party. In 1903 the party split into two factions – the larger and more radical of which was known as the Bolsheviks and the smaller as the Mensheviks. As the twentieth century entered its first decade, the corruption and incompetence of the Tsar's regime were humiliatingly exposed by defeat at the hands of the Japanese in the Russo-Japanese War (1904-5). More significant than the military defeats, however, was the massacre of 22 January 1905, St Petersburg's 'Bloody Sunday'. Demonstrators led by a priest, Father Gapon, attempted to present a petition to the Tsar, but were attacked and slaughtered by troops and police. The reaction was to be the regime's first taste of popular power: shocked by the outrage, the new industrial working class took to the streets and the empire was rocked by strikes and disturbances which the army could not stamp out.

The revolution of 1905 persuaded the Tsar to issue the famous October Manifesto which granted, in very general terms, the liberties of person, conscience, speech, meeting and association. It also promised an elected parliament, the Duma; but its powers were severely circumscribed, and were to be whittled away over the ensuing years. As Witte, the Tsar's prime minister, observed, there was 'a constitution, but a conservative constitution and without parliamentarism'.

Although the traditional attitude to the Tsar as the 'little father' of his people was still widespread, tsardom itself was under challenge as never before. Unease continued. In late July 1914, during the state visit of the French President Poincaré, the barricades were again going up in St Petersburg.

The situation was transformed when Germany declared war on Russia on 1 August. Those who had been building barricades knelt among the crowds outside the Winter Palace, before proceeding to sack the German embassy. Scenes of wild patriotic joy submerged discontent as people of all classes rallied round the flag against the Central Powers.

The war proved to be a succession of costly defeats for Russia, and the Russian people's original enthusiasm was replaced by despondency and then anger. Although victories were won against the Turks and Austrians, they were overshadowed by the disasters which resulted whenever the Russians faced the Germans, underlining the corruption and incompetence of tsardom. By the end of 1915, some two million Russians had been killed or captured without there being anything to show for it.

The horrific loss of life was accompanied by the loss of territory. Russian Poland, Lithuania and parts of Western Russia were overrun by the Central Powers. Worse still, under the strain of war the railway system broke down, and railways were the only means of transporting men and bulky items like munitions and food across the vast expanses of the empire. The cities were flooded with refugees from the lost provinces – it has been estimated that there were a million of these unfortunates in St Petersburg (renamed Petrograd in 1914) and Moscow by the end of 1915. Nothing had been done to prepare for such an eventuality. Problems of food, employment and accommodation swelled to crisis point. Many Russians abandoned hope that the regime could fight the war to a successful conclusion. This demoralization was not confined to civilians but spread to the army.

In order to restore the morale of his battered armies, the Tsar dismissed the Grand Duke Nikolai Nikolaievitch and took his place at the front as Commander-in-Chief. This proved a disastrous mistake: Nicholas's presence made not one iota of difference, and the continuing defeats now reflected directly upon the Tsar himself.

Nicholas had left the government in the hands of his German Tsarina, Alexandra, who was suspected of being in league with the Germans and thus provided a useful scapegoat. To make matters worse, she was as widely believed to be under the thumb of Rasputin, a peasant monk with healing powers who had shown himself able to restore the haemophiliac Tsarevich where the doctors had failed. Rasputin influenced the Tsarina in her choice of ministers and it was rumoured that she was one of his mistresses. Nicholas and Alexandra were increasingly despised, and there were cases where peasants walked out of church when prayers were offered for them.

An Anglo-French mission was sent to Russia in December 1916 in an attempt to stimulate the Russian war effort. Its members found a lack of confidence in the Tsar and could see little to suggest that Russian efforts in 1917 would be any more effective. In December, Rasputin was assassinated by a group of nobles, and members of the imperial family were implicated. The fact that the Tsar could not protect one so close to his family as the monk had been merely emphasized his own power-lessness.

The Allied mission's recommendations came too late to help the Tsar. On 10 March 1917 rioting broke out in the food queues in Petrograd. Army units sent to quell the trouble sided with the rioters, some going so far as to murder their officers. The disorder spread and by 12 March the imperial government had lost control. A cabinet government was formed under Prince Lvov and the President of the Duma, Rodzianko, which disbanded the old ministry and arrested some of its members. In Britain, perhaps inspired by wishful thinking, the March Revolution was seen as a *coup d'état* engineered by the army's high command and members of the Duma with the objective of ensuring a more effective prosecution of the war.

While these momentous events were taking place, Nicholas was with GHQ at Mohilef, on the River Dnieper, between Minsk and Smolensk. Realizing that this was more than a mere food riot, he decided his presence was needed near the capital. On 13 March he set out by train for the Summer Palace of Tsarskoye Selo on the outskirts of Petrograd, but his plans were disrupted by revolutionary railway workers. His train was eventually diverted to Pskof, some 125 miles to the west of the capital.

The situation had gone far beyond Nicholas's control. A deputation led by his generals visited him at Pskof and urged him to abdicate in order to preserve both Russia and the army. An account of the meeting reaches us from the lips of Vitali Szulgin, the head of the Black Hundred, the group which specialized in terrorizing Jews under the tsarist regime, and a member of the deputation: 'Nicholas II was deep in a game of chess and did not want to be distracted. When he learnt the object of their visit, the Tsar did not try to conceal his joy: "At last, it's over!" "What do you expect?" Szulgin added. "He was the biggest idiot in the whole dynasty." '[1]

Nicholas signed the abdication papers in his railway carriage on 15 March, standing down in favour of his brother, the Grand Duke Mikhail Alexandrovitch, and abdicating in his son's name as well as his own. After meeting Rodzianko, the President of the Duma, the Grand Duke Mikhail also abdicated when it became clear that his personal safety could not be guaranteed. As to the future, he left that to be considered by an elected constituent assembly. Not merely the monarch but the monarchy had fallen.

Nicholas's British and French allies were quick to abandon him. They had been presented with a *fait accompli* and were more concerned with fighting and winning a war which by 1917 had turned into a brutal struggle for survival. For this they needed the Russians, under whatever government, and they could not afford to alienate the new regime. Following the events in Petrograd, it was expected that the Russian war effort would now be pursued with new vigour and efficiency. The overthrow of the Romanovs was also depicted as a triumph of democracy which would strengthen the Allied hand when dealing with neutrals like the United States, who had been reluctant to join Allied ranks when they included the tyranny of tsardom. The Allies paid their respects to the Tsar as a loyal friend, after which he was quickly forgotten as another year of bloodletting got under way.

All the same, British consciences were pricked by Miliukov, the Provisional Government's first Foreign Minister. On 19 March he asked the British Ambassador, Sir George Buchanan, whether the British would be sending a ship to convey Nicholas and his family to safety in Britain, taking it for granted that this would be done. After all, he was more than just a loyal ally; he was the first cousin of King George V, while Alexandra had been Queen Victoria's favourite grandchild. Buchanan was taken unawares as no arrangements had been discussed, much less prepared; and he had, perforce, to reply in the negative and forward Miliukov's question to the Foreign Office.

After his abdication, Nicholas had returned to GHQ from where he was escorted to Tsarskoye Selo to be reunited with his wife and family. Alexandra had been under house arrest in the Summer Palace since 21 March. The family was to remain there in relatively genteel confinement until August 1918.

Nicholas was an honest man with a simple outlook on life. He was devoted above all else to his country and his family. He was dutiful and hard-working but was not blessed with the ability to read people's characters. He was rather reserved and disliked familiarity, and he inspired awe rather than fear in those who met him. According to the family's English tutor, Charles Sydney Gibbes, he was 'methodical in his habits, he could not bear anyone to touch his things'.

His wife was a stronger, more aggressive person who appeared haughty and distant to those who did not know her personally. Gibbes described her as 'kind-hearted, extremely fond of homely secrets, she liked to prepare surprises'. As she grew older she became increasingly religious and fatalistic. She was devoted to her husband.

Their eldest daughter, Olga, was fair with golden-brown hair and had inherited her father's striking blue eyes. Gibbes considered her 'innocent, modest, sincere and kind, but easily irritated; her manners could be a little brusque'. She was the most spiritual of the Tsar's daughters, preferring simplicity, solitude and her books. She was not noted for her practicality. She was closer to her father than her mother, though she was unable to disguise her attachment to those she loved.

Tatiana, the second daughter, was tall and elegant but also tended to be haughty and reserved, with a strong sense of duty. Gibbes found her pensive, and observed that 'it was impossible to guess her thoughts, even if she was more decided in her opinions than her sisters'. She combined this with an independent streak and was the natural leader among the Tsar's children, though perhaps a touch over-zealous in her dealings with her siblings, a fact which earned her the nickname of 'the governess'. She was her mother's favourite and confidante, and favours from their mother would certainly be granted if the children approached her through Tatiana.

The third daughter, Marie, was strong and broadly built. She was the most considerate member of the family and the most sociable. Gibbes recalled that she was 'simple and fond of children; a little inclined to laziness; probably she would have made an excellent wife and mother'.

Anastasia was the youngest and the most ungraceful of the four girls, but she compensated for that with her ready wit which made her the family comedian. She was an excellent mimic, ever ready to raise laughter at the expense of the more pompous or obsequious members of the court. Gibbes felt that 'it seemed as if her mental development had been suddenly arrested', although the only basis he gives us for this view is that Anastasia was only in the first stages of playing the piano and painting; we can only surmise what else might have helped to shape this opinion.

Nicholas and Alexandra's only son, Alexis, suffered from haemophilia, which meant that the normal rough and tumble of young boys could all too easily threaten his life. Although intelligent and observant, he was less than eager when it came to study. Gibbes observed that he was 'influenced only through his emotions; he rarely did what he was told, but obeyed his father'. His mother doted on him, which made her putty in his hands. He had a habit of collecting all sorts of oddments – nails, paper-clips, pieces of string – on the grounds that they might come in useful one day.[2]

There were other relatives among the great family of European monarchs who could be expected to take more than a passing interest in the fate of the Romanovs. Nicholas was related to the German Kaiser, Wilhelm II, who with his grand ideas about the dignity of royalty could be expected to try in his usual ham-fisted manner to ensure that no harm came to his Russian relatives. Nicholas was also related to the Danish royal family, as was the Tsarina. Her brother was the Grand Duke Ernst of Hesse; but with Russia at war with Germany there was only the slimmest hope that the German part of the family could achieve anything, and an even slimmer prospect of the Romanovs accepting help from such hands.

There were signs of British interest in these early days. The rumour ran abroad that Nicholas had been arrested, and Buchanan was instructed to ask if there was any truth in the story. This he did on 21 March 1917. Miliukov's reply was evasive, for although Nicholas had been deprived of his freedom of movement, he was at perfect liberty in private. Buchanan had little opportunity to quibble over this since the Foreign Minister switched the conversation to his previous request, fully expecting to hear that a British cruiser was on its way to relieve the Provisional Government of its embarrassing responsibility. Needless to say, no cruiser was ever sent.

The Provisional Government had more pressing problems to face. It had thrown itself behind the war effort, but its conduct of the war proved to be no more successful than its predecessor's. There were domestic rivals at home as well. The new government was largely composed of educated liberals and moderate socialists, but the real foot-soldiers of the Revolution had been the soviets, local councils of workmen and soldiers. They had first appeared in the 1905 Revolution and had now resurfaced to direct the Revolution at local level. They were staunchly socialist and under the stresses of war Bolshevism had made great inroads among them. Meeting in the Smolny Institute in Petrograd, formerly a school for aristocratic young ladies, they were effectively a rival government.

The main Russian war effort in 1917 was a grand offensive along the length of the Eastern front. It was a disaster. The only worthwhile success was won by the forces under General Kornilov, but these gains were swiftly lost when the Central Powers counter-attacked. One alarming feature was the increasing unwillingness of many Russian soldiers to fight. The army was awash with Bolshevik propaganda and most of the men simply wanted to go home.

Demands from the more radical soviets and the extremists in Russian politics for the Tsar to be put on trial alarmed the Provisional Government, and the new head of government, a liberal lawyer named Alexander Kerensky, made one more attempt to discover what the British were doing about the question raised by Miliukov. To Kerensky's surprise and disappointment, Buchanan, with tears in his eyes, told him that the British government had resolved not to provide a refuge for the Romanovs. Kerensky solved, or postponed, the problem by sending the family to the Siberian city of Tobolsk, well out of the immediate reach of extremists in Petrograd. On 14 August the family and forty-five attendants boarded the imperial train and set out across Russia. At every halt on the way they were warmly received, with no animosity shown towards them. They arrived at the Governor's House in Tobolsk on 19 August.

The Provisional Government now faced a new crisis in the form of a military *coup*. Many of the senior generals had lost all confidence in its efforts to conduct the war. With Kornilov at their head, they attempted to march their troops on Petrograd and overthrow the Provisional Government. Neither Kornilov's troops nor the railway workers shared his ambitions and the *coup* collapsed, farcically, in the face of their opposition. Superficially it looked like a victory for the Provisional Government, but the army had been the only body which had kept the Bolsheviks underground and that could no longer be counted upon.

With the watchwords 'All power to the soviets' and 'Make peace with your legs, take land with your hands!', Lenin – who had returned to Russia in April 1917 – spread his influence even more deeply among the soviets and among the industrial workers and soldiers. With the Provisional Government unable to count on the army, the time was ripe for him to make his move. On 7 November 1917, the Bolsheviks struck. The Provisional Government was put to flight and the newly elected Constituent Assembly was dissolved by force. One of the Bolsheviks' first moves was to try to deliver the peace they had promised: therefore they declared an end to the war and began disbanding the old army. An armistice was agreed with the Central Powers, and negotiations for peace began in the shattered Polish city of Brest-Litovsk.

For the Romanovs, the Bolshevik seizure of power represented a real threat. The most immediate indication of the temper of the new regime was a heavy cut in the money paid for their subsistence, and the family was placed on soldiers' rations. Most of the retainers who had accompanied the family from Tsarskoye Selo had to be dismissed. Worse was to come when the guards who had been responsible for them were dismissed and replaced by Red Guards from the Siberian cities of Ekaterinburg and Omsk.

Negotiating peace terms with the Bolsheviks was anything but straightforward. They were not like the governments of old Europe, who would be prepared to face defeat and settle as best they could with the loss of some frontier provinces. The Central

Powers originally demanded Russian Poland, Lithuania and Western Latvia from the territories of the Russian empire, but for ideological reasons the Bolsheviks refused to surrender territory or people to the imperialism they so hated. They sent a new negotiating team to Brest-Litovsk, led by the new People's Commissar for Foreign Affairs, Leon Trotsky.

Trotsky had been the last chairman of the St Petersburg Soviet in 1905, and held the same post in 1917, so his revolutionary credentials were perfect. He advocated a policy of 'neither war nor peace', and he summed up his stance towards the negotiations with the rhetorical question, 'What diplomatic work will we have?' He provided the answer: 'We will publish a few revolutionary proclamations to the peoples, and then shut up shop.' Trotsky's oratory made good propaganda for the Bolshevik dream of international revolution and reduced the negotiations to a farce, but it did not bring peace. He overplayed his hand when, on 28 January 1918, he announced that the trifling was over and Soviet Russia was unilaterally declaring the war to be over. The assembled diplomats and generals of the Central Powers were stunned into silence, broken only when the representative of the German General Staff, Max Hoffmann, muttered *'Unerhort!'* ('Unheard of!')

The response of the Central Powers was predictable. They renounced the armistice and ordered their armies forward – only now there was no Russian army to oppose them. Huge expanses of territory fell to them, and it required all Lenin's skill and energy, plus the threat of his resignation, to force the idealists to face reality and accept the German peace terms.

The new terms were far harsher than the old. Not only was more territory surrendered to the Central Powers than had been demanded in January, but Soviet Russia had to agree to evacuate the Ukraine and Southern Russia. These savage terms were signed on 3 March 1918 and were to dominate Russia's foreign relations for most of the rest of the year. The forces of the Central Powers advanced over 500 miles into the evacuated land and reached Rostov on the Sea of Azov on 8 May. The disaster was overwhelming.

The peace emphasized the Bolsheviks' weakness in the face of

German military might and led directly to the creation of the Red Army, the original purpose of which was to fight further German depredations rather than to crush internal opposition to the Bolsheviks. Such opposition as they faced within Russia in early 1918 was weak and disorganized, but with the Treaty of Brest-Litovsk that was to change. Many Russians felt the humiliation of the peace very deeply and resolved to fight on – but against the Bolsheviks as much as against the Germans. The left wing of the Social Revolutionary Party (hereafter the LSR) had been allies of the Bolsheviks until the peace was signed, but in a move that was to have far-reaching consequences later in the year they split with them over the peace.

On 4 March 1918 a puny force of 140 British marines landed at the port of Murmansk in North Russia, with the objective of preventing it from falling into German hands. It was the beginning of what was to become a sizeable intervention by the British over the following twelve months.

3

MURDER MOST FOUL?

While the clouds of invasion and civil war were gathering over European Russia, the Romanovs remained helpless spectators in Tobolsk. There was no indication about what the new revolutionary government intended to do with them, and all they could do was to wait upon events.

The evening of 22 April brought the waiting to an end. A column of horsemen arrived unannounced at the Governor's House, led by Special Commissar Vassily Vassilievitch Yakovlev. There is little reliable information about Yakovlev: for eight brief days he featured in the Romanov tragedy, but of his activities before his arrival in Tobolsk and his ultimate fate nothing definite is known. What is known is that he carried authority and could produce impressive documentation to establish that he was acting on the direct orders of the Bolshevik Central Executive Committee or TsIK, the Bolshevik equivalent of the Cabinet in most governments. Since his arrival had been unannounced, and the reason for his presence in such a sensitive place was unknown, he aroused considerable suspicion among the guards. However, if Yakovlev's documents did not altogether allay their fears, they did at least persuade them to listen to him.

The new arrival spoke first of all to Colonel Kobylinski, the official commander of the guard. Kobylinski's authority over the Red Guards was superficial at best, for discipline was slack and it was all that he could do to maintain the barest pretence of order. One of his problems lay in that the guard was divided into two factions – one from Omsk, deep in Siberia, and the other from the industrial city of Ekaterinburg, on the Siberian side of the Ural Mountains. Both factions were jockeying for control of the imperial family, and tension ran high.

The guards remained suspicious because Yakovlev had not revealed the purpose of his arrival at the Governor's House. He did not do so now, leaving them to discuss among themselves whether his credentials were all they appeared to be. When he next met them, he skilfully played upon their rivalry and won over the detachment from Omsk. The leader of the Ekaterinburg faction was jeered for spreading alarmist rumours of escape plots; he left the meeting sullen, angry and humiliated, which was to have repercussions later on. Only after he had left did Yakovlev reveal his mission to the guard committee. He had come to take the imperial family away from Tobolsk, though he does not appear to have told the committee of guards where he was taking them or for what purpose.

Yakovlev then met the Tsar. Unlike most Bolsheviks, he was polite and respectful. When he told Nicholas to be ready to leave later that night the first and only clash of wills occurred, with the Tsar simply stating, 'I refuse to go.' Yakovlev overcame this by gently but firmly telling him that he would either have to take him by force or resign – and that if he resigned, Moscow would send someone less scrupulous to take his place.

Nobody knew where the imperial family were to be taken, but it was generally believed that they were to be taken first of all to Moscow and then, via Riga, to Scandinavia, from where they were to go to Britain. This opinion was founded on statements by Colonel Kobylinski, Prince Dolgoroukov, the Tsar's aide-de-camp, and Dr Botkin's two children: according to Gleb Botkin, the doctor's son, he was told the news by his father, who had heard it from Kobylinski, who had been given it by Yakovlev himself. Kobylinski had been told that the Soviets had promised the Germans that they would release the family:

> But the Germans have had the decency not to demand that the imperial family go to Germany. Accordingly it was decided that we shall be sent to England. To satisfy the masses, however, we are to pass through Moscow where a short trial of the Emperor will be held. He will be found guilty of whatever the revolutionists care to accuse him, and be condemned to deportation to England.[1]

This information is at third hand so it is not entirely reliable, but it does tally with the fact that, since the Tsarevich was sick and could not travel, Yakovlev had decided to leave him behind in the care of three of his sisters and return in eleven days – the time it took to make the round trip to Moscow and back. Reliable or not, this version of events was accepted and welcomed by Kobylinski and the Botkins. The Tsarina, on the other hand, was torn between two fears. She needed to stay with her sick son and she also needed to be with her husband in case it was planned to make him sign the infamous Treaty of Brest-Litovsk, thereby endowing it with a symbolic value which would make it more palatable to many Russians. She had always regretted not being at her husband's side when he received the deputation which asked for his abdication. She sincerely believed that she could have dissuaded him from signing, thus averting the possibility of civil war and the breakdown of Russian society. In the end she decided to go with her husband.

At 4 a.m. on 27 April the party set off. With Nicholas and Alexandra went their third daughter, Marie, Dr Botkin, Prince Dolgoroukov, the valet Chemodurov and two servants, Siednev and Demidova. Travelling by sleigh because of the snow, Yakovlev made all the speed he could – as well he might, given the attitude of the commander of the Ekaterinburg detachment. The latter had already informed his home base of what was happening by telegraph.

The nearest railway station was at Tiumen, which was reached on 28 April. There Yakovlev left them to send a telegram to

Moscow. A train was already waiting with steam up, and once the party was aboard it pulled out as if it was going to Moscow on the line through Ekaterinburg. This was one of two rail routes to Moscow from Tiumen. The other ran through Omsk – and it was this latter route that Yakovlev actually planned to take. The train slipped back through Tiumen with all lights doused and onto the Omsk route. By this means Yakovlev hoped to deceive the Ekaterinburg detachment, who still did not trust him and whose leader was smarting from the reception he had been given at Tobolsk. But the deception failed: the Ekaterinburg detachment was too alert and news of what had taken place was sent by telegraph to Ekaterinburg. The local soviet's reaction was swift. Yakovlev was declared a traitor and an outlaw, and a telegram was sent to the Omsk Soviet warning them to turn the train back.

As they approached Omsk, Yakovlev learnt from railway workers of the reception that was awaiting him. He halted the train and went into the city to try to argue his way through, but this time to no avail. The attempted deception probably tipped the scales against him and aroused, at the very least, intense suspicion. There was no alternative other than to travel back through Ekaterinburg. As soon as they reached Ekaterinburg, the Romanovs and their servants were taken off the train and sent straight to the Ipatiev House, while Prince Dolgoroukov was taken to the city prison. They arrived at their last place of confinement on 30 April, though nearly a month passed before the rest of the family joined them. The guards at Tobolsk were changed yet again, and the remaining members of the family and their servants were treated with insolence bordering on brutality before they rejoined their parents and sister on 23 May.

The most curious aspect of this tale of double-dealing is that Yakovlev, the outlaw and traitor, was allowed to walk free. It does not fit into any of the likely explanations of what had happened. He had to explain himself to the Ekaterinburg Bolsheviks and evaded their wrath by producing once again his documentation from Moscow and the tapes of his telegraph messages. Yet despite having aroused their suspicion and hostility, they seem not to have checked his *bona fides* with

Moscow – which remains, arguably, the biggest riddle in the proceedings.

It is clear that the Ekaterinburg Soviet was expecting the arrival of the Romanovs. They had already commandeered as their prison the villa of Nikolai Ipatiev, an engineer, who was abruptly ordered to leave, and erected a pallisade around it. It was then renamed the 'House of Special Purpose'.

That a deception was being practised is beyond doubt – but who was practising it and who was being deceived? It has been argued that it was part of an elaborate plan to avoid surrendering the Romanovs to the Germans by leading them to believe that Moscow had done its best to comply with their wishes – only to be thwarted by the independent and unpredictable action of the local communists, over whom the TsIK had at best only the loosest form of authority. It could equally be argued that Yakovlev was acting entirely on his own initiative and in contravention of any orders he had been given, or even that he was a German agent. The list of possibilities is endless, and no one guess is any more convincing than another.

No one ever got an opportunity to interrogate Yakovlev about his startling mission. His disappearance needs to be noted because of the dubious circumstances which surround it. Summers and Mangold found that Yakovlev had deserted to the White Russians – 'Whites' being the collective term for the Bolsheviks' opponents during the civil war into which Russia was now being drawn – and that two formal requests were made by the later investigators into the fate of the Romanovs that he should be made available for questioning. After a six-month delay he was finally, due to the persistence of the investigators, brought for questioning – only to be lost by the troops escorting him as a result of a 'mistake'. The precise nature of the mistake has never been revealed. Neither has Yakovlev's subsequent fate. According to one report he was killed while fighting the Bolsheviks, while another said that he was 'shot by mistake'.[2] We simply do not know the truth, and it may well be that we are not meant to know.

The scenario that sees Yakovlev as the dupe of a cunning plot engineered by Sverdlov, the chairman of the TsIK and thus the head of state in Moscow, and the hardliners in Ekaterinburg gains support from Edvard Radzinsky's research in the recently opened Soviet archives. Radzinsky is a Russian playwright who has investigated the murder over the past few years, and the telegrams he discovered in those archives show that Yakovlev genuinely believed that he was taking the Romanovs to Moscow but was unaware that Sverdlov had already decided to imprison them in Ekaterinburg as an act of petty spite, designed to cheat the popular Trotsky of his dream of a show trial where he, Trotsky, would be the 'People's Advocate' against 'Nicholas the Bloody'.[3]

Nor had Yakovlev been killed by the Whites. Radzinsky tells us that he fled to Harbin in China, where he assumed the name Stoyanovich and worked as an adviser to Sun Yat-sen, the Chinese revolutionary. However, he remained an agent of the Cheka. He returned to the Soviet Union in 1927 but was arrested, then temporarily vindicated, only to disappear into Stalin's Gulag in 1938, never to be seen again.[4] He and his motives are an extraordinary part of this story, but by no means the most extraordinary.

The villa in which the Romanovs were incarcerated was a two-storey brick building, set against the slope of a hill near the centre of the city. Ekaterinburg itself had been a thriving industrial centre with 80,000 inhabitants, but the combination of war, famine and burgeoning civil war had considerably reduced its population. Nicholas and Alexandra were confined together in one of the six upstairs rooms, and they shared this room with their son once he had been reunited with them. The four girls shared another room, and the commandant of the guard, Alexander Dimitrievitch Avdiev, and his deputy, Alexander Mikhailovitch Moshkin, occupied another of the upstairs rooms.

The pallisade was reinforced by a second which cut the house off from the outside world, except by one gate. The guard was composed of men from two local factories – the Syssert factory and that of the brothers Zlokazov. The guard was divided into two sections, an outer and inner guard: the former was drawn from the ranks of local Red Guards, who were not allowed inside the house. To complete the isolation, the upstairs windows of the house were whitewashed.

Conditions were the harshest yet faced by the family. They were originally allowed thirty minutes every day for exercise in the garden, but this was later cut to five minutes as the regime stiffened. Nicholas used to carry out his frail son for his ration of fresh air. The family were permitted no privacy: they were not even allowed to relieve themselves in private, one of the guards always being present.

In the evenings the Tsar's daughters were made to play the piano for the guards, who were often drunk and sang revolutionary songs calculated to offend the pianists. Food was sent across from the local soviet. It was plain and repetitive, and the meat dishes were usually either chops or rissoles.[5] More and more of the servants were arrested, until only four were left, along with the kitchen boy, Leonid Siednev. Chemodurov, the valet, had been taken ill on 24 May and transferred to the city prison. He and young Siednev were to survive.

Although Avdiev's regime was noteworthy for its coarseness, drunkenness and petty pilfering, it did have one redeeming feature in that nuns from the local convent were permitted to bring eggs and dairy produce from the monastery farm to the house, chiefly for the benefit of the Tsarevich. This had been arranged by Dr Derevenko, the boy's physician, who had come to Ekaterinburg with his patient but had unaccountably been allowed to settle and live unhindered in the city and even to establish a medical practice there. He seems to have had some sort of understanding with the Bolsheviks; this was one of the points the later investigators were to seize upon as suggesting that Avdiev and his men were too easy-going and becoming too close to the prisoners. The claim was used to explain the replacement of the guard on 4 July.

The new guard was more sinister. They were members of the Cheka (*Chrezvychainaya Komissiya po Borbe s Kontr-Revolutisnei i Sabottazhem* – Extraordinary Commission for the Struggle against Counter-Revolution and Sabotage, the forerunners of the KGB) and most of them were Letts. Strictly speaking, a Lett was a native of Latvia or Lithuania, but by 1918 it was being more loosely applied to provincials and even foreigners in communist service. Some of the 'Letts' in the Ipatiev House are known to have been German, Hungarian and Ukrainian. The Letts were noted for being cold-blooded, disciplined and loyal. Their commanders in the house were Yakob Yurovsky, a local communist, and Prokopy Nikulin.

No reliable testimony has survived from among the guards about life and conditions in the house under the new regime. The original guards were confined to the exterior of the house and were not allowed upstairs at all, and Avdiev and Mochkin were both arrested. A new machine-gun post was mounted in the attic and a sentry was always stationed in the back garden. On the same day that the new guards took their station, the Regional Commissar for War, Chaya Goloschekin, hurried off to Moscow. He returned on 14 July, on which day a Mass was held in the house for the family. On about that same day, an aeroplane flew over the house, greatly alarming the guard – or so the British High Commissioner for Siberia, Sir Charles Eliot, was later told. He feared it may have led the guards to kill the Tsar.[6]

In the early hours of 17 July, two of the neighbours heard shots from within the house. The family vanished and were never seen alive again. During the next few days Yurovsky and his men were busy in the forest, near the neighbouring village of Koptiaki.

4

THE SMOKING GUNS

The first news the outside world heard about the fate of the Romanovs came from a Bolshevik wireless communiqué on 18 July 1918, ironically sending its message from a station close to the Summer Palace at Tsarskoye Selo. The doleful communiqué announced that the Tsar alone had been shot and blamed the advance of the Czech Legion on Ekaterinburg for the decision to shoot him. It went on to say that his wife and son had been taken to a safe place but did not mention his daughters. The salient part of the communiqué read:

> Chairman Sverdlov announced receipt by direct wire of advice from the Ural Oblast Soviet of the shooting of former Tsar Nicholas Romanov. In recent days, the danger of approach of Czechoslovak bands posed a serious threat to Ekaterinburg, the capital of the Red Urals. At the same time, a new plot of counter-revolutionaries was exposed, which aimed at tearing the crowned executioner from the hands of the Soviet government. In view of all these circumstances, the Presidium of the Ural Soviet decided to shoot Nicholas Romanov, and this was carried out on 16 July. The wife and son of Nicholas have been sent to a safe place.

This was broadcast on 18 July, but an earlier communication had already been sent to the Foreign Office in London, on 17 July, by the British Diplomatic Agent in Moscow, Robert Bruce Lockhart, who sent a telegram. His brief message read: 'Ex-Emperor of Russia shot on night of July 16th by order of Ekaterinburg local Soviet in view of approaching danger of his capture by Czechs. The Central Executive at Moscow has approved (? their) action.[1]

The Czechs mentioned in the official communiqué and in Lockhart's telegram were the Czechoslovak Legion, which had been formed in Russia in 1914 from Czechs living in Russia and prisoners-of-war from the Czechoslovak units of the Austro-Hungarian army. They had chosen to fight alongside their fellow Slavs for the liberation of their country from the Austro-Hungarian empire; the Legion had grown in size as the war continued and more Czech prisoners and deserters joined it. By 1917 the Legion had the strength of an army corps, and its men had proved to be skilful and courageous fighters.

The Revolution had left them untouched. They had no stake in Russian politics and could hardly be disbanded like the old Russian army since a return to their homeland would result in their being punished for bearing arms against their Austro-Hungarian overlords. With the agreement of the Soviet government, they set out across Russia for Vladivostok, from where they intended to sail to France to continue their struggle in the trenches of the Western front. This was the last thing the Germans wanted to see, and they pressed the Bolsheviks to intern them. The Bolsheviks had no desire to help the Germans and in any case were glad to see the back of the Czechs; moreover, they were hardly strong enough to halt the movement of such a large force of determined men.

The situation changed dramatically as the result of a brawl on 14 May 1918 between the Czechs and their traditional Hungarian enemies at Cheliabinsk in western Siberia. The Hungarians were prisoners-of-war returning to Austria–Hungary, and as they passed the trains carrying the Czechs in the opposite direction one of them was stupid enough to throw a bottle at them. The incident soon escalated into a full-scale brawl. It might have been speedily forgotten, but the Bolsheviks were still being pressured by the Germans: an exasperated Trotsky over-reacted and ordered local Red Guards to disarm the Czechs and press them into service in Red army labour battalions.

The Czechs, of course, resisted and on 25 May fighting broke out along the length of the Trans-Siberian railway, with the Red Guards soon finding themselves outclassed and outfought by the experienced and highly motivated Czechs. By the beginning of June 1918 most of the railway and the city of Vladivostok were in Czech hands. Where the Czechs had driven out the Bolsheviks, local White governments took their place. The domestic opponents of the Reds, or Bolsheviks, in the civil war, the Whites were an uneasy mixture of Social Revolutionaries, Conservatives (Kadets), landowners, Cossacks, former army officers and anyone else who loathed the Bolsheviks. The army officers soon became the dominant group – there were no less than 8,000 of them in Siberia alone – and they were progressively to alienate their civilian allies as time went on. In the meantime, however, they started to raise a Siberian army to join the Czechs against the Bolsheviks.

The Czechs and the Whites then marched westwards to link up with other Czech contingents marching to join them from European Russia. Between them lay Ekaterinburg. Contrary to popular belief – which reflected the urgency injected into Bolshevik communications – their advance on the city was painfully slow and deliberate, and the Reds would have had time to remove their special prisoners if they wished. Ekaterinburg fell to the Czechs and Whites only on 25 July 1918.

During their last days in the city, the Bolsheviks gave the inhabitants no further information about the fate of the Romanovs beyond that contained in their final wireless communiqué. On 20 July Goloschekin, the Regional Commissar for War, announced the execution of 'Nicholas the Bloody' to a public meeting in the city theatre. At least one person greeted the announcement with a cry of 'Show us the body!' Of course, the commissar could not do so. Red Guards then began to put up posters in the city proclaiming the Tsar's execution, ending with the words 'The family of Romanov has been sent to another and safer place'. No sooner had they been put up than other Red Guards began to tear them down.

Five days later the Whites entered Ekaterinburg and a sea of confusion. There were the official statements of the execution. There were reports from eyewitnesses of unknown reliability, which said that not only the family but Nicholas himself had been secretly moved away from Ekaterinburg. There was the evidence of murder – bullet holes and the swab marks where, presumably, blood had been washed away in the Ipatiev House. And there was the testimony of one of Ekaterinburg's citizens, Fyodor Gorshkov, to the effect that the whole family had been murdered, though how reliable his testimony was is unclear – he said he had heard the news from Court Investigator Tomashevsky, who had learnt of the deed either from an eyewitness or someone close to the Bolsheviks. Who Tomashevsky was is not at all clear, and no real effort seems to have been made to trace him or to hear his story at first hand.

What looked ominously like confirmation of Gorshkov's story was the discovery of burnt debris near the Four Brothers mine in the forest near Koptiaki. This was found by local peasants, who had gone to the mine largely out of curiosity after the Reds had left. The debris included the remains of clothing and shoes, and among the ashes some pieces of jewellery. Some of the debris was taken to the White authorities in the city by Lieutenant Andrei Sheremetevsky, a White officer who had been hiding in the village. The jewellery was recognized as having belonged to the women of the imperial family.

Rumour ran rife. Nobody was at all sure what to believe. Dr Botkin's son, Gleb, who had an indisputable personal interest in discovering what had happened to the imperial family, found near-anarchy in the city. Dr Derevenko told him that the traces of murder in the house were a Bolshevik ruse and maintained that the family could not have been murdered. The White Commandant of Ekaterinburg, the Persian Prince Riza-Kuli-Mirza, refused to believe that the Romanovs had been murdered and showed young Botkin secret reports from investigators which said that the family had been taken to a monastery in neighbouring Perm province and then sent to Denmark. There is no way of knowing how reliable these reports were, but Botkin found them 'most unconvincing'.[2]

The confusion and rumours were not confined to Ekaterinburg or to Russia. In London *The Times* reported an account by *Pravda*, the official Soviet newspaper, of the Tsar's execution, according to which Nicholas was shot in a riding school outside the city: his executioners were his guards, who had acted on their own initiative and only informed the local soviet at the last moment.[3] *The Times* chose to doubt the date of 16 July as the date of the shooting and referred to another, more probable version which gave the date as 1 July. What this other version was and why it was considered more probable, we are not told.

The date of 1 July is of interest because the Danish Legation in Petrograd wired home that the execution appeared to have taken place on 1 July: they repeated the story that the local soviet had taken the initiative and then reported their action to the central government, which then proceeded to approve it. Precisely what the Danish source was it is impossible to know, but as a neutral power whose royal family was related to both the Tsar and Tsarina their information cannot be dismissed out of hand.[4]

In Sweden, *Svenska Dagblad* reported on 3 August that Nicholas's murder had been premeditated because he was seen as a standing danger to the Revolution; and went on to say that his brother, the Grand Duke Mikhail Alexandrovitch, had escaped from detention and was working to restore the monarchy.

It was against this background, compounded by the confusion and the tortuous politics of the civil war, that the White Russians began their official investigations into the disappearance of the Romanovs. It was one of those investigations which provided the orthodox account of the murder of the family – an account which was even, to some extent, to colour Bolshevik thinking on the subject.

5

THE ORTHODOX VIEW

The first inquiry into the disappearance of the Romanovs was established in July 1918 by Prince Riza-Kuli-Mirza, the White Commandant of Ekaterinburg, who ordered a commission of officers to start work on the case. Some of these officers came from the St Petersburg Military Academy, which had been re-located to Ekaterinburg by the Bolsheviks. Working alongside, but apart from, the Officers' Commission was the White army's Criminal Investigating Division which was normally responsible for counter-espionage in the army's rear. The civilian judiciary was, naturally, in disarray under the twin stresses of Bolshevik rule and civil war, but the Officers' Commission had had a civilian judge attached to it at the army's request. Once the judiciary re-established itself, the city prosecutor instructed the judge to begin an entirely separate civilian inquiry. The judge was Examining Magistrate for Important Cases Alexander Nametkin. He was the first of three judges to head the civilian judicial inquiry, and it was that inquiry which ultimately gave the massacre theory its orthodoxy and the stamp of official acceptance. The papers and results of the efforts of the other two teams have never come to light.

Nametkin began work immediately, and during the short time

in which he was responsible for the case he searched both the Ipatiev House and the Four Brothers mine with its incriminating debris. He went to the mine on 30 July, when Red army troops were reported in the forest nearby. The mine stood in a clearing in the forest and could be reached either by a track leading off the Ekaterinburg–Koptiaki road or by walking through the forest from the nearby railway line which led from Ekaterinburg to Perm. The shaft was thirty feet deep, and it was flooded with water when Nametkin visited the site. The duty of pumping the mine clear devolved onto his assistant, N. N. Magnitsky, but it was a long-winded job which required the use of a barge steam-engine.

There were three classes of Examining Magistrate in the Russian judiciary, and Nametkin belonged to the most junior class. The Ekaterinburg Public Prosecutor, Alexander Kutuzov, evidently decided that a case of this magnitude needed the services of a judge rather than an examining magistrate and approached the Ural Regional Court to provide one. Judge Ivan Sergeyev was chosen, and he was sworn in on 7 August 1918 and replaced Nametkin. Between 11 and 14 August, he carried out a further thorough examination of the Ipatiev House. It was under his jurisdiction that most of the important material discoveries were made and the mineshaft finally cleared. On searching it the investigators found nothing but cinders and miscellaneous debris, including the bones of a bird – the only bones to be found.

Sergeyev then interviewed all the available witnesses, including Mikhail Ivanovitch Letemin of the Red Guards at the Ipatiev House. Letemin had not been present when the shooting took place, but he had been told about what had happened by one of his colleagues, Andrei Strekotin. The priest who had said Mass for the Romanovs on 14 July, Father Storozhev, was also interviewed, but neither his companion, Deacon Buimirov, nor Father Meledin, who normally said Mass for the family, was interviewed. Perhaps neither of them was in Ekaterinburg at the time – there is no information on this point.

There were many stories to be checked from the mass of partial evidence available, including those tantalizing reports that were already in the hands of Prince Mirza. All of these, whatever their import, had to be followed up and analysed, and their reliability assessed. Sergeyev was to dismiss all of them as fabrications. He did not hurry to draw his conclusions, but allowed them to develop as the evidence was found. At the beginning of October he could not be at all definite in his findings. He told Sir Charles Eliot that:

He dismissed as fabrications all stories respecting discovery of corpse, confessions of soldiers who had taken part in the murder, and on the other hand all narratives of persons who declared that they had seen the Emperor after July 16th.

He would only say that on the whole he thought chances were 4 to 3 that the Emperor was dead.[1]

In December, however, Sergeyev gave an interview to Herman Bernstein, a journalist from the *New York Tribune*, to whom he said:

I do not believe that all the … people, the Tsar, his family, and those that were with them, were shot there. It is my belief that the Empress, the Tsarevich and the Grand Duchesses were not shot in the house. I believe, however, that the Tsar, Professor [*sic*] Botkin, the family physician, two lackeys and the maid, Demidova, were shot in the Ipatiev House.[2]

We must contrast this with the statement of his successor, Court Investigator for Specially Important Cases Nikolai Alexeyevich Sokolov, that Sergeyev had no doubt that all the prisoners in the Ipatiev House had been murdered. Sokolov stated that 'In his report No. 106, sent to the Supreme Command on 1 February 1919, and delivered to General Dietrichs, he stated this quite categorically.'[3]

Two points need to be made immediately. Sergeyev was dismissed on 23 January and had to surrender all his material to General M. K. Dietrichs, a staff officer at White headquarters who was now to direct the case. This was done on 25 January

1919 in the presence of Valery Jordansky, the official prosecutor. That would have been the time to submit a final report,
not after the material had been out of the judge's hands for six
days. And when Summers and Mangold located one of the original copies of the dossier in the United States, which was
supposedly a complete record, there was no report No. 106 in it.

Yet the most important question that arises is the most
obvious: what had happened between the interview with
Bernstein in December 1918 and late January 1919 which could
have so drastically altered Sergeyev's views? There is no record
of any new evidence to account for it and, in fact, Sergeyev had
begun work on a dramatic new lead when he was sacked – a lead
which certainly did not indicate that all of the family were murdered.

Behind Sergeyev's dismissal lay an ominous change in White
Russian politics. The chaotic mixture of 'governments' that had
sprung up in the aftermath of the Bolsheviks being driven out
was never going to fight the common enemy successfully. Most
of these authorities had banded together under two of the
most representative organizations, Komuch and the Provisional
Siberian Government (PSG). Komuch was an SR Government,
which held sway to the west of the Urals with its capital at
Samara. The PSG was an uneasy combination of Kadets and
conservative Siberian regionalists (*oblastniki*). The two governments existed in a state of rivalry – which inhibited the PSG from
helping the Komuch to resist the Bolshevik offensive which
eventually overwhelmed them.

Under pressure from the Allies and the Czechs, the rivals
agreed to work together. A state conference at Ufa led to the
creation of the Provisional All-Russian Government (PA-RG).
The new government formed a five-man Directory to act as its
executive, but this child of the enforced marriage was quickly
smothered by the military. On the night of 17 November, the
White army overthrew the PA-RG and the Directory in a military coup. The conspirators invited Admiral A. V. Kolchak to
head the new government – not because of any outstanding
abilities on his part, but because he was the only senior officer of
the old school who was in the area of the White's capital, Omsk.

The coup was, in effect, an illegal seizure of power which put the officers of the White army into power.

Shortly after the seizure of power, stories of how the Tsar and his family had met a grim end began to spill out from Omsk. The sea change was noted by the British, with Eliot reporting that the Vice Consul in Ekaterinburg stated that, at the end of November 1918, officials were coming to the conclusion that the whole family had been murdered as well as Nicholas.[4] Prince Lvov, the first head of state of the original Provisional Government, had also been a prisoner in Ekaterinburg and claimed that he had been in the cell next to the Romanovs when they were murdered. According to him, they had been tied to chairs and bayoneted repeatedly throughout the night before being finished off by revolver shots.

Yet Lvov had never been in the Ipatiev House, still less in a room next to the Romanovs: he had been confined in the city prison. The story could not stick, so a new version was contrived. This time Lvov claimed to have heard from an unnamed judge who was investigating the crime that the chances were 99 out of 100 that the family had been murdered. Apart from the contradiction between these two stories, there was only one judge working on the case – and his view, in October 1918, had been that the chances were 4 to 3 that the Tsar had been killed.

It was then announced that the entire family had been shot. The Whites produced statements by 'the Tsarina's manservant', who had been imprisoned by the Bolsheviks shortly before the murder but had succeeded in escaping. The whole story was riddled with the most ridiculous errors – including the claim that the facts of the murder had been established by a commission of inquiry appointed by the Siberian government and composed of two professors from Tomsk University and members of the Tomsk and Ekaterinburg judicial benches. There had never been a commission of inquiry, let alone one composed of such distinguished individuals.

Even more absurd was the creation of 'the Tsarina's manservant'. There was no such person in Ekaterinburg, never mind one who had succeeded in escaping from the Bolsheviks. There was only the old valet, Chemodourov, who neither escaped nor said anything remotely along these lines.

The stories emanating from Omsk grew increasingly sordid. On 5 December 1918 the French Secret Service were fed a report that the Romanov women had been tied to chairs and systematically raped and abused before being murdered. By the end of January, the story had been changed, but again the French were used as carriers of the news. Général Janin, head of the French Military Mission in Siberia, forwarded another blood-curdling account according to which the Tsar had been shot by a Lett called Biron, while the women were again repeatedly raped over several days before being murdered.

How Sergeyev reacted to this is unknown. He simply disappeared from the scene and was reputedly caught and shot by the Bolsheviks. Sokolov, his successor, was officially appointed to his new post on 7 February 1919 and began work on the material passed to him by General Dietrichs. He did not reach Ekaterinburg until the end of March.

It is important to note, before going any further, that the Judicial Inquiry never actually produced a report. Findings based on its work – or, more accurately, some of its work – were eventually published in two books, respectively written by Nikolai Sokolov and General M. K. Dietrichs. The latter exerted a powerful and not always benevolent influence on the case. He had been with the Czechs when they captured Ekaterinburg and was an officer of the old regime, a reactionary and devoted monarchist. His relationship with Sokolov was a peculiar one, the roots of which lay in the tangle of White Russian politics. In January 1919 he was a staff officer with the White high command and directed the judicial inquiry. It may seem odd that a military officer should have any sort of power to intervene in a case conducted by the civilian judiciary, but White rule in Siberia was far closer to a military dictatorship than a Western democracy. Although Dietrichs and Sokolov were in broad agreement, there were differences between them which later culminated in the General forcibly seizing Sokolov's files and such material evidence as he had collected during the White retreat in Eastern Siberia. Many of the files were returned to Sokolov later but several remained in the General's possession. Even today their whereabouts are unknown except to a small group of White Russians – one of whom, N. G. Ross, was permitted to publish a book based on this collection in West Germany in 1987.

Sokolov remained in Ekaterinburg until July 1919, when the surviving Whites fled from the advancing Red army. He continued to work on the case even after he, like so many other White Russians, had been driven into exile. He died in France in 1924.

In Ekaterinburg, he conducted another search of the Ipatiev House between 15 and 25 April, during which bullet holes, bloodstains and graffiti were found which the earlier investigators had – apparently – missed.

Three more of the Red Guards who had been on duty at the house were found and interrogated, two of them by Sokolov. These were Philip Proskuryakov, who was interrogated between 1 and 3 April, and Anatole Alexandrovitch Yakimov, who was subjected to the same process between 7 and 11 May. Like Letemin, neither man had been an eyewitness, and they could only relate what they were told by other guards. But the gist of the testimony was the same – that the whole family had been cold-bloodedly murdered.

One further guard, Paul Spiridonovitch Medviedev, was in a different category. He claimed to have actually seen the corpses of the victims immediately after the killing – but typhus carried him off and deprived Sokolov of the chance of interrogating him in person.

The scientific reports on the bullets and stains found in the house now came into Sokolov's possession, but they added little real knowledge beyond the types of weapons which were used and the fact that human blood had been spilt in the room.

Most of Sokolov's work, however, was concentrated around the Four Brothers Mine area where the burnt debris had been found earlier. He expected to find the remains of the family here, for as he told the family's French tutor Pierre Gilliard, the Reds had had four days in which to dispose of the bodies. It was common practice among the Bolsheviks to dispose of the bodies of assassinated enemies by dumping them down a mineshaft and then hurling grenades or other explosives down on them. This is precisely what had happened to the indisputably royal victims at Alapaevsk – Grand Duke Serge Mikhailovitch, his secretary Theodor Romez, the Grand Duchess Elizabeth Feodorovna, and the three sons of the Grand Duke Constantin Constantinovitch, John, Constantin and Igor, together with a nun, Barbara Yakovlevna.

From 23 May to 17 June a concentrated search was conducted of the mine and its immediate area. Additional debris was found, but although such high expectations hung on the search the results were disappointing. The next stage was to extend the area of the search, and a zone of twenty hectares around the mine was subjected to a methodical search from 6 June to 10 July. Again, the results were worthless. Nevertheless, there was what appeared to be one stroke of luck – on 25 June the body of Jemmy, the Grand Duchess Tatiana's dog, was found at the bottom of the shaft.

This was the only corporeal find that could indisputably be attributed to the Romanovs. Various bones found could only draw the opinion from an expert that he 'could not exclude the possibility that they might be human'. A finger which, Sokolov claimed, was the Tsarina's, and the upper part of a set of false teeth, which were believed to have belonged to Dr Botkin, did not amount to conclusive evidence.

Ultimately Sokolov felt justified in concluding that the whole family had been murdered in the early hours of 17 July 1918 in the Ipatiev House. Besides the remains mentioned above, he based his conclusion on a degree of coincidence in dates; the testimony of the four Red Guards; the debris at the mine; the marks and stains in the Ipatiev House; evidence that a heavily laden lorry had passed along the track from the city to the mine and back; and a telegram in which the chairman of the Regional Soviet told the Secretary of People's Commissars in Moscow that the family had shared the same fate as its head. As for the failure to find the bodies, Sokolov explained that the murderers had destroyed them without trace by incinerating them in petrol and acid. According to Sokolov, Yurovsky was the man responsible for the murders. Since the 1920s this has been the orthodox account of the end of the Romanovs.

The Sokolov version was reinforced by the fact that Yurovsky boasted of killing the family for the rest of his life, and it received startling confirmation when, in 1989, the Soviet Union permitted the publication of his official account in the West. In November that same year another two accounts of the murder, by the Lett brothers Alexei and Mikhail Kabanov, were published by *Komsomolskaya Pravda*.

Despite this seemingly unimpeachable evidence, the orthodox doctrine has not escaped serious criticism, not least because of the flaws and contradictions in the evidence. We must now turn from the orthodox doctrine to the heretical accounts.

6

THE HERETICS

It is hardly surprising that the orthodox view of the fate of the Romanovs has attracted a good deal of criticism, if only because Court Investigator Sokolov left so many loose ends and so many unanswered questions that any genuinely critical reader could not fail to have profound reservations about his conclusions. Part of this no doubt was due to the exceptionally difficult conditions under which the investigation laboured, but even after allowance has been made for that, weaknesses remain in both the evidence and his treatment of it.

The most comprehensive modern criticisms have been made by the American lawyer John F. O'Conor, whose *The Sokolov Investigation* first appeared in 1971, and the investigative journalists Anthony Summers and Tom Mangold, the authors of *The File on the Tsar*. To an extent both books rehearse some of the familiar alternatives to the orthodox position, yet both present solid grounds for reopening the debate. The most important of these is the undeniable fact that Sokolov deliberately suppressed material evidence which contradicted the chosen position. While this suppressed evidence does not necessarily prove a case for the survival of the Romanovs, it does mean that the conduct and conclusions of the investigation are highly questionable.

39

The fundamental flaw in Sokolov's case lay in that his instructions dictated his findings from the very start. Whereas his predecessors investigated what had happened to the Romanovs, he was ordered to prove that they had been murdered. In his book Sokolov quotes Admiral Kolchak's order to this effect:

> By these presents I order all places and persons to fulfil, absolutely and precisely, all lawful demands of Court Investigator for Specially Important Cases SOKOLOV, and to assist him in the fulfilment of the duties imposed upon him by my command in connection with the conduct of a preliminary investigation of the murder of the former Emperor, his family, and of the Grand Dukes.
>
> Admiral Kolchak[1]

Sokolov was not, then, an impartial and even-handed investigator. There was no case for him to investigate other than murder, which made him less an investigator than a prosecuting counsel. This was in keeping with the drift of White politics of the time, as evidenced by the clumsy murder stories that were circulated from Omsk in December 1918, and the reaction to a White officer, Gregory Ptitsin, who submitted an Intelligence report to Kolchak's headquarters in 1918 which cast doubt upon the massacre theory. According to Ptitsin,

> I reported what I had learnt to the commanding admiral who said we were all to assume that the Tsar had been killed, and hoped that would stop all the jerks searching for him. We were told to tell everyone he was dead, and that's what we continued to do.[2]

No doubt Kolchak preferred to sweep the whole Romanov case under the carpet while he got on with the serious business of winning the civil war and creating a new and virile Russia.

The heretics could point to a number of serious flaws in examining Sokolov's evidence. The testimonies of the guards were at odds in many important respects – including no less than five entirely different versions of the last words said to the Tsar, the timing of the shootings, the positions in which the victims were standing or sitting, the means by which the corpses were carried out of the house, and the appearance of the victims.

The key witness who was actually supposed to have seen the bodies is arguably the most unconvincing of all. Paul Spiridonovitch Medviedev surrendered to the White army outside Perm at Christmas 1918 and, we are asked to believe, promptly confessed to his part in the murders. He died in prison on 25 March before Sokolov could interrogate him, and there are three different explanations of his death. Officially he died of typhus, but Summers and Mangold found that a Staff Captain Belotserkovsky told a friend in exile that 'I hit him once too often'; on the other hand Sir Thomas Preston, who was the British Consul in Ekaterinburg and worked closely with the Whites, told them that Medviedev's confession had been extracted by torture, which eliminates it from consideration as reliable evidence.[3]

Medviedev is supposed to have been interrogated twice, and Sokolov prints the transcripts of two interrogations in his book. There is some confusion over when the second interrogation actually took place, but more suspicious than that is that it was reputedly undertaken by Sergeyev, who had been sacked a month previously. When and how did he conduct a second interrogation? Was there in fact a second interrogation?

Summers and Mangold presented convincing evidence that there was not, in the shape of an anxious letter from Prosecutor V. F. Jordansky, who was keeping a watching brief on the case for Nikander Mirolyubov, the Public Prosecutor of the Kazan Court, under the jurisdiction of which Ekaterinburg fell. The letter, written on 28 March 1919, posed the question of whether there had been something underhand about the unaccountable death of such a key witness, and finished by observing that 'this is also unsatisfactory because, although he was questioned thoroughly according to what facts were known at the time, he should have been questioned a second time ...'[4]

Sokolov's discovery of bullets, bullet holes and blood stains which had escaped Sergeyev's notice also falls under suspicion. It was not simply a case of Sergeyev having failed to notice them, but three independent British observers must have missed them as well – Sir Charles Eliot, Consul Preston and Captain Francis McCullagh, an Intelligence Officer attached to the Whites. Similarly, more blood stains appeared in the accounts of supporters of the massacre theory than were seen by any of the other witnesses.[5] It was also discovered that Pierre Gilliard, the family's French tutor, had altered his original account of the condition of the murder room and confessed to destroying documentary evidence of value to the case.[6]

One fact that argues powerfully against any of this being accidental is the close involvement in the case of Robert Wilton, as an aide to Sokolov and an ardent supporter of the massacre theory. Wilton was a correspondent for *The Times* in Siberia, but he was more than that. Summers and Mangold were able to examine his staff file at *The Times* which showed that he had travelled to Siberia with the co-operation of British Military Intelligence. They also found a letter from Brigadier-General Sir George Kynaston Cockerill, Director of Special Intelligence, informing the newspaper's editor that 'the object of his journey is political', and that Wilton had been sent £1,100 through government channels.[7]

Wilton's presence and influence might have been no more than passing interest had he not quarrelled publicly with Commandant Joseph Lasies at Ekaterinburg Station. A French Deputy and, like Wilton, a journalist, Lasies was also a member of the French Military Mission and was conducting his own inquiries into the Romanov case. Their fiercely contrasting views came to a head in an angry exchange on the station platform on 18 May 1919, with Lasies arguing that the massacre theory's biggest weakness was the complete absence of bodies. Wilton walked away, apparently at a loss for an answer, but then came back to explain the disappearance of the bodies with the claim that the Bolsheviks had destroyed them with fire and acid – precisely the same conclusion that Sokolov was to reach.

That Sokolov and Wilton were working in conjunction with the complicity of the British Foreign Office is made clear in Sokolov's report to Mr Bannon of that ministry, now held in the British Library. He wrote: 'I feel compelled to tell you that I particularly consider it necessary to draw attention to the confidential nature of my information as I am still engaged in similar work and have in my possession other information which is not known to Robert Wilton.'[8]

Wilton went on to shout to the still sceptical Lasies, 'Commandant Lasies, even if the Tsar and the imperial family are alive, it is necessary to say that they are dead!' What, if anything, did Wilton's connection with Military Intelligence have to do with this extraordinary outburst?

Destroying the bodies by fire and acid was certainly a novel way of dealing with the major flaw in the massacre theory – the absence of the bodies – and it was one which Sokolov found acceptable. In fact it is scientific nonsense. It was physically impossible for anyone to destroy so much flesh and bone by these methods in the time available to the Bolsheviks, and it is amazing that so many apparently intelligent people were prepared to accept such an explanation.

Much of the same can be said about the discovery of the body of the Grand Duchess Tatiana's dog, Jemmy, at the foot of the Four Brothers mineshaft on 25 June 1919. The investigators claimed that it had been dumped there after being slaughtered by the Bolsheviks, though why they should have done so when pyres fuelled by acid and petrol, allegedly capable of utterly destroying eleven human bodies, were immediately available is a question that has never been answered. Summers and Mangold showed that it was impossible for the body of the dog to have been so well preserved had it been slain by the Bolsheviks. Its condition suggested that it was killed only a week or two before it was found – in other words, that the dog had been killed and planted by the Whites to provide 'evidence' for the gullible.[9]

The possibility of further White disinformation is suggested by the telegram from Alexander Beloborodov, the chairman of the Regional Soviet, to Nikolai Gorbunov, the secretary of the Council of People's Commissars in Moscow, announcing the deaths of the whole family. The telegram reads: 'Tell Sverdlov family suffered same fate as head officially family will die in evacuation.'

As O'Conor observed in *The Sokolov Investigation*, the

precise meaning hinges on where the punctuation is placed.[10] If a full stop is placed before the word 'officially' then the message reads that the family was killed, but the excuse for their deaths would have been that they perished – perhaps by accident or while trying to escape – during the evacuation of the city. Alternatively, if the full stop is placed after 'officially', it reads as if they were 'officially' killed along with Nicholas, but in fact were to be murdered elsewhere. Whichever the case, the word 'officially' indicates that the story of the death of the Romanovs was going to involve a deception.

The real significance of the message is that it was never acted upon, in either context. At no stage did the Bolsheviks in either Moscow or Ekaterinburg make any official statement about the death of the family, during the evacuation or at any subsequent time during 1918. The only official statement was that the wife and son of Nicholas had been taken to a safe place. If the telegram was genuine, what happened to the 'official' statement about their deaths? The telegram suggests that the version to be fed to the public was planned and arranged between Ekaterinburg and Moscow, and that the timing of the subsequent communiqué would not permit any change in the arrangements. Was the telegram another White invention?

Summers and Mangold found evidence to suggest that it was. The text of the message was out of alignment with the heading, which would not have been the case had they been typed at the same time by the same person. The message carried Beloborodov's handwritten signature at the foot: it does not match the only other example of his signature known to us – quite apart from which, telegrams do not transmit handwriting. Despite this, the telegram – with its impossible handwritten signature – is, according to Edvard Radzinsky, in the former Soviet archives. It was never entered in the outgoing cables book, which would normally have been the case. Finally, the telegram remained undeciphered until September 1920, even though the code was well known. What lends suspicion to the whole affair is that Sokolov was able to advise the man who eventually succeeded in decoding it that the words 'family' and 'evacuation' would probably appear in it. These words were not used by the

Bolsheviks in their other communications, so it is reasonable to ask whether Sokolov knew the content of the message in advance because it was a White forgery.

The most important revelation made by the heretics was that Sokolov and his colleagues had deliberately suppressed a mass of information which indicated that the Romanovs had not been murdered but secretly moved from Ekaterinburg, and that the women at least had reached Perm, just to the west of the Urals. Much, if not all, of this material was found in the Sokolov dossier by Summers and Mangold. Had Sokolov found this evidence unconvincing or wanting, he would have been obliged to point out its flaws. He did not. The evidence was simply suppressed.

There were accounts from witnesses which spoke of the family being moved by rail from Ekaterinburg during the night of 16–17 July 1918, but none was nearly so convincing as a body of testimony which reported the Romanov women in the city of Perm after that date. A nurse, Natalya Mutnykh, swore she had seen the Tsarina and her daughters in Perm in September 1918. She was interrogated three times, and during her final interrogation, on 2 April 1919, she said she had seen the Tsarina and three of her daughters in Berezin's rooms on Obvinskaya Street in Perm.

Ivan Girschfeld, a German refugee, had been told that two of the Tsar's daughters were being held in Perm, but he had not seen them himself and his testimony was weakened by the fact that it was uncorroborated hearsay.

The wife of one of the communists who was allegedly guarding the women, Glafyra Malyesheva, said she had seen one of the Tsar's daughters and had Romanov napkins in her possession. The girl she had seen had been pointed out to her as one of the Romanovs – though in all probability Glafyra Malyesheva would have been unable to tell a female Romanov from any other well-to-do young lady of the time, while the napkins could easily have been looted from the Romanov possessions in Ekaterinburg.

There was also a history teacher, Yevgeniya Sokolova, who had heard from the families of leading communists that the

Romanov women were in the city, but like Girschfeld's statement this was uncorroborated hearsay.

Several witnesses, however, spoke of an unusual incident on the railway at Siding 37, to the north-west of Perm, where a young woman was recaptured after an escape attempt. She was reputed to have been the Grand Duchess Anastasia, the youngest of Nicholas's daughters. There were no less than eight witnesses to this, so there is no doubt that an incident of some kind had occurred. The witnesses were Maxim Grigoryev, Tatiana Sitnikova and her son Fyodor, Ivan Kuklin and Matrina Kuklina, Vassily Ryabov, Ustinya Varankina and the doctor who treated the captured woman afterwards, Dr Pavel Utkin.

Can we trust all this evidence to the effect that the Romanov women had been moved to Perm? Certainly much of it needs to be viewed with considerable caution. The testimony of Girschfeld and Sokolova was founded on hearsay, and Girschfeld spoke of only two of the daughters being in Perm. Mutnykh and Malyesheva were both related to communists, Mutnykh's brother being the secretary to the Ural Regional Soviet, while Malyesheva's husband was a local communist. Neither of them was in a position to identify the women they saw personally, and both relied on what their menfolk are supposed to have told them – and it is as well to remember that every kind of rumour and fantasy about the Romanovs abounded in Russia at this time. And all too often, of course, prisoners will tell their interrogators what they think they want to hear. The two women could well have latched on to one of the rumours and accepted what they were told in that light.

Malyesheva's account gains some support from her mother-in-law having confirmed that her son had told her that the Tsar's family were held in Perm – but her testimony is vague, and her son did not give her any concrete details, replying to her questions about where they were that they were kept 'in rooms'. It is hardly conclusive evidence.

The witnesses to the incident at Siding 37 present a far stronger case. None of them was a communist, but neither were they in a position to identify the young woman independently. Nevertheless, Tatiana Sitnikova and her son were told by the Red troops,

for what it is worth, that the young woman was Anastasia, and
some of the witnesses picked out Anastasia from a collection of
photographs. It is of course possible that the soldiers were
playing a joke on credulous peasants or that they actually
believed the young woman was Anastasia – but that cannot be
said about Dr Utkin's testimony.

Dr Utkin had treated a young woman at Cheka headquarters
in September 1918, at the very time that the incident at Siding 37
took place. His patient identified herself to him by saying, 'I am
the daughter of the ruler, Anastasia.'[11] The description he gave to
the Whites bore a reasonable similarity to Anastasia, and there
was no question that he did treat some young woman: his
prescription was traced in the chemist's shop and, as the doctor
had claimed, the mystery patient was identified solely by the
letter 'N', a technique Dr Utkin had resorted to on the
instructions of the Cheka.

This did not in itself make his patient Anastasia and even if she
had been who she said she was, that did not prove that the other
Romanov women were in Perm with her. There were frequent
cases of young Russians passing themselves off as members of
the imperial family. One individual, Boris Soloviev – an
embezzler who was married to Rasputin's daughter and almost
certainly betrayed monarchist organizations to the Bolsheviks –
made a profitable business out of pretending that the Romanovs
had escaped. On that basis he persuaded several prosperous
Russians to part with substantial sums in order to help members
of the 'family' escape to China, even going so far as to provide a
young woman to play the part of a grand duchess departing for
safety for the benefit of those he so ruthlessly gulled.

Be that as it may, the crucial fact is that Sokolov suppressed
all this evidence – perhaps because it had been discovered by the
rival CID, though in view of his connection with the British
through Robert Wilton it is unlikely that that was the only
reason. The Perm testimony *is* valuable up to a point, but so
much of it is partial, circumstantial or open to different
interpretations.

In 1991 a grave was discovered in the forest outside
Ekaterinburg and it was claimed that this was the grave of the

47

Romanovs. If it is, then it means that the heretics were wrong. There are, however, good reasons which indicate that the remains are not those of the imperial family. The grave was located from the protocol or testimony written in 1920 by Yakob Mikhailovitch Yurovsky, the family's last jailer and ultimately their executioner. It is worth looking at this protocol, for it includes evidence that everything might not be so clear-cut.

Yurovsky wrote that the execution was carried out on orders from Moscow which reached him in a coded telegram on the early evening of 16 July 1918. The story behind this telegram is important, for Edvard Radzinsky found a telegram from the Regional Soviet at Ekaterinburg to the TsIK which had been received on 16 July 1918. It informed Moscow that the execution of the Romanovs could no longer be postponed because of the precarious military situation. Civil war was raging, the Czecho-slovak Legion and the White Russians were closing in on Ek-aterinburg and the Bolsheviks were preparing to evacuate the city.

There was no record of any reply, other than Yurovsky's state-ment, but Radzinsky's researches led him to an obscure journal, *Construction Gazette*, in the issue for 11 August 1957 of which he discovered an article about Alexei Akimov, who had been Lenin's bodyguard. One of Akimov's duties was to carry Lenin's particularly important telegrams to the telegraph office and to bring back a copy of the telegram and the telegraph tape. On one occasion, the article stated, he had asked for the copy and tape but the operator had refused to surrender them, and Akimov had forced him to give them to him at pistol point.

Radzinsky then tracked down Akimov's autobiography in the Museum of Progress Factory in Kuibyshev. In it Akimov wrote that the telegram in question was the order from Sverdlov to kill the Romanovs. What gives rise to doubt about this story is the melodrama of Akimov having to threaten the telegraph operator with his pistol. Why did the operator refuse to surren-der this particular message and no other? It is unlikely that he could have read the message as it was in code, nor is it probable that he was privy to the secrets of the code. The story simply does not ring true.

Yurovsky said that one of the guards tried to finish off one of the daughters with his bayonet, but was unable to pierce her corset. The story of at least one of the girls being bayoneted to death is not new, and it contains one weakness which casts doubt over the story. The corset stays of the Romanov women were found by the Whites after they had captured Ekaterinburg, and none of them bore any signs of violence. Yet Yurovsky is specific on this point, as are other Red Guards whom Radzinsky quotes.

When writing about the disposal of the victims' bodies by the Bolsheviks, Yurovsky says that when they were transporting the corpses by lorry to their eventual resting place, they came across a group of 'about' thirty-five people who turned out to be members of the Ural Executive Committee, and who themselves were expecting to kill the Romanovs. It was they who began loading the bodies onto horse-drawn carts, on which they were to carry their grisly cargo into the forest. In other words, there were thirty-five other individuals who not only saw but handled the bodies. It is inconceivable that they would have been able to keep silent about such sensational news, which would have spread throughout the city like wildfire: yet neither the Whites nor any of the foreign consuls in the city reported such a story. Nor is it at all clear how the members of the committee came to learn that the Romanovs were to be killed when the decision to murder the Romanovs was supposed to be secret.

The most obvious flaw in Yurovsky's protocol occurs when the burial party reached a disused gold pit after the lorry had got stuck in mud near the village of Koptiaki, on its way to the intended burial spot. Here, according to Yurovsky, the bodies were stripped and dumped into the pit which was, he tells us, 3½ *arshine* (8 ft 2 in) deep – one can only marvel at the murderer's precision in this matter. Hand grenades were then dropped on the bodies to tear them apart. In fact eleven bodies would have filled a sizeable proportion of the available space in a pit of this size; had hand grenades been lobbed in at random, as these allegedly were, they would turn the bodies – and the bones – into bloody wreckage.

Grenades achieve their effects in two ways – by blast and by the splinters torn from the disintegrating case. Three levels of damage would have resulted: there would have been pocking of the skin, similar to the damage caused by the pellets of a shotgun fired from some distance; there would have been heavier pocking of the bones, and in some cases the bones would have been thoroughly holed, with long cracks appearing in the skulls and teeth knocked out; finally, there would have been still heavier wreckage, with some parts of the bodies being simply blown away. The only human remains which were found in the vicinity of the gold pit were part of a finger and the top half of a set of false teeth which had reputedly belonged to Dr Botkin.

I consulted an expert in the British army, who has seen the effects of blast on the human body in Northern Ireland and the carnage wrought by grenades in training accidents. Given the circumstances outlined by Yurovsky, he said that it would have been impossible for all the skulls to escape undamaged, and that at least four of them would bear obvious traces of fragmentation damage, with any head which was near the detonation being completely blown away. None of the skulls or bones found in the forest grave bear the marks of such damage.

Lyudmila Koryakova, the archaeologist who directed the work in the forest, told the *Sunday Times*, which broke the story in the West in May 1992, that

It is clear that those shot were lying down at the time. One of the skulls shows a bullet wound through both temples. There are traces of blows from bayonets. The facial parts of the skulls are destroyed, many bones are broken, while others [are] crushed as though a lorry drove over them.[12]

The damage to the faces is commensurate with their being beaten by rifle butts, but Yurovsky does not say that this was done to the Romanovs. What is squarely at odds with Yurovsky's account is the categorical statement that the victims were lying down at the time. It is also at odds with every other account of the murder. Yurovsky wrote that two chairs were brought into the murder room and the ailing Alexei, the Tsar's son, sat down on one while the others were made to stand in a row. All the various accounts of the murder have the majority of the victims standing up, though some maintain that two or three of them were sitting down. Yet here it is *clear* that they were all lying down. It is likely that the excavation team has discovered the remains of some of the hundreds of other victims of Bolshevik murder at the time.

These are the third set of supposed Romanov remains to be found in the same forest in nearly as many years. First off the mark, in 1989, was Geli Ryabov, a former policeman in the Ministry of the Interior turned thriller-writer. Using Yurovsky's protocol, he traced a collection of bones which he maintained were the remains of the Romanovs, though it soon became clear that they were not. In July 1991 nine skeletons were found by an official search team led by none other than Lyudmila Koryakova. The team, formed from senior scientists, lawyers, historians and police, worked under an armed guard in the same area in which Ryabov had made his discovery. Forensic scientists claimed that the quantity and quality of the find was such that they could conduct tests which would make it possible to say for certain whether the remains were those of the Romanovs. Vadim Viner, a historian investigating the fate of the Russian royal family for a society of New-York-based Russian aristocrats, was sceptical about this find as well as that of Mr Ryabov. He believed that the bones found by the official search team were those of an industrialist and his family who were murdered and their bodies dumped outside the city in a deliberate attempt to deceive investigators. In any case, two bodies are missing from this find as eleven people were supposed to have been murdered in the Ipatiev House.

The May 1992 discovery turned out to be the same bones as those found in July 1991 and presented as a dramatic new discovery. The publicity surrounding this latest find skirts the fact that the remains have been subjected to extensive forensic tests, and apparently finds nothing odd in the fact that after nearly a year the only evidence of identity that the scientists can produce are a series of computer projections which cannot be considered conclusive evidence.

Two aspects of this matter need to be borne in mind. The whole business was engineered by former communist politicians to try to exorcise their own murderous past and ease the transition of the new Russia into the community of modern states, and anything which could help secure support for their bid to join the Western world would be welcome. Those involved were, until very recently, loyal communists, and it is unlikely that they would be able to shed that culture in the space of so short a time. The new presentation of this old material is no more than old wine in new bottles and needs to be regarded with considerable scepticism.

The story took a new twist when, in June 1992, it was reported that two bodies were missing from the grave – that we were, in fact, back to there being nine bodies instead of eleven. The body of the fourteen-year-old Tsarevich was not among them, nor was the body of one of the daughters. The suggestion that a fourteen-year-old haemophiliac could have survived the treatment the family suffered on the night of 16–17 July 1918 really is stretching the point too far. There is not even a slight possibility that he could have survived.

Plans to reinter the bones with a majestic state funeral in St Petersburg are already far advanced, suggesting that these bones are to represent the Romanovs irrespective of whether they are their bones or not, and irrespective of whether all of the bones belong to the family. The Russians regard this as a symbolic act to mark the end of communism, and indeed the timing of these discoveries seems to have been dictated by reasons of state rather than by historical accuracy.

Ryabov's discovery was announced just as President Gorbachev was about to meet Queen Elizabeth II, Nicholas II's first cousin twice removed; the find of July 1991 came shortly before another meeting of the two leaders; and now, when Boris Yeltsin is desperately trying to restore his country and hoping for Western support, such remains – whosoever they are – assume a new importance.

If these remains are not those of the Romanovs, then the heretics still have a case and the Perm testimony lies at the heart of it. Summers and Mangold suggested that the key to the Perm testimony lay in the efforts that were being made by Imperial Germany to help the Romanovs, and that the women were kept alive as pawns in Soviet–German relations. This is not an entirely persuasive theory, but before we look into it we need to explore the tangled web of relations between Russia and Germany.

7

THE KAISER'S WILL

The treatment by Summers and Mangold of the Perm testimony – that some of the Romanovs were seen alive after they were supposed to have been murdered – hinges on the connection they drew between it and German attempts to aid the family. Their hypothesis was that the Bolsheviks kept the women alive for use as bargaining counters in Soviet–German relations, on the grounds that Germany would refrain from using her overwhelming military might to crush the infant workers' republic while there was still a hope that the Romanov women could be released into German hands. This was ultimately dependent on the character of the German Kaiser, Wilhelm II, whose code of chivalry excluded any idea that harm should come to his fellow sovereigns.

Wilhelm was related by blood and marriage to Nicholas II, but was even more closely related to the Tsarina, Alexandra, who was his first cousin; both of them were grandchildren of Queen Victoria. The two emperors wrote to each other frequently, but Wilhelm was not the easiest of relatives, and his tactlessness often offended the Romanovs. He was devoted to the idea of absolute monarchy and tried to influence his younger relative accordingly, but his advice was not always wanted or useful and was too often delivered in a patronizing manner. On one occasion Wilhelm nearly succeeded in upsetting the whole structure of alliances in Europe when he persuaded the crestfallen Nicholas to sign a secret treaty of alliance with him at Björkö in Sweden, on 24 July 1905, after the Tsar's humiliating defeat at the hands of the Japanese. However, the treaty did not meet with the approval of either emperor's ministers – Bülow, the German Chancellor, actually went through the motions of resigning to bring his royal 'master' to heel – and it came to nought.

Such an initiative was perhaps typical of the imaginative but unstable Kaiser. At once impetuous and indecisive, his character was summed up later by his former friend Prince Philipp zu Eulenburg-Hertefeld, who was to write:

> ...the Kaiser's hyper-vivacious nature in fact knows *only the superlative*. To him something is either: magnificent, splendid, incomparable – or: atrocious, infamous, intolerable. The intermediate notes desert him *entirely* (I mean if he is expressing his feelings), whenever he chooses his words. That is why his speeches always impressed *strongly* – and offended strongly.[1]

Wilhelm held romantic notions of chivalry, at least so far as his fellow sovereigns were concerned. It was this side of him, perhaps, that was stirred by an approach from the Danish royal family to help rescue the Tsar and his family after the March 1917 revolution. Wilhelm warned Kerensky that he would hold him personally responsible if so much as a hair from the head of the imperial family was harmed. He also let it be known to the Provisional Government that if the British sent a ship to carry the Romanovs to safety he would order his navy to refrain from attacking it, and he even offered to provide an honour guard.

Yet given the thousands dying in the trenches and the almost fanatical hatred of the Kaiser in Britain, it might have been wiser for Wilhelm to have contented himself with a simple offer of safe passage. As it stood, no British monarch or government could even consider the proposal, for while revolution had so far triumphed only in Russia, there were ominous stirrings in both Britain and Germany. Had co-operation between the two monarchs over a family matter such as this become public, the consequences could have been alarming.

Once the possibility of transporting the family to Britain had been abandoned, there was little more that Wilhelm could do, since Russia and Germany were still at war. A year later, however, with the Bolsheviks in power, a peace treaty signed between the Central Powers and Russia, and a German diplomatic legation resident in Moscow, the prospects of effective German help looked brighter. The surviving records suggest that Wilhelm had no intention of abandoning his relatives to the whims of the revolutionaries; indeed, as soon as the Treaty of Brest-Litovsk was signed, a German mobile column raced across southern Russia to Dulbert in the Crimea, where members of the imperial family, including the Tsar's mother and both his sisters, were being held. The column arrived just in time: a party of Bolshevik extremists from Yalta was attacking the château in which they were being held when the Germans arrived and drove them off.[2]

Nothing as dramatic as this occurred to Nicholas II and his family. The Kaiser's genuine concern for the Romanovs has led some to think that the peace treaty provided a secret means for effecting their release into German hands. Rumours long persisted that there was a secret codicil to the Treaty of Brest-Litovsk whereby the Bolsheviks were to surrender the family to the Germans. Wilton described how a member of the household at Tobolsk read gossip about it in a newspaper.[3]

The story was resurrected in 1971 by Peter Bessell, the former MP for Bodmin, who claimed that he had been given privileged access to American official documents which showed it to be true. His story was taken up by an American journalist, Guy Richards, in his book *The Rescue of the Romanovs*.

There do appear to have been secret clauses to the treaty, an account of which is to be found in the Public Record Office at Kew.[4] There were five such clauses, requiring the cancellation of a Bolshevik decree concerning land and private property, the disbandment of the Red Guards, the opening of a port to the

Germans in north Russia, the occupation of unspecified towns and districts by the Central Powers to ensure that the Bolsheviks complied with the peace terms, and the formation of a government which would have the confidence of the whole country and be able to regulate relations with foreign states.

No mention was made of the Romanovs, nor is it likely that a peace treaty between five states would involve itself with what had become by then largely a family matter. As it was, the Germans were unable to enforce the existing secret clauses listed, so it seems unlikely that – even if such a clause had existed – they would have been able to force the Bolsheviks to surrender the imperial family.

All the same, some Russians saw the Germans as potential saviours of their country from the ravages of the Bolsheviks, and many looked to the Kaiser to save both Russia and the Tsar. In April 1918, Count Benckendorff, the former Grand Marshal of the Tsar's court, wrote to the new German ambassador, Count von Mirbach, to request the Kaiser's direct intervention. Von Mirbach sounded less than impressed, judging by his reply: 'The fate of the Tsar is a matter for the Russian people. We now have to concern ourselves with the safety of the German princesses on Russian territory.'[5]

The 'German princesses' were the Tsarina and her sister, the Grand Duchess Elizabeth Feodorovna. The latter was a favourite of the Kaiser, and if any of the Romanovs seemed likely to benefit from German aid, she was the prime candidate. There were other German princesses who had married into the Russian imperial family and while the Germans did try to help them, their interest was centred on the Tsarina and her sister.

The German role has been the subject of much debate, but neither the supporters nor the opponents of the theory that the Germans had succeeded in keeping the Tsarina and her daughters alive appear to have consulted the official German records on the subject.

These show that von Mirbach had been as good as his word, assuring the German Foreign Office, on 11 May 1918, that he had approached the People's Commissars and been told that 'the German princesses will be treated with every consideration', and would not be subjected to unnecessary petty annoyances or threats to their lives.[6]

On 14 June 1918, he reported that members of the imperial family were obliged to go to the Crimea without delay, and that the Tsar's mother and the former Generalissimo, the Grand Duke Nikolai Nikolaievitch, were among those being sent.

Greater urgency was added to the German efforts by the Czech advance on Ekaterinburg and reports that there had been an attempt by counter-revolutionaries to free the imperial family, during which one or more members of the family had been killed or wounded. The information received by the German government over this episode highlights the major problem the Germans faced when trying to help the Romanovs – they had no independent sources of their own and were totally dependent on the Bolsheviks for all news. Joffe, the Bolshevik representative in Berlin, and Chicherin, the People's Commissar for Foreign Affairs, both assured the Germans that the Czechs had cut the telegraph and railway lines to Ekaterinburg and they had no information. It was only on 26 June 1918 that Chicherin told von Mirbach that the counter-revolutionary attempt had been crushed and the Tsar had not been injured.[7]

However, von Mirbach was assassinated on 6 July, and further negotiations about the Romanovs devolved upon Dr Kurt Riezler, a Bavarian career diplomat who had been a confidant of von Bethmann-Hollweg, the German Chancellor at the outbreak of war, and was now serving as counsellor in the Moscow Legation. Riezler was sick at the time and had much else on his hands beside which the Romanovs paled into insignificance.

The negotiations over the Romanovs do not merit so much as a mention in Riezler's diary or papers, which were published in 1972. The published version does, however, make clear that the Germans were deeply involved with Russian monarchists, Kadets and officers in plotting the overthrow of the Bolsheviks. Neither the German Foreign Office nor the army expected the Bolsheviks to survive. What needs to be emphasized is that July 1918 was a month of dire crisis for the Bolsheviks, during which their rule trembled on the brink of the abyss. The assassination of von Mirbach was the first indication of this, and it signalled an attempted coup by the Left Social Revolutionaries which almost succeeded. Chaos reigned in Moscow, and the Social Revolutionaries actually captured Felix Dzerzhinsky, the head of the Cheka. Only their failure to press home their initial advantage ruined their chance.

The day was saved by the timely intervention of the Letts in the shape of the Latvian Rifle Division, the crack unit of the embryonic Red army. Riezler described them as the praetorian guard of the communists, and considered that, apart from the matelots who were thoroughly revolutionized, they were the only worthwhile force the Bolsheviks had at the time, as the soldiers of the Red army were completely demoralized. Like other provincial units of riflemen, they had been raised for war service, but the combination of radical local traditions, German occupation of their homelands and insulation from the old army by their language led them to maintain their cohesion and discipline – their regiments were, in effect, the only homes these men had.

Their commander, Colonel Vatsetis, was summoned to an empty and gloomy Kremlin on the night of 6–7 July. Matters were at such a pass that Lenin faced him with a simple, direct question: 'Comrade, can we hold out until morning?'[8] Vatsetis moved quickly and decisively, regrouping his forces in the Moscow area and surprising the Left Social Revolutionaries with a speedy and effective counter-attack. Moscow had been saved, but the threat remained outside the capital.

Boris Savinkov – for long a revolutionary opposed to the Tsarist regime, but then the War Minister under Kerensky – had formed a corps of ex-officers into the 'Union for the Defence of Fatherland and Freedom', which seized and for a time held the provincial capital of Yaroslavl, a mere 175 miles from Moscow. A potentially greater threat came from Colonel Mikhail Muraviev, Chief of Staff of the Red Army on the Volga and a Social Revolutionary, who attempted to march his forces westwards against both the Germans and the Bolsheviks – only to be killed in a Bolshevik ambush.

Nor were these the only problems that the Bolsheviks were facing. The Right Social Revolutionaries and Mensheviks were aligning themselves with the Allies and the war against Germany, and the Bolsheviks themselves thought they would not survive. Riezler told Hintze that 'The Bolsheviks are dead' on 19 July,[9] but the representative of the German High Command in Moscow, the anti-Semitic Major von Bothmer, noted Trotsky's earlier comment of 13 June, '*Wir sind eigentlich schon tot*'[10] ('We are really dead already'). That two men on different sides of the fence could independently draw the same conclusion from the circumstances surrounding them speaks graphically of the Bolsheviks' plight.

The German Foreign Office documents show that the Germans were well aware of that plight and were seeking to mend their fences with the other political groups in Russia – only by fomenting a German-oriented counter-revolution could they hope to prevent the expected counter-revolution from being a complete triumph for the Allies.

One week after the murder of von Mirbach, the representative of the Foreign Office at the German High Command, Freiherr von Lersner, explained that everybody in Moscow expected the Germans to invade. Hopes were high among those on the right who favoured a German orientation for Russia, and Lersner reported, 'Should the German orientation indicate that they would strike against the Bolsheviks, could they calculate on receiving active German military help? You must say something positive to these people, otherwise you will lose all their confidence.'[11] The Germans spent the summer and autumn of 1918 toying with the various groups and ideas, but without ever deciding on any one plan.

One of the reasons why the Germans never got beyond this stage was the fact that they needed a quiescent Eastern front as much as the Bolsheviks needed peace with the Germans. The Germans had stripped the Eastern front of troops and sent them to the Western front, where they were fighting to give Germany overall victory in the war. Once Germany's military position in the West changed from the offensive to the defensive in the summer of 1918, the High Command needed every man it could get to stave off defeat. Von Hintze, the Under Secretary at the German Foreign Office, put his finger precisely on the problem when he countered arguments from the army for a new adventure in Russia:

> What, after all, do we want from the East? The military para-
> lysis of Russia. The Bolsheviks are doing a better and more
> thorough job of this than any other Russian party, and without
> our devoting a single man or one mark to the task. We cannot
> expect them or the other Russians to love us for milking their
> country dry. Let us rather be content with Russia's impo-
> tence.[12]

This fact dominated Germany's ability to do anything in Russia and demonstrates that the picture of helpless Bolsheviks trembling before overwhelming German military might is an oversimplification. That it is an oversimplification has an important bearing on the interpretation of the negotiations between the Germans and Bolsheviks over the Romanovs.

Court Investigator Sokolov tells us that, three years later, Riezler received him in Berlin on 14 June 1921 and 'acquainted' him with the contents of German Foreign Office files on the Romanov case. He gave him copies of four documents which Sokolov published: these indicate that negotiations continued, but their outcome is left firmly in the air. However, the German initiative went beyond these four documents and the files of the German Foreign Office enable the course and outcome of the negotiations to be charted.

After the communiqué announcing the shooting of the Tsar, Germany's Moscow Legation asked Berlin on 20 July 1918 whether an earlier approach to the Bolsheviks for favour for the Tsarina should be repeated with emphasis. It warned against extending these representations to the Tsarevich since the Bolsheviks were well aware that the German orientation sought to place the Tsar's brother, Grand Duke Mikhail Alexandrovitch, in the foreground as Tsarevich. Moreover, the Bolsheviks distrusted the Germans because of their support for counter-revolutionaries, which the Bolsheviks had learnt about from 'revealing communications' with the White General Krasnov.[13]

Yet continuing German pressure brought what appear to be important implications in respect of the Perm testimony, for Riezler reported on 24–5 July that:

> Chicherin said yesterday on my inquiry [that] we should look at whether the lives of the German princesses including the Tsarina had been secured, that he knew that the Tsarina had been brought to Perm. It is unlikely that Chicherin is telling the truth in this question. Chicherin avoided any assurance, he only meant she could not go to Italy until she was proved to be not guilty. The attitude of the government over this question was dangerous for the princesses.[14]

Riezler took immediate steps to confirm Chicherin's statement by requesting the Soviet government to pass on a telegraphic greeting from Princess Irene, the wife of the Kaiser's brother, Prince Henry of Prussia. However, three days later Riezler was telling the German Foreign Office that the Soviet government had to instruct the local Perm soviet to pass on the greeting, but the move could prove dangerous for the Tsarina. He would also try to find another means to pass the message on to Perm. No acknowledgement was ever sent to Princess Irene.[15]

It all has the appearance of a Bolshevik deception, and deception becomes all the more probable when we turn to Bolshevik statements about other members of the imperial family. On 31 July 1918, the new German ambassador to Russia – the former Chief Secretary to the Treasury, Helfferich – reported that the Soviet government had stated that Grand Duke Serge Mikhailovitch was in Perm.[16] In fact his broken body was lying in a mineshaft at Alapaevsk in Siberia.

The body of Grand Duchess Elizabeth Feodorovna – the favourite of the Kaiser – also lay there, yet the Germans had been told she was living, impoverished, at her palace in St Petersburg. This information reached a very high level, or so we might judge from a telegram sent to German friends of the Grand Duchess by the Kaiserin Augusta, which read: 'All cordial thanks and warmest greetings according to latest news Elizabeth [is] in very critical [and] helpless position because wealth confiscated.'[17] Indeed, Under Secretary von Hintze also wrote to the same friends, advising them that the Foreign Office lacked reports about the Grand Duchess but hoped that her poverty had been relieved through gold having been sent to her.[18]

Deception lay at the very heart of communist philosophy. We have already seen it in play when Yakovlev was duped. Yet it gained its impetus from the very highest level, for as Lenin remarked to Dzerzhinsky, 'The West are wishful thinkers, we will give them what they want to think.' This has been a trait reflected in all dealings with communist governments in the present century, a trait which has led to words being given a double meaning, as when 'peace' comes to mean the unopposed supremacy of the Soviet Union, or when corrupt party dictatorships are passed off as democracies. It should alert us to the probability of forgery in Soviet historical sources and the testimonies of the servants of the Soviet state.

Obvious Bolshevik prevarication over the issue continued. Riezler had been a sick man during the summer of 1918 and was eventually recalled in August. His replacement, Hauschild, continued the effort to free the Tsarina and her daughters. On 29 August he reported that he had again seen Karl Radek, an Austro-Hungarian subject from Galicia who worked as the Soviet Foreign Ministry's European expert. Chicherin, Hauschild said, had long been promising to put the matter of the release of the Tsarina and her children before the Central Committee but had never done so. Radek introduced a new factor into the negotiations by proposing that the Bolsheviks should receive compensation for releasing the Tsar's family in the shape of the Germans releasing Leo Jogisches, the Polish Social Democrat leader and Spartacist, who was under arrest in Berlin. Radek said he wanted to put the proposal before Lenin that same day and suggested that negotiations should be opened on that basis.[19]

Hauschild returned to the task on 10 September 1918. He was told that both Chicherin and Radek had no objection in principle to the release of the imperial family, but compensation would have to be found in the form of the proposal of 29 August. Hauschild stressed the need to bring the family to Moscow since they were exposed to danger in Perm from which the central government was powerless to protect them. Radek promised him that the Bolsheviks desired to do this and Hauschild observed, 'In the light of the growing influence that he has won, I hope that this step will be carried out.'[20]

Significantly, all reference to the imperial family being in Perm had been dropped by the Bolsheviks when Hauschild next spoke to them on 13 and 14 September. He spoke to both Chicherin and Radek, only to be told that they would have to investigate a report from the front that the Tsarina and her children had been lost in the evacuation of Ekaterinburg. Radek said – rather lamely, one imagines, in the light of his previous statements – that he 'supposed that the Red Guards with the mentioned prisoners, whereabouts still unknown, were scattered and that news of their present location on this side of the front would shortly be received'.[21] Hauschild forwarded this astonishing statement without commenting on the obvious contradiction between it and the information he had been given before.

Parallel negotiations were taking place in Berlin between officials of the German Foreign Office and Joffe, the Bolshevik representative. On 10 September Joffe repeated to Nadolny, the Foreign Office representative, that compensation would be required and, if the Germans were concerned about the Tsarina, then he could be equally concerned about Karl Liebknecht, the imprisoned Spartacist leader. Nadolny resolutely rejected this and suggested to his superiors that the Germans should stop pursuing the issue and leave it in the hands of the Spanish.[22]

Nadolny's reference reflected the fact that the German diplomatic effort had foundered and the Germans were now relying on neutral Spain to effect the release of the Romanovs. The first steps towards this end were taken by the King of Spain, Alfonso XIII, on 3 August 1918 – Ratibor, the German ambassador in Madrid, informed Berlin that King Alfonso was making a personal effort to obtain better conditions for the family.[23] However, his telegram did not reach Berlin until 5 August, and by then the Spanish ambassador in Berlin, L. Polo de Bernabé, had taken matters a stage further with a handwritten letter which offered the King of Spain's hospitality to the imperial family once their freedom had been achieved.[24]

The Spanish attempt seems to have been sabotaged from the start by the Bolsheviks. On 8 August Ratibor was again wiring to Berlin, this time to tell the Foreign Ministry that the Russian Military Attaché in Madrid was warning him that the initiative had not come from King Alfonso, but from the Allies who wished to have the Tsarina brought to them at Archangel, rather than see her pass into German hands.[25] However, the proposal came to naught as the King explained to Ratibor at an audience on 12 August. Alfonso explained that he could not achieve anything through the Entente powers since the Russian government lacked the desire to co-operate. The King also raised the question of the Romanovs in the Crimea, offering them refuge as well as the Tsar's immediate family.[26]

It was also on 12 August that the Kaiser – presumably after consulting the various other family members and other legitimately interested parties – agreed to Alfonso's proposal of hospitality for the Romanovs, perhaps hastened by two further approaches from the Spanish ambassador.[27]

Despite the King's suggestion to Ratibor on 27 August that vigorous steps should be taken in Moscow to hasten the move of the Tsarina and her children to Spain, diplomatic wheels still turned slowly. An unnamed official from the German consulate-general in St Petersburg told Berlin only on 26 August that he was now acting in combination with the messenger from the Spanish Legation there, and that they would be travelling to Moscow in the course of the week to open negotiations with Chicherin.[28]

The Spanish–German alliance on the issue increasingly turned on the fate of the four Grand Dukes – Paul Alexandrovitch, Nikolai Mikhailovitch, George Mikhailovitch and Dmitri Constantinovitch – arrested and confined in the Peter and Paul fortress in St Petersburg. Spurred by desperate appeals on their behalf from the Grand Duchess George in England and Queen Olga of Greece in Switzerland, attention was increasingly diverted from the Tsarina.

By the second half of September the joint attempt was looking increasingly hopeless and the Germans were ready to follow Nadolny's recommendation and pass responsibility to the Spanish. Under Secretary von Hintze summed up the position on 17 September 1918:

> The Russians have rejected our approach as interference in Russian affairs, unless we equally were to allow Russian intercession on behalf of certain troublesome personalities in Germany. This obviously has to be turned down. Besides, the authorized Russian representative, Herr Joffe, maintains that the Grand Dukes are not held as hostages but have been arrested for their own safety. Also, death sentences may no longer be handed out by local authorities, as has happened frequently to date, but only by the Centre in Moscow. According to our hitherto accepted experiences, our intervention would hinder rather than help the Grand Dukes, so we will leave it to the governments of the neutral states to intercede. With regard to the Tsarina, the Spanish intervention is not without prospects.[29]

No reasonable hope can be maintained that the Spanish attempt prospered. The surviving documents show that it petered out without receiving either a firm refusal or any degree of acceptance. The Bolshevik response that such appeals were interference in Russia's internal affairs were standard practice by this time. The Bolsheviks had played a dangerous game in biding their time until the Germans were quite unable to influence the situation, raising new obstacles at every stage, prevaricating in a Byzantine manner, and not once being open about the truth of the situation. It was a game they played well and won.

The testimony of the German agents Markov and Cornel which Summers and Mangold used to support the theory that some of the imperial family had survived the massacre in Ekaterinburg and were being moved about Perm province by the Bolsheviks is material that needs to be treated with considerable circumspection. Spies are not beyond telling their employers what they want to believe, nor are they above flights of fantasy. Had the testimony they supplied been valid then we would reasonably expect to see it reflected in the reports of the German Foreign Ministry, or in the correspondence with the Kaiser and other members of the Prussian royal family. It is noteworthy by its absence. Indeed, arguably the chief feature of the German documents is that they clearly show there was a complete absence of any form of independent information, that the Germans were, in fact, slaves of the Bolsheviks in this respect. Moreover, when we look at this form of testimony in the light of the evidence the Whites gathered in Perm – where so much of it came from communist sources – the suspicion grows that the Germans were fed what the Bolsheviks wanted them to believe. This is entirely in keeping with the experience of British Military Intelligence in the First World War, which consistently found the Germans clumsy and easily duped.

The limitations on what the Germans and the Kaiser could achieve were starkly displayed by the murder of the Tsar. They had been unable to do anything and were taken completely by surprise. At no stage did they resort to force or threaten to use it on behalf of the Tsar, nor did they do so on behalf of his family. German military supremacy was not unfettered and did not represent the overwhelmingly decisive position ascribed to it by Summers and Mangold.

Under the circumstances of July 1918, the Bolsheviks' decision to murder the Romanovs is readily understandable. Faced with the prospect of their own imminent destruction, they no longer had anything to gain from keeping these representatives of their class enemies alive. Threatened as they were in their own backyard, a symbolic blow against the symbols of the *ancien régime* made perfect sense. Once the situation had been restored, they could afford to play the Germans along, thus averting any consequences that the truth might have entailed.

Unhappily for Anna Anderson, the Anastasia claimant, there is nothing in the German files to suggest that Anastasia escaped. It might be argued that as the Germans had no independent source of news about what was happening in Ekaterinburg they would not have known whether Anastasia had escaped or not. That argument is sound so far as it goes, but information ought to have reached the Foreign Ministry from the German military commands through whose territory she would have had to pass if her escape route was as she described. There is nothing from Oberost, the German Headquarters in the East, that supports this and the file from the German army on the murder of the Tsar was – apparently – not deemed sufficiently important to warrant copying for British researchers. However, there is one other source where information might be expected to exist and that is in the files of the German consulate in Romania where the claimant stated that she had successfully made her identity known and where she allegedly lived in a property belonging to the consulate and gave birth to a son. The files of the German consulate in Romania are not large, and they contain not one reference to the Romanovs.[30] There is no mention of Anastasia, nor of any woman claiming to be Anastasia identifying herself to the staff of the consulate.

This was borne out by the murder of other Romanovs at Alapaevsk, the day after the murder of the Tsar and his family. The victims were the Grand Duke Serge, Grand Duchess Elizabeth Feodorovna, three sons of the Grand Duke Constantin Constantinovitch, Serge's secretary and a nun who was Elizabeth's constant companion. As we have seen, the Grand Duchess was one of the 'German princesses' referred to by von Mirbach, and a particular favourite of the Kaiser. Any prospect of successful German intervention was shown to be an empty promise by the murders at Alapaevsk.

8

THE VATICAN INTERVENES

Some of those who have doubted the official account of what happened to the imperial family have raised the possibility – based on some partial and rather scrappy evidence – that assistance for the Romanov women came from an unexpected quarter, namely the Vatican. Summers and Mangold felt that there might be something to it; since the story has never been properly investigated, it needs to be examined to see just how far the Vatican's interest went and whether it led to anything concrete, or whether it is merely another of the many red herrings that litter this case.

The files from the British Mission to the Vatican make it clear that the Holy See tried to persuade the Bolsheviks to release the Romanov women. The first hint that anything was being considered by the Pope reached Arthur Balfour, the British Foreign Secretary, in a telegram from the Count de Salis, the British plenipotentiary and ambassador extraordinary to the Vatican. That part of the message dealing with the Pope's initiative read:

Cardinal Secretary of State informed me yesterday that the Pope, preoccupied with regard to the fate of the Russian Grand Duchesses, was trying to obtain the liberation of the

Empress and her four daughters and their transfer to a safe place outside Russia; an appeal was being made to the Central Empires to support these efforts and the Pope was prepared to meet any expenses.[1]

De Salis told the Foreign Secretary that he had replied to the Cardinal Secretary of State, Cardinal Gasparri, that 'so far as I could judge steps to alleviate the position of the imperial family could not but be welcome to the King and to His Majesty's Government'.[2] The reply from London might best be described as laconic: 'Your telegram No. 46. Your reply approved.'[3]

It is worth noticing in passing that de Salis was a secret service diplomatist who was well connected to Europe's aristocracy. His son was to follow in his footsteps and a little more than twenty years later was to figure as the Duke of Windsor's aide-de-camp when the Duke toured secret French military establishments during the phoney war.

This correspondence took place one month after – according to the conventional wisdom – the Romanov family had all been brutally murdered. In itself that proves nothing, except that most people were keeping an open mind about whether the family were still alive or not – which, as we have seen, reflected the uncertain and confused situation which the Whites found in Ekaterinburg. What is curious, and unsettling, is that after this brief exchange there is no further communication on the subject in the British files. If the Foreign Office was being kept abreast of the progress of the Papal efforts – and we are entitled to assume they would be, given that such steps 'could not but be welcome' in Britain – then someone saw fit to ensure that no information reached the public about it.

There are, of course, other sources which can be consulted beyond those official British papers deemed suitable or harmless enough for the public to see. These sources reveal diplomatic activity on the Romanovs' behalf, involving participants as diverse as the queens of the United Kingdom and Spain, the imperial Austro-Hungarian government and the German empire. The involvement of Queen Mary, the wife of George V, provides positive proof that the House of Windsor did not abandon their Russian cousins to the tender mercies of the Bolsheviks, as the official record would have us believe. Since nothing has ever been released which sheds light on her initiative, the implication that material on the Romanovs has been deliberately withheld in Britain is inescapable. How far did this initiative go, how was it conducted and what else was being done besides?

In view of the secrecy still prevailing in Britain, the obvious channel through which to pursue this initiative is the Vatican itself. I was told that in 1968 the surviving documents concerning the case had been transferred from the Vatican's Secret Archives to the *Prima Sezione – Rapporti con gli Stati* of the Secretary of State's office. They were subsequently assigned to the *Seconda Sezione*, where they remain today.

The collection originally formed part of the former *Congregation Degli Affari Ecclesiastici Straordinari* (Concerning Extraordinary Ecclesiastical Affairs), and the present archivist, Monsignor Marcello Camisassa, tells me that the surviving papers are really only a small collection, a *posizione* or digest kept to illustrate the attitude of the Vatican. As a result, the collection is by no means as informative as the historian would like. The documents reflect the humanitarian stance adopted by the Pope, Benedict XV, formerly Cardinal Della Chiesa. A reformer who was bent on modernizing the Church, Benedict XV was particularly noted for his peace initiatives during the First World War and for his concern for prisoners-of-war, so his humanitarian approach towards the Romanovs was not unexpected.

According to the documents, the Papal initiative originated with the Czech man of letters, Jean Greméla, who was in exile in Paris. On 3 August he wrote to the Vatican to suggest that now the Tsar had been assassinated, the question of saving the family – including the 'celebrated generalissimo' the Grand Duke Nikolai Nikolaeivitch – needed to be faced. Greméla was clearly well informed, for he observed that the queens of Spain and England were adding their efforts in this direction, and he hoped that the Pope would add his voice to the pleas for clemency so that their collective intercession might lead to the liberation of the family.[4]

He went on to refer to another letter he had written to the Vatican in January 1918, in which he had appealed for Papal intervention on behalf of the Tsar and his family. The *posizione* does not contain this letter, nor does it allude to any action which may have been taken by the Vatican in response to it.

The fact that Britain's George V was not the kind of monarch who was prepared to throw his relatives to the wolves is reflected in the activity of his wife. Since we are denied British document-ary evidence of this initiative it is difficult to comment on it; suffice it to say that the King's protection was extended to sovereigns who were more distantly related to him than Nicholas and Alexandra had been, including some who had only recently been his enemies. The case of the Emperor Charles of Austria–Hungary substantiates this. In 1919 the young em-peror and his family were living in straitened circumstances in the Austrian countryside. Starvation was a real threat, as were marauding bands of discharged soldiers from the old imperial army, who now lived by plundering the countryside.

A British officer, Lieutenant-Colonel Edward Lisle Strutt of the Royal Scots, was sent to act as bodyguard for Charles and his family. His vigorous presence helped in many respects, even to the point of bending diplomatic propriety to ensure that Charles could leave the new Austrian republic without abdicating. This was achieved by threatening the Republican government with renewal of the wartime blockade unless they dropped their de-mand for abdication. Strutt had no authority whatever to threaten such a course.[5] George V extended his own personal protection to the family and sent three memoranda to the Holy See asking it to exert any influence it might have to restore Charles's former estates and property.[6]

None of this provides evidence that the King moved heaven and earth to help the unfortunate Nicholas and his family, but it does suggest that some steps were taken, and that these steps – whatever they might have been – were quite in keeping with the King's character and the context of the time.

Such of the Papal effort that is revealed by the archive resolved itself into two main channels. One was through Monsignor Val-prè, the Apostolic Nuncio in Vienna, and the other was through

Monsignor Pacelli, the future Pope Pius XII who was then the Apostolic Nuncio in Munich. Identical letters were sent to them on 11 August 1918, saying that 'the extremely sad fate' of the Tsarina and her daughters had aroused 'profound pity' in the heart of the Pope. Both were instructed to approach the governments to which they were accredited – Valprè the Austrian and Pacelli the German – asking them to use their good offices to secure the release of the family and their removal from Russia. Should they succeed, the Holy See might, if needed, look after the 'dignified maintenance' of the imperial refugees.[7]

The nuncios were sent another message which is not altogether clear and illustrates the problems of dealing with a digest, which is what the *posizione* represents. The text of the message reads: 'Your Holiness wishes to add also the name of the Dowager Empress Marie Feodorovna to the persons he recommended with my cipher No. 187.'[8]

It is not clear whether the Tsar's mother, the Dowager Empress Marie Feodorovna, had her name added as one of those who were appealing for mercy, or whether she was one of those for whom mercy was being sought. Since the telegram was sent in August 1918, it is likely to be the former, as by that time the Tsar's mother was living under the relative security provided by the Germans. What is unhelpful is the lack of information about telegram 187 – without No. 187 we cannot know who was asking for what.

Both Papal Nuncios pressed ahead with their tasks. By 13 August Valprè had consulted with Count Burian, the Austro-Hungarian Foreign Minister, and by 14 August Pacelli had written to Hertling, the German Chancellor. Burian informed Valprè that the kings of Spain and Denmark were already pursuing the subject, but that he would broach the matter with the Emperor Charles as 'the most desirable wish' and give him an answer.[9] Certainly, Germany was the strongest member of the Central Powers, but the Vatican preferred to deal with the Austrians, because the Dual Monarchy was a Catholic state. Pacelli wrote to Hertling on 12 August 1918 and his letter survives in the German Foreign Ministry files. It stresses that the plight of the imperial family had 'moved the heart of the Holy Father to profound sympathy' and explained that the Pope sought to liberate them and lodge them outside Russia. Pacelli went on to appeal for German support, but he may well have been disappointed in the reply he got. Under Secretary Baron von dem Bussche wrote to say that the King of Spain had already made an identical offer and had already taken steps with the Russian government to gain the desired result. Von dem Bussche promised to let the Pope know if the Spanish proposal succeeded; he was never able to keep that promise.[10]

It is clear from an exchange between Treutler, in the Royal Prussian Legation in Munich, Hertling and Pacelli in October 1918 that the Germans attached no weight to the Pope's initiative. Treutler wrote to Hertling to tell him that Pacelli had received a telegram from the Cardinal Secretary of State expressing astonishment that Under Secretary von Hintze of the German Foreign Ministry had not mentioned the Pope's request at a meeting of the Ministry's steering committee on 24 September, while he had dwelt on the pains King Alfonso had taken. The German reply was intended to be conciliatory, but it cannot have provided much satisfaction for either the Papal Nuncio or the Cardinal Secretary of State. It explained that the papal initiative was not regarded as illusory, but the King of Spain had acted 'a long time before' the Pope (in fact it was less than two weeks before). Under Secretary Hintze, the reply explained, had not mentioned the papal action as the discussion paper that had been prepared had been modelled around the King's proposal. Whoever wrote the letter – the signature is illegible – offered the further excuse that there had been recent changes in personnel at the Foreign Ministry and he hoped that the affair would calm down and not become the subject of any more official correspondence.[11] It provided cold comfort at best.

At this point direct evidence of the Vatican's efforts on behalf of the imperial family die away. Instead, the documents in the archive devote their attention to correspondence about the plight of the Grand Duke George, also a prisoner of the Bolsheviks. Von dem Bussche of the German Foreign Ministry informed Cardinal von Hartmann, Archbishop of Cologne, that proposals to alleviate the lot of 'The Grand Prince' had been forwarded to the Soviet government, which had rejected the intercession 'as an unwarranted interference in internal Russian affairs'. The Russians disputed that the Romanov princes were being held as hostages; rather, they argued, they were being held to protect them from the mob. The Soviet representative, however, was prepared to suggest to the People's Commissars that the imperial family be sent to the Crimea. Von Hartmann translated the message into Italian and forwarded it to the Cardinal Secretary of State.[12]

An unsigned letter of 21 September 1918 conveys the same message from the German Foreign Office – as does another of 29 September from Cardinal von Hartmann, who then goes on to discuss at length the security of Church property in the German-occupied territories on the Western front.

Correspondence between the British primate, Cardinal Bourne, and the Cardinal Secretary of State about the Grand Duke George, all of it from the month of October 1918, completes the contents of the archive. The only indication that it provides about the fate of the imperial family looks ominous. In a letter dated 28 October 1918 the Cardinal Secretary of State tells Bourne that the Pope had never ceased to be interested on behalf of the family and prayed that the Austro-Hungarian government would be able to contact informed Bolsheviks through its consul in Moscow; however, the Bolsheviks were failing to respond to these efforts, and the consul was having trouble getting details of the family's whereabouts. This letter coincides with Bolshevik evasiveness towards the Germans and their initiative. It seems reasonable to conclude that both the Vatican and the Germans were the victims of a smooth deception.

That the writing was obviously on the wall for both the German and Austro-Hungarian empires by October 1918 indicates that the Bolsheviks simply played for time and waited until the Central Powers were no longer in a position to influence the position through their military superiority. It does not, however, explain why records of correspondence between the Vatican, Valprè and Pacelli cease as early as August 1918. Summers and Mangold found newspaper reports which suggested

75

that the Vatican had achieved the impossible, and that Moscow had agreed to the release of the Tsarina and her daughters; Archbishop Freiherr Dr Repp was to make sure that the release was carried out as agreed and accompany the Romanov women to their new home.[13] Yet these newspaper reports were from August 1918 – and it is not as if newspaper reports are especially reliable, least of all in wartime. We may well ask why, if there was any truth in these reports, the Vatican continued the negotiations as late as October. Moreover, we have already had examples of the unreliability of reports from newspaper sources in the question of the murder at Ekaterinburg.

The likelihood that the Central Powers and the Vatican had been the victims of a calculated deception is reinforced by the fact that the Vatican officially recognized the White government in Siberia as the legitimate government of all Russia on 28 October 1918, just as the final papal efforts on behalf of the Romanov women were being recorded in the *Archivio*, and just as the Austrian consul in Moscow was making his last desperate attempts. That the Vatican should extend unequivocal recognition to the Bolsheviks' mortal enemy strongly suggest that it realized there was no hope left for its humanitarian approach and that the Romanovs were beyond all earthly help, however spiritually inspired its source.

9

TSAR IN WAITING

The Germans despised the Bolsheviks, but found them necessary allies in keeping their Eastern front quiet. The evidence from the German Foreign Ministry's files shows that they did not expect their uncomfortable allies to remain in power for very long and they were seeking new surrogates to take their place. There were few contenders as most Russians still regarded the Germans as enemies and loathed the humiliating peace of Brest-Litovsk. Opinion among politically active Russians had divided into two camps, the larger of which, known as the Allied orientation, pressed for the continuation of the war against Germany in conjunction with the Tsar's British and French allies, now joined by the United States. The smaller faction – the German orientation – was composed mainly from former officers and monarchists who felt that the best way to rid their motherland of the Bolsheviks was to form an alliance with Germany. One of the baits held out to them by the Germans was the restoration of the monarchy in Russia, but there was little unity on who was to wear the imperial crown.

Nicholas II had abdicated in favour of his brother, the Grand Duke Mikhail Alexandrovitch, who surrendered the throne himself within a matter of hours. He was known to be very ambitious

and had a better claim to the throne than any of the other contenders. However, he disappeared from his rooms in a hotel in
Perm on the night of 12–13 June 1918. Court Investigator
Sokolov concluded that he had been kidnapped and murdered by
the Bolsheviks in the forest outside the city that same night. His
English secretary, Brian Johnson, was supposed to have been
murdered with him. Sokolov's version received confirmation
from one of the murderers, Andrei Vasilievich Markov, who gave
his version of the murder to the head of the Perm (Communist)
Party Archives in 1965, one year before his death. It was found,
and extracts from it published, by Edvard Radzinsky.[1]

According to Markov's account the murders were the
brainchild of Myasnikov, the chairman of the soviet in the
nearby town of Motovilikha. Markov, the Chief of Police (V. A.
Ivanchenko) and two workers, N. V. Zhuzhgov and Kolpash-
chikov, organized the killing with the knowledge and complicity of the chairman of the provincial Cheka, P. Malkov.
Markov stated that Mikhail Alexandrovitch protested when the
gang entered his room and demanded that he went with them,
claiming he was ill and demanding to see a doctor and Malkov.
The murderers were not to be denied and forced the Grand Duke
out of the hotel where he was put into a phaeton, with Johnson in
another. A short way outside Perm, the vehicles were stopped
and Zhuzhgov ordered the victims to get out. Johnson was shot
in the temple by Markov as soon as he got out; the Grand Duke
was wounded by Zhuzhgov and ran towards Markov, begging to
be allowed to say goodbye to Johnson. Markov shot him in the
head at close range. The bodies were hastily concealed under
twigs, until Zhuzhgov and 'a very reliable policeman' returned
to the site and buried them the next night. At the end of the
interview, Markov told the archivist that he went to Moscow,
where, 'with the help of Sverdlov he was received by Lenin,
whom he told about the event'.[2]

Markov's account is not as convincing as it first appears. It is
not corroborated by any of the others he named as accomplices,
and the story of the abduction could have been drawn from
Sokolov or any later history which relied on him. Nothing is
known about any meeting between Markov and Lenin. More

serious than that, it is contradicted by the official evidence in the files of the German Foreign Ministry.

The first substantial indication that Sokolov had been mis-led – or had concealed vital evidence – is found in a telegram from Armin von Reyher, one of the staff at the German con-sulate-general in St Petersburg, dated 15 June 1918, two days after the Grand Duke had disappeared. It was sent to Prince Henry of Prussia, the Kaiser's brother, who had been given per-sonal responsibility for the Romanov case. It read:

I have learnt that His Imperial Highness was in Perm almost one month ago and held under close arrest at first and then with the permission he held he moved into a hotel with his secretary, where His Imperial Highness proved to have much sympathy on the part of the people ... I have learnt from a trustworthy source that the Grand Duke has been brought by ship to Rybinsk (a town on the Upper Volga), which was certainly a result of the struggle with the English and French subsidized Czechoslovakians, that stands under the supreme command of the French Major Comte de Lubersac.[3]

It could hardly be more at odds with the White and Bolshevik versions. If von Reyher's message is true, then it raises a lot of very important questions – but is it true?

The telegram does not stand in isolation; the German files continue with more correspondence indicating that the Grand Duke was alive, or at least that the Germans considered him to be alive. The next significant document is a telegram from Count Wilhelm von Mirbach, the German ambassador in Moscow who had also received information that Mikhail Alexandrovitch was alive. He was concerned about the impact the news that the Grand Duke was co-operating with Germany's enemies would have on the monarchists whom the Germans saw as a potential pro-German government in place of the Bolsheviks. The tele-gram read:

Use of Michael Alexandrovitch by the Entente has made a considerable impression on the generals and officers of the

79

groups inclined to us in these places. In [the] latest week there has been a noticeable holding back of the tide.[4]

On the same day von Mirbach sent an appraisal of the possible candidates for a German-inspired restoration of the Romanovs. As we have seen, the Germans maintained close links with the Russian monarchists and were heavily engaged in plotting with them. On 3 July von Mirbach considered the possible contenders for the throne. At the head of the list he placed Nicholas's son, Alexei, and in his case von Mirbach recommended a regency under the Grand Duke Nikolai Nikolaievitch. Even if the chance arose for the restoration of Nicholas II, von Mirbach thought his position hopeless since he had very few supporters. Alternatively there were hopes for a regency under the Grand Duke Paul, an uncle of Nicholas II, or perhaps his son Dmitri. Yet von Mirbach had to record that there was more support in Russia for Mikhail Alexandrovitch taking the throne.[5]

After the Bolsheviks had announced the shooting of the Tsar, the question assumed a new importance. We have already noted Riezler's comments on the difficulties posed for the monarchists by German pressure on the Bolsheviks for consideration to be shown to the young Alexei.[6] By 22 July the pressure was mounting on both the Germans and the monarchists, for a proclamation had been published under Mikhail Alexandrovitch's name in Omsk in Siberia, claiming the throne for himself. The issues were highlighted by one of the German delegates in Kiev, the capital of the 'independent' Ukraine – which was in fact a German puppet state – and the centre of monarchist activity. Berckheim, the delegate, telegraphed to Berlin that the monarchists in Kiev were worried about the whereabouts of Mikhail Alexandrovitch. They thought, he reported, that

he is with Dutow or in Omsk. His Omsk proclamation is generally regarded as a forgery. However, his weak character would not rule out him going over to the Entente. That would bring Russian officers of Monarchist inclinations into a difficult position. General Brusilov, former Commander-in-

Chief, thus sent a captain-lieutenant known to me personally to the Grand Duke, to skilfully hold him back from an Entente orientation. With the assistance of the head of the Caspian Sea Fleet Ivan Feodorovitch Schmidt, former assistant of the commander of the port of Libau, contact can be established by reference to Herr Treitck of the consulate-general of Petersburg.[7]

What the Germans and the Russian monarchists who were seeking German support were so concerned about was the risk of the Grand Duke becoming a pawn in the hands of the British and French. If he did, then such power as the principle of legitimacy had in any question of succession to the throne would be thrown into the scales against both of them. Berckheim's message also tells us something about how the Grand Duke was taken to the Upper Volga, since that river empties into the Caspian Sea; and the River Kama, which runs through Perm, flows into the Volga south of Kazan. As if to emphasize the fact, von Reyher repeated his message of 15 June on 23 July.[8]

Dr Riezler added more information to complicate the position of the Germans and Monarchists. On 22 July he telegraphed that the Grand Duke was indeed in Omsk[9], and followed this with a wire which showed just how confused the monarchists were by the news, which was now – apparently – further complicated by the Grand Duke's decision to retire from the political stage.

At the last meeting the group had – telegram No. 541 from this place – (Brusilov is its military leader) on the question that according to a message Mikhail Alexandrovitch had refused every active post. The group is nevertheless indeed worried because of the validity of the legitimacy principle in that they do not become suspicious of each other. They saw Mikhail on the other side of the Czechoslovakian front and the more important Tsarevich threatened by Bolsheviks, but would gladly get the Tsarevich in their hands fearing meanwhile to endanger his life by means of a local coup or kidnapping attempt.[10]

The material in the German files cannot be readily dismissed as rumour or the result of a Bolshevik deception. The Germans were getting their information from at least three separate places – the embassy in Moscow, the consulate-general in St Petersburg, and their delegation in Kiev – and the evidence was to grow stronger.

The most decisive statements came from the consulate-general in St Petersburg. The first of these is a telegram to the German Foreign Ministry on 25 August 1918, which states that according to what was known in the consulate-general, a letter to Prince Henry should have passed on hard, reliable news that Mikhail Alexandrovitch and the son of the Grand Duke Constantine had been rescued. The letter would appear to have gone astray, for on 8 September a copy was forwarded to both the Chancellor and the Kaiser as a result of inquiries having been made in St Petersburg. The letter, dated 24 August, was from Armin von Reyher and read:

> Today I have received the completely reliable and exact news that His Imperial Highness the Grand Duke Michael is healthy and has been found in safety. Received data on his living in freedom which I am not at liberty to communicate to you.
>
> As to the son of the late Grand Duke Constantine, he is rescued and not shot as the accursed Bolshevik official claims.[11]

Not only is this a categoric statement that Mikhail Alexandrovitch was alive and well, it emphasizes the Bolshevik penchant for lying that we have already noted. It suggests that nothing that comes from communist sources is to be trusted in the Romanov case. The German sources would appear to be reliable since the different German delegations were all reporting the same information, and von Reyher's letter of 24 August stated that the information was 'completely reliable and exact'. Not only that, but it gets support from both British and Swedish sources. On 26 August 1918 – just two days after von Reyher's letter had been written – British agent ST12 sent news that 'A Swede arrived from Omsk reports that the Grand Duke Michael Alexandrovitch is living in the Governor's House in Omsk with the imperial Russian standard flying; with guards and procedure as in old regime days'.[12] This confirms an even earlier message from Sir Conyngham Greene, the British ambassador in Tokyo, who received his information from the General Staff and the Military Attaché. A one-line note read: 'A counter-revolutionary movement headed by Grand Duke Michael has started at Omsk.'[13]

German plans to restore a monarchy favourable to Germany were also known to the British. The British Naval Attaché in St Petersburg informed the Admiralty on 29 June 1918 that the Germans proposed to 'declare' a monarchy in Russia and re-negotiate a peace settlement with the new regime with terms that were more favourable to Russia than those of the Treaty of Brest-Litovsk. The Naval Attaché continued:

Candidate for Throne is Grand Duke Michael and a high German Agent has already been sent to Perm to open negotiations but Grand Duke Michael has temporarily disappeared. My informant, a Russian officer whose name must remain secret, has lately travelled much and has been in touch with peasants says unless further famine is threatened the crisis will be in July and it is then Germans will declare Monarchy, in August new harvest will be available and all this will be put down to new Monarchy Regime.

He considers Monarchy only means of saving situation and in view of German purpose it would seem such is the case and that it would be to Allies advantage to forestall Germans.[14]

This could mean that the rescue of the Grand Duke from Perm was a deliberate political move to thwart German plans and to embarrass them in their dealings with the pro-German monarchists in European Russia. As the documents cited above show, it achieved a good part of its purpose. The monarchists of the German orientation in Kiev should not be confused with monarchists of an Allied orientation in Siberia. The latter hated the Germans as deeply as they hated the Bolsheviks; while they might have thought long and hard about whether to restore the monarchy, they were certainly not going to put a German puppet on the throne.

Despite the knowledge indicated in these British sources, Britain's official files on the murder of the imperial family contain very little about Mikhail Alexandrovitch. There is a report that he had been seen in Shanghai in 1919, but the report is swiftly discredited. Was it a deliberate false trail to throw researchers working on the fate of the Romanovs off the scent? The exclusion of the rest of the evidence and the known withholding of many documents suggest that this may well be true. The motive existed in the shape of the support Britain gave to the Kolchak regime, which, when it came to power in Siberia, seems to have excluded the Grand Duke from any form of political activity. As the British were among the warmest supporters of Kolchak they must have acquiesced in this, if not inspired it. The Great Powers were playing for enormous stakes in Russia at the time of the civil war, upon the outcome of which their own survival depended in 1918. Both the British and the Germans were fishing in dark and dirty waters.

In the autumn of 1918 the Bolsheviks tried to spread disinformation about the Grand Duke. The German Foreign Ministry was sent a report from the army's headquarters in the field on 21 September which informed them that 'Red newspapers in Petersburg of today reported Grand Duke Michael Alexandrovitch was arrested 10 *versts* from the Chutowski Sawod (Ural area) and brought to Perm'.[15] The sender, Oberleutnant Bauermeister, signed off with the phrase '*Geht wie immer*', which does not translate readily into English; its nearest approximations might be 'Always the same' or 'Not a problem'. In either case it could suggest contempt for the report, but it could equally be interpreted as signing off in a friendly if informal manner. Whatever the case the Germans do not appear to have attached any credence to the report, and with good reason since it was entirely false. The Grand Duke had not been captured by the Bolsheviks, and we can only speculate about their motive for spreading the story. Perhaps they wanted to quash the effect that stories of the Grand Duke being alive might have on the mass of the citizens of Russia, but much depends on the degree to which the Soviet government was responsible for inspiring the report.

Plots for a restoration centring on the Grand Duke continued through the autumn. The German envoy in Riga forwarded an account of discussions he had had with a German Balt, Baron Rosen from Reval, who was on his way to Kovno where a monarchist mission was to negotiate with the influential German Chief of Staff in the East, General Max Hoffmann. According to the envoy, 'The principals plan a dictatorship of the generals and former army leader Leschitski, [and] shall prepare the Grand Duke Michael, the brother of the Tsar, to ascend the throne.'[16] Hoffmann's diary and private papers shed very little light on these proceedings – just as they are silent on many other sensitive matters – but his published diary does give a glimpse of the train of thought among the German army's leaders:

We could have advanced to the lines Smolensk–Petrograd, and once arrived there we could have formed a new government which would simply maintain the fiction that the Tsarevich was still alive, and we could have appointed a regent for him. I thought at the time of the Grand Duke Paul, with whom, through his son-in-law Colonel Durnovo, the Commander-in-Chief in the East had been in connection. The Provisional Government could then have been transferred to Moscow, where in my opinion it would have been a simple matter to sweep the Bolshevik government away.[17]

This was never more than a dream, for while it might have been possible to drive the Bolsheviks from St Petersburg and Moscow, it was quite another thing to provide the large army of occupation the Germans would have needed to maintain the new government in power. This was the fatal flaw in all German plans in the East in 1918, for while their forces were so concentrated on the Western front they did not have adequate strength to reap the harvest which beckoned so enticingly from Russia. They needed – and did not have – significant support from large sections of the Russian people, a fact which applied to the case of the imperial family as much as it did to other German ambitions in Russia.

Apparent eyewitness confirmation that Mikhail Alexandrovitch was alive and well surfaced in October – bringing in its train the usual complications for German relations with the Russian monarchists. The message, from the German delegation in Kiev, opens with the startling words:

> According to a communication from Shuvalov, the Grand Duke Michael Alexandrovitch is in safety in Siberia in the hands of the 'Siberian Government'.[18]

'Shuvalov' was Count Alexander Shuvalov, a trusted aide and spokesman for Skoropadski, the Hetman of the 'independent' Ukraine which survived by virtue of German support. The 'Siberian Government' was the Provisional Siberian Government, the conservative partner in the Provisional All-Russian Government. Skoropadski had the Grand Duke's morganatic wife, the Countess Brassowa, to contend with as well as the Russian monarchists infesting his capital; official confirmation of the Grand Duke's survival by his personal aide raised problems for the Germans once again. The message continued by proposing that the Germans got permission for the Countess to leave Kiev with the ultimate purpose of being reunited with her husband, since German support for Skoropadski's policy of Ukrainianization was losing them ground among the monarchists – the monarchists in Kiev were evidently as anxious to keep the Russian empire together as were their political cousins in Siberia. This was subject to the condition that she should not fear disfavour from the Danish Court through her connections with the Germans.

Much of the rest of the documentation concerning Mikhail Alexandrovitch deals with the question of permitting the Countess Brassowa to travel to Copenhagen via Germany to be reunited with her ten-year-old son, George. The Germans feared that the Countess would be received with disfavour at the Danish Court, and hesitated to let her proceed. They eventually relented, and on 30 October 1918 Under Secretary Baron von dem Bussche of the Foreign Ministry wired her that she could go, the responsibility for her travel to and through Germany resting with Oberost, German Military Headquarters in the East. It was not to be. A little more than a week later Germany had collapsed and the country was wracked by revolution, so these plans fell apart. The Countess eventually escaped from Russia at the end of the year via Constantinople, being carried to Malta aboard the British warship HMS *Agamemnon*. She was never to see her husband again.

After this there is little definite news about the Grand Duke. The Kolchak *coup* put an end to any hope that might have existed for a restoration under his banner. Kolchak seemed determined to carry out his task of creating a new, militaristic Russia without the Romanovs and seems to have forced Mikhail Alexandrovitch into the background. Nearly a year later, on 15 September 1919, a German newspaper, *Volkisches Zeitung*, carried a story that an impostor was claiming to be 'the Grand Duke Michael Alexander' in Siberia. Comment was passed on the story by an official of the German Republic's Foreign Ministry. It is instructive in more than one sense:

In the summer of 1918 the Grand Duke Michael was in Perm [and] was actually liberated by officers of Kolchak. He lived a long time in Barnaul in Altai-territory and for the time being in the surroundings that Kolchak deemed fit. He gave assurance that the Grand Duke Michael would play no future role in the political life of Russia. He is the typhoid of the degenerate Romanov. His wife, a divorced Mrs Brassowa, was in Petersburg with the consulate-general in connection with him. She was saved with German help. She lived for a time in Copenhagen with her son from her first marriage.
The newspaper story has to be typical sensationalism.[19]

This suggests that Kolchak found the Tsar's brother a potential embarrassment, and while he did not have him assassinated, he ensured that he was politically impotent – perhaps in exchange for guarantees about his safety. It is equally possible that Kolchak was keeping secret the news that the heir apparent was alive, with the aim of bringing him forward in the event of a

White victory and thus establishing the legitimacy of the new regime – the need to keep the support of those Social Revolutionaries who had sided with him would certainly give him the motive for discretion. Either eventuality would explain the devious handling of the White enquiry into the murder of the imperial family at Ekaterinburg.

However, we are descending into the realms of speculation here. Either explanation is plausible, even credible, but both lack the documentary evidence to establish them as fact. Precious few original documents from Kolchak's government survived to reach the West, which means it is impossible to explain Kolchak's attitude except in terms of guesswork based on probabilities, and that can never provide a conclusive argument.

The German documents so far studied do not explain what eventually happened to Mikhail Alexandrovitch. It is known that he never rejoined his wife, the Countess Brassowa, in the West. Did he perish in Russia? The late G. N. Tantzos, who told Summers and Mangold that he had studied the 1916 diary of the Dowager Empress Marie in Moscow, advised me in a telephone conversation on 29 March 1991 that the Grand Duke was in Omsk in 1919 and had ridden towards the front when the Red army was closing in on the city. He was caught and killed by a Red patrol. He stated that the information was held in one of the War Office files on operations in Siberia, but I have never been able to find this material despite an extensive search. Moreover, I regard Tantzos's information as suspect since in February 1991, in company with Mr Alexander Anderson, I scoured all the museums and archives in Moscow and Leningrad for the diary of the Dowager Empress – and nobody had ever heard of it! Tantzos claimed that he had studied the diary in the then Central State Archive of the October Revolution. Staff at the centre willingly permitted Mr Anderson to look at the records of people who had studied at the Centre from 1983 to 1985 (Tantzos claimed he was there in 1984) and his name was not on the register. It looks as if Tantzos was in the habit of telling researchers what he thought they wanted to believe. The question of what happened to the heir apparent remains open, like so much else about the family of Tsar Nicholas II.

10

HM PREFERS ...[1]

Only one other state had the same powerful combination of political and personal interests in the welfare of the Romanovs as Germany. For the British the stakes were, if anything, higher since the Tsar had been a loyal ally and on more than one occasion had ventured his armies on disastrous campaigns to help his embattled allies. There was a debt of honour here, though this could never outweigh the more serious consideration of the Anglo-French need to keep the Eastern front open.

As we have seen, Miliukov, the Provisional Government's Foreign Minister, made two attempts to persuade the British to send a ship to take the imperial family to Britain. After his second request, on 21 March 1917, the Imperial War Cabinet in London considered the question on 22 March. Their deliberations were closely followed by a meeting that same day at Downing Street with the Prime Minister, David Lloyd George, the Chancellor of the Exchequer, Andrew Bonar Law, the Permanent Under Secretary at the Foreign Office, Lord Hardinge, and Lord Stamfordham, the King's private secretary. It was decided that an invitation should be sent to Nicholas, offering him asylum in Britain for the duration of the war, and this was duly telegraphed to Russia that same day. However, Sir George

Buchanan, the British Ambassador in St Petersburg, was instructed to emphasize that the invitation had been made at the request of the Provisional Government.

It was not long before George V changed his mind. The available documents show that this was caused by the political situation in Britain. The strain imposed by the war had provided a fertile soil for the seeds of unrest, and revolutionary ideas and sentiments were flourishing. During the spring of 1917 tremors of revolutionary unrest were being felt in Britain as well as in the rest of Europe – so much so that General Sir William Robertson, the Chief of the Imperial General Staff, felt obliged to write to the commander of the British armies in France, Field Marshal Sir Douglas Haig, that 'I am afraid there is no getting away from the fact that there is some unrest in the country now as a result, partly, of the Russian Revolution. There have been some bad strikes recently, and there is still much discontent.'[2]

Such fears were reflected in the King's having second thoughts about the wisdom of inviting his cousin to Britain. He expressed his initial doubts, on 'general grounds of political expediency', in a letter from Lord Stamfordham to Arthur Balfour on 30 March. Balfour was able to sidestep the royal reluctance by gently pointing out that it would not be possible to withdraw the invitation unless the position in Russia changed. This only applied a momentary brake to his sovereign's new course. He returned to the subject again, apparently prompted by letters from Lords Carnock and Beresford which stressed the gathering opposition to the Tsar coming to Britain.

The Tsar had long been regarded as a bloodthirsty tyrant who lived a life of luxury while his people toiled without rights of any kind. The Russian occupation of Poland, the repression of movements for domestic reform and decades of rivalry over Russian expansionism in the Middle East and Asia, which were seen as a threat to British India, together with tension over Russian ambitions towards the Dardanelles, had combined to create deep seated anti-Tsarist feeling.

On 6 April the King had Stamfordham write tWo more letters to Balfour. The first highlighted the domestic political difficulties that would result from bringing the Romanovs to Britain and drew attention to the socialist character of the opposition to the proposal. The second letter was even more explicit, specifically referring to an article in the magazine *Justice* by the socialist H. H. Hyndman which condemned the invitation and implied that it had originated with the royal family. The King's anger is clear from the sentence: 'And Hyndman is the person that Mr Henderson [Labour member of the War Cabinet] told the King he wished to send to Russia as one of the representatives of our socialists in this country!'[3]

This effectively undermined any remaining inclination on the part of the War Cabinet to keep the invitation open. Buchanan was advised to evade the issue on the grounds that

> There are indications that a considerable anti-monarchical movement is developing here, including personal attacks upon the King. Part of the ground of the attacks is that he supported the Ex-Emperor and King Constantine of Greece. It is thought that if the emperor comes here it may dangerously increase this movement.

The message added that indications of British concern for the family's welfare might weaken the British position in dealings with the Provisional Government, and it was suggested that it would be a better idea if the Romanovs could go to France instead.[4] On 15 April Buchanan replied that he entirely shared this view.

It is easy to criticize the King for callousness towards his cousin, but such a view is superficial. The crisis of the war was approaching, and it was vital above all else to maintain national unity. Risking that unity, and possibly costing the country the war, was not a viable option. Whatever the King did was bound to be wrong: had he secured the release of the Romanovs, no doubt those same critics who charged him with cowardice would have accused him of selfish obstinacy in putting family interests above the national interest at a time when thousands of his more humble subjects were being slaughtered in the trenches.

Besides, in the spring of 1917, there was no immediate danger to the Romanovs. On the contrary: the Provisional Government had shown itself solicitous for their welfare and their concern was used to justify their rejection of Buchanan's suggestion of 16 April that the family should be sent to their palace at Livadia in the Crimea, where Nicholas himself hoped to retire. Prince Lvov told Buchanan that he feared the family would be seized by revolutionary railway workers *en route*, a risk he dared not take.

That the King did what he felt was right in the circumstances would command general acceptance were it not that attempts were made to mislead posterity. Even Lloyd George and Buchanan were drawn into this sorry story – the latter by a threat to stop his pension if he told the truth, a threat which was not revealed until his daughter published it after his death.[5]

In his *War Memoirs* Lloyd George fastens the responsibility for the failure of the British offer on the shoulders of the Provisional Government. Answering post-war criticism that Britain had done nothing to help the Tsar, he wrote: 'That is untrue. The fact is that at no time between his abdication and his murder was he free to leave Russia. An invitation to take refuge here was extended by the British Crown and Government. The Czar was unable in the event to avail himself of it, even had he been anxious to do so – and of that we have no evidence.'[6] He went so far as to quote Buchanan on the issue, even though he knew the former ambassador could not be honest about it: 'Our offer remained open and was never withdrawn. If advantage was not taken of it, it was because the Provisional Government failed to overcome the opposition of the Soviet.'[7]

He added that this was the real history of what had happened, but we now know that it was anything but. Alexander Kerensky gave the lie to this in his book on the murder of the Romanovs, published in Paris in 1936. He approached Buchanan in June 1917 for information about when the ship which Buchanan had discussed with Miliukov would be coming to fetch the Tsar and his family. Kerensky said that Buchanan informed him, with tears in his eyes, that the British government had finally refused to provide a refuge.[8] Kerensky observed that this was due solely to considerations of British internal politics.

The attempt to disguise the responsibility for the decision in London must raise the question of how much more is still being disguised or concealed. There seems little ground for dispute that the British later resumed their efforts to get the Romanovs to safety – but that was after the situation had been transformed by the Bolshevik seizure of power in November 1917. Until then there had been no direct threat to the family, but the new regime was cast in an entirely different mould to its predecessor.

That the Romanovs recognized the fact and appealed to George V for help is established by a letter the Tsarina sent to the King via the family's English tutor, George Sydney Gibbes, who ghosted a letter for her since the family's correspondence was examined by the Bolsheviks. It was addressed to Miss Margaret Jackson, who had been one of the Tsarina's childhood governesses, and under the guise of an innocent, friendly letter lay an appeal for direct and practical help which even included a diagram of the layout of the Governor's House at Tobolsk for the use of any rescue party that might be sent.[9] We only know about this plea at all because Gibbes kept the draft among his papers and confirmed that it was indeed an appeal for help. The original, in common with so many other documents relating to this case, has disappeared. It was probably this letter which inspired renewed British efforts to save the family.

Summers and Mangold were able to interview the then heir to the Russian throne, the Grand Duke Vladimir Kirilovitch. They raised the subject of rescue attempts, and they relate that 'Vladimir hedged, but admitted knowing Lied, and added: "There were plans, distinct from monarchist plots, while the imperial family were at Tobolsk, and they involved George V and others . . .".'[10] No trace of these plans remains in the British files, but the fact that 'Lied' is mentioned could be important since Summers and Mangold argue that a rescue mission had been mounted by a Norwegian explorer, businessman and adventurer called Jonas Lied, who was on good terms with the Bolsheviks. They pieced the story together using Lied's diary and the memory of an English friend of his, Ralph Hewins.

Lied was mysteriously summoned to London in the early spring of 1918 for discussions with senior members of the British Intelligence hierarchy, including Colonel Frederick Browning, the aide to the head of SIS, Lord Robert Cecil of the Foreign

Office and Captain Sir Reginald 'Blinker' Hall, the brilliant Director of Naval Intelligence. He was also briefly introduced to the Prince of Wales. Until Lied met the Grand Duke Mikhail Mikhailovitch, a cousin of the Tsar who was in exile in England because of a morganatic marriage of which Nicholas had disapproved, he had no idea of the purpose of the summons or the talks. Lied discovered that the Grand Duke was director of a plan to rescue the imperial family and had contributed £800 towards the costs of the mission, but with the proviso that his part in it should be kept secret.[11]

The plan sought to ferry the family downstream from Tobolsk aboard one of Lied's cargo boats to the Norwegian's sawmill depots on the Kara Sea, where they would rendezvous with a Royal Navy torpedo boat. The boat was then to race north for the Arctic and thence to Britain. Lied believed the scheme to be practical and blamed its abandonment on a veto exercised by Lloyd George. This seems unlikely; it is more probable that the family was transferred to Ekaterinburg before any decision could be made.

Whether or not the Lied mission was ever considered is less important than that plans were undoubtedly being laid. Apart from Lied, there was another mission which was centred on an officer in the Royal Flying Corps (RFC) called Steven Bertholt Gordon-Smith. He was the son of Philip Smith, an exporter of Ukrainian wheat to Britain who had married a Russian, Nadia Kavolaska, and settled in Taganrog before the war. The family had flourished there and moved in exalted circles, including the imperial family. Steven grew up able to speak fluent Russian and with many friends and contacts in Russia.

After four years at Trinity College, Cambridge, he married and worked in the Cornish tin-mining industry before joining the Foreign Office. On the outbreak of war he was commissioned in the South Staffordshire Regiment but was invalided out with that scourge of the Western front, trench foot, in 1915. Unable to serve in the infantry, he joined the RFC, where his linguistic ability led to his secondment to the Imperial Russian Air Force. He won Russia's highest award, the coveted Order of St George; further decorations included the Orders of St Vladimir and St

Anne. So many Smiths were killed in the war that he found he had been reported dead or missing several times; so to avoid the distress to his family he adopted his wife's surname, creating the double-barrelled name of Gordon-Smith.

His second wife, now Mrs Eykyn, told me how she came to know of her late husband's brief involvement in the Romanov case. She knew nothing about it until shortly before their wedding in October 1938 at St Paul's in Knightsbridge. Steven and the vicar, the Reverend Eric Hamilton, later Dean of Windsor and chaplain to the Queen, greeted each other as old friends in fluent Russian. Gordon-Smith told her afterwards that they had both served in Russia during the war and that he had been attached to the British Military Mission with orders to 'rescue the imperial family at all costs'.

As is the case with 'deniable' operations of this kind – deniable operations are those of which the government can deny all knowledge if anything goes wrong – Gordon-Smith was left entirely to his own devices so far as arranging the rescue was concerned. Once he had succeeded in rescuing the family, he was to fly them to Archangel where a British submarine would be waiting, though he was left to find the aeroplane for himself! However, for reasons which he could never discover, he received orders to abandon the attempt and to return via Stockholm.[12]

Is the foundation for this story reliable? Mrs Eykyn was not in good health, but her mind was clear and sharp. I found her wary, and while willing to talk to me about her late husband she did not expect me to accept what she said as gospel truth – whereas fantasists tend to exude self-confidence and a conviction that they are party to some great secret. When I cross-questioned her in an attempt to find flaws and discrepancies in her testimony which would indicate that either she or her late husband had invented the story, I found none; on the contrary, I was presented with a seamless robe, with none of the attempts to embellish the story and create explanations to fit awkward facts which characterize tales that stem from hyperactive minds. Mrs Eykyn simply stuck to what she knew.

When I asked her whether it was possible that her late husband had invented the story, she replied, with conviction, 'In a way, all Russians do. In a typically Russian way. That you'd understand – but not on anything like this. Not on anything like this. No, never!'[13]

A major stumbling block was the question of Gordon-Smith having to find an aeroplane in Russia to fly the family to Archangel. In the spring of 1918 that was not as absurd as it sounds. Brigadier-General George Hill had made a reputation for himself as one of the most capable British Intelligence Officers in Russia at the time. That spring, relations between the British and the Bolsheviks were quite good, as the British were still hoping that the Bolsheviks would turn against the Germans and lead Russia back into the war. Hill advised the Bolsheviks on the organization of their secret service and actively co-operated in local resistance to the advance of the Central Powers in February 1918. He made such an impact on the Bolshevik leadership that he was invited to the Party Congress and Trotsky personally appointed him Inspector of Aviation – with unrestricted access to airfields and aeroplanes.[14]

The ability to mount a rescue mission existed – and, more importantly, the will to do so was there, though it was only when the danger to the Romanovs became real and pressing that earlier diplomatic reluctance was set aside. It is clear that nothing was achieved while the Romanovs were at Tobolsk. The transfer of the family to Ekaterinburg made it much less likely that any rescue attempt would succeed, but it did not mean that efforts were abandoned. In spite of all the difficulties, one last attempt was made.

I I

A DIARY IN OXFORD

Evidence that a last desperate attempt to save the Romanovs was mounted by the British at the behest of George V is found in the diary of Colonel Richard Meinertzhagen, CBE, DSO, one of the most colourful and charismatic officers to have served in the British army. He had made a name for himself as head of Intelligence with the British forces in East Africa and Palestine. In 1917, in Palestine, he had planned and executed a daring operation in which he rode out alone to the Turkish lines and, pretending to be wounded by the fire of a Turkish patrol, dropped a carefully prepared haversack containing fictitious plans for a British offensive against the town of Gaza, a key position in the Turkish lines. The Turks fell for the bait and reinforced Gaza, only to find that the British stroke fell at Beersheba at the other end of their lines. The deception resulted in the complete defeat of the Turks and the capture of Jerusalem before Christmas.

In 1918 Meinertzhagen was working with MO2 in the Directorate of Military Operations at the War Office in London, the nerve centre of the British military effort. Here he was responsible for the campaigns fought in Mesopotamia and Palestine, and for military developments in Afghanistan and India. Despite being attached to the Directorate of Military Operations, he did not relinquish contact with Intelligence, in which he had made such a mark. It was typical of the British organization of the General Staff that divisions between Intelligence and Operations were not hard and fast, so that on occasion sections of the Directorate of Military Operations served as a cover for Intelligence work. In Meinertzhagen's case it was this aspect of his work which brought him into contact with Russia.

In January 1918 a new section at the War Office was created with the designation MIO, formed from personnel drawn from MO2 and one of the subsections of the Directorate of Military Intelligence, MI2(c). It was directly responsible to the Director of Military Intelligence, Lieutenant-General Sir George Macdonogh, and its concerns were all matters relating to Russia, Romania, Siberia, Central Asia, the Caucasus, Persia and Afghanistan. It sought to combine the functions of Intelligence and Operations in one body, with the primary task of manipulating the chaotic situation in Russia to the advantage of the Western allies, chiefly by organizing and directing anti-German elements in Russia into an effective replacement for the Eastern front. Meinertzhagen's part in this was the raising and direction of an Intelligence service in Russia.

As head of his section, Meinertzhagen had to visit the King periodically to keep him, as head of the armed services, in touch with developments in the theatres of war for which he was responsible. This was a practice common to all heads of section at the War Office. Reporting for one of these audiences in the spring of 1918, Meinertzhagen was surprised to find his friend Hugh Trenchard, Chief of Air Staff, waiting to see the King as well. Their joint presence was no accident, as the King soon made clear. Meinertzhagen tells us that:

King George opened the conversation by saying he was devoted to the Tsar (his cousin) and could anything be done about rescuing them by air as he feared the whole family would be murdered. Hugh was very doubtful as the family must be closely guarded and there was no information regarding landing facilities for aircraft. I said I thought I could find out about that and perhaps arrange for a rescue party to bundle at least some of the royal prisoners into an aircraft. But it was taking a great risk as failure would entail the murder of the whole family.[1]

The diary states that Meinertzhagen discovered that although the Tsar and Tsarina were too closely guarded for any rescue to have a chance of success, he felt that he might be able to rescue some of the children. On that basis, according to Meinertzhagen's entry for 18 August 1918, the operation went ahead. 'On July 1st everything was ready and the plane took off. Success was not complete and I find it too dangerous to give details. One child was literally thrown into the plane at Ekaterinburg, much bruised and brought to England where she still is.'[2] Meinertzhagen had no doubt about the fate of the rest of the family. He mentions their murder on no less than three occasions in this one extract.

As it stands, Meinertzhagen's diary entry is the first time that anything resembling concrete evidence of a British rescue attempt has emerged. It is also the only account which tells us anything about how the operation was engineered. Yet how reliable is it?

Meinertzhagen was dynamic and decisive, a man of action to whom philosophizing and the stifling atmosphere of committee work were alien. Instant decision and immediate action were his specialities – qualities that may have been inculcated by his headmaster at Aysgarth School, who drummed into the boys in his care the importance of acting rather than talking, though by the time Meinertzhagen went to Aysgarth he was already displaying a boisterous and adventurous spirit. Be that as it may, Aysgarth taught him discipline and the need to direct his energy towards a given goal and to stick to that goal, undaunted by the strength of any opposition.

The habit of instant decision and immediate action remained with him all his life. As he wrote in his eighty-second year, 'deep reflection, weighing pros and cons and consultation with others is often impossible and sometimes dangerous. I believe it is better in an emergency to do something not quite perfect than to sink into deep reflection or consult others and let the moment for action pass for ever.'[3]

Such an attitude fitted him very well in the early years of his military career, when there was abundant scope for initiative. Influenced by the Prusso-German model, the army of the time encouraged this, expecting its officers to take the initiative and do something even if proved wrong by subsequent events. It is an attitude that many academics, whose reputations are founded upon study and contemplation, simply cannot come to terms with, and this is reflected all too often in a faulty and partial perception of both the man and his diary.

Such an attitude proved a hindrance when Meinertzhagen rose to higher rank: he had to work as one of a team, and his independent line made him as many enemies as friends. He recorded how Lieutenant-General Sir William Thwaites, Director of Military Intelligence in 1919, told him that

The trouble with you, Meinertzhagen, is that you look just a little farther ahead than most of us, you know you are right and you persist in telling us all we are wrong. On this occasion I feel you are right, but if the team is to work smoothly, your unorthodox views must take second place even if they are perfectly correct. And if you can't fit into the War Office machine you run small chance of getting on.[4]

The problems that Meinertzhagen – and his colleagues – experienced because of this lust for action and instant decision were instrumental in wrecking his promising career as Chief Political Officer in Palestine in 1919 and 1920. His single-mindedness and his insistence on the truth poisoned relations between him and his superiors, and led Field Marshal Lord Allenby to demand his recall. The issue which inspired this breach was Zionism, which Meinertzhagen had embraced with all the ardour of a convert: given his character, his new enthusiasm could only spell trouble. He was unable to reconcile his urge for direct, immediate solutions with a deeper, more subtle approach, which more often than not demanded committee work, discussion, intrigue and explanation.

As might be expected, Meinertzhagen invariably saw things in stark blacks and whites, omitting the details and tiresome complexities which completed the picture. More often than not this

resulted in a narrowness of outlook and an intolerance of others
whose opinions differed from his own, leading him sometimes to
exaggerate their opinions and faults into something far worse
than they actually were.

This simplicity, which Thucydides considered to be the mark
of a noble nature, was a distinctly mixed blessing. It made him
inflexible and strongly prejudiced, direct and ruthless, a man
who was very much a loner and apparently driven by some inner
demon. According to one officer who served with him he was
stern, single-minded and relentless.[5] On the other hand, he got
things done, more often than not successfully. According to his
own account, he was once told by a distinguished soldier that 'I
"rushed my fences". Maybe I do, but I often surmount them.'[6]

Even with these faults, Meinertzhagen was an excellent
soldier and continues to enjoy a golden reputation in the successor to his old regiment, the Royal Fusiliers, and more to the
point in the present context within the Secret Intelligence Service.[7] His achievements were considerable, by whatever yard-
stick they are measured, and his memory is rightly honoured.

Despite his achievements, his diaries – or, rather, the published versions – have been criticized as the product of fantasy.
The late Malcolm Muggeridge considered that 'they would be a
monument to his fantasy self'.[8] More scholarly critics have
pointed to his controversial accounts of the time he spent with
T. E. Lawrence at the Paris Peace Conference in 1919 (in which
Meinertzhagen alleged that Lawrence had exaggerated his own
part in the Arab revolt), suggesting that they are unreliable later
revisions of his diaries which are not to be trusted.[9]

Yet those who dismiss the diaries as the work of an unreliable
fantasist are making precisely the same error for which
Meinertzhagen can be justly criticized: they are looking at the
diaries in plain blacks and whites, without taking into account
the nature of the diarist. Moreover, many Arabists and devotees
of T. E. Lawrence are influenced by the need to 'prove'
Meinertzhagen wrong, since to admit otherwise would com-
promise the favourable impression of Lawrence that they seek to
portray.

It is not as if Lawrence was a simple character whose own

version of events is utterly reliable. He always inspired considerable controversy, and serious doubts have been cast on his
account of the Arab revolt in *The Seven Pillars of Wisdom*. These
doubts have not only been raised by scholars writing many years
after the event, but were at large among members of the Intelligence services. When Meinertzhagen lunched at Brooks's Club
on 9 March 1960 with General Sir James Marshall-Cornwall
and Harold Nicolson, Lawrence came up in the conversation:
according to Meinertzhagen, all three deemed him a fraud and
'an utter little humbug'.[10]

Of course, Meinertzhagen's critics might answer, his dairy was
fantasy, too – but they would be wrong as Marshall-Cornwall
expressed identical views, though in more delicate language,
when I spoke to him on 10 September 1980. He is not the only
member of the Intelligence services who has expressed that same
opinion to me.

One of the problems scholars seem to encounter in
Meinertzhagen's diary is the inability to reconcile the often
pedantic language of the academic world with Meinertzhagen's
simple, robust style. Referring to the celebrated Ronda incident
of 1930, when Meinertzhagen led the Spanish police in a raid
which resulted in the slaughter of all the members of a communist cell at Ronda in Spain, his latest biographer, Mark Cocker,
observed that 'Many of Meinertzhagen's descriptions of the
events in Ronda have the ring of fiction'.[11]

This is true, but Meinertzhagen's naive, almost novelistic
style was typical of the man and is constant throughout his diary.
He was not a scholar and tended to despise the scholarly as pale,
spineless creatures given to prevarication and indecision. His
own schooling and background had emphasized action and decision, at the expense of intellectual pursuits. He commented on
'the complete lack of instruction I received in my own language
as a boy'[12] and recognized this as a handicap. His leisure reading
was largely restricted to novels, and his mode of expression
naturally followed suit.

The manner in which the diary was written resulted in various
anomalies which have provided ammunition for those who have
looked at it with a view to discrediting its author. It must be

recognized from the outset that the diary was not an authentic contemporary record in the accepted sense. Given his vigorous, active life, Meinertzhagen would have found it impossible to keep an exact account of his doings. The diary was typed, and it would hardly have been practical to haul a typewriter and paper round some of the most awkward and inaccessible places on earth.

If the diary is not an authentic daily record, what does it represent and how did it come to be written? The answer is surprisingly simple, and goes a long way towards countering claims that the diary was a later revision, conjured up by Meinertzhagen in his old age. In response to my inquiry about the way the diary had been written, Mrs Theresa Searight – who, as Theresa Clay, enjoyed a long and intimate friendship with the Colonel and was his literary executrix – told me that 'R. M. was a great one for destroying "paper" and I have never seen any drafts'. The diaries, she said, had been in typescript for as long as she knew Meinertzhagen, which was from 1927 or 1928. His various adventures abroad were initially recorded as roughly pencilled accounts, which were typed up when he could find the time – which may have been weeks or even months after the events. She said that the rough pencilled accounts were then 'presumably destroyed'.[13]

Instead of being an immediate and contemporary account, there would sometimes have been a considerable delay between an event and Meinertzhagen entering it into the diary. This made it more likely that he would embellish the rough notes from memory – a dangerous process for a man like Meinertzhagen who, on his own admission, had a terrible memory. In 1910, after spying on the fortifications of Sebastopol, he noted that such work was not for him: 'I feel a perfect wreck, tired out both morally and physically. It also requires too great a memory capacity for men of my calibre.'[14]

On these grounds we would be justified in expecting the diary to contain a number of minor errors where Meinertzhagen's memory had let him down. This does not invalidate the document as a historical source; it means that more care is needed when studying it than some of his critics have taken. Had they taken the trouble to find out how the diary was written, many of the minor discrepancies on which they seize – perhaps as a result of being over-eager to discredit Meinertzhagen – would be placed in their true perspective and a sounder evaluation of the document have been reached.

Even more caution is required when it comes to the published versions of the diary – and since they are readily available, they have been understandably mined by scholars for a variety of purposes. They contain additions to and omissions from the original document, as a result of which they are not reliable. They have unquestionably been subjected to later revision, though not as much as Meinertzhagen's critics would have us believe; they have been manipulated on occasions to protect particular people and, inevitably, the shadow of the Official Secrets Act hangs heavily over them. There are also some additions, where the Colonel dredged his memory to fill out the original picture, though examples of this are not particularly common. As a result, the published diaries are a flawed tool for the historian.

While the published diaries may be flawed, the flaws should not be exaggerated by sometimes shoddy scholarship. A case in point is the entry for 8 April 1919, published in Meinertzhagen's *Middle East Diary*, in which he stated that T. E. Lawrence blamed three admirers – David Hogarth, Lowell Thomas and Ronald Storrs – for 'pushing him into the limelight'. Critics have avidly seized on this passage as 'proof' that the dairy was a later reconstruction, carefully doctored to run Lawrence's reputation down. It is claimed that the entry must be fraudulent since Lowell Thomas did not open his film show on the Middle East campaign, which made a hero of Lawrence, until later in 1919, and that Meinertzhagen could not possibly have known about this influence as early as April of that year.

A moment's thought puts this into perspective. Meinertzhagen was not blaming Lowell Thomas for the publicity surrounding Lawrence: he was recording, briefly, Lawrence's own observations on the subject. Meinertzhagen may not have known about Lowell Thomas at the time, but Lawrence did and he told Meinertzhagen about the situation – or what the complex

Lawrence wanted him to know. The entry should be seen for what it is: a précis of Lawrence's comments on the influences behind him.

Meinertzhagen's diary was a private document, and when he decided to publish parts of it later in his life he accepted that his views and feelings at the time of writing would necessarily colour what he had written:

> Diaries are more accurate in facts than in opinions and criticisms, the latter often being made before all the facts were known. To write a diary as a future historical document is suspect, because, in a day-to-day account of events, the whole picture cannot be seen. As history a diary is not reliable, for events are recorded amid the human reactions which they invoked and without calm assessment.[15]

He tells us that his diary was created from a wish to 'observe, record and explain', a wish impressed on the young Richard by the philosopher Herbert Spencer, a friend of his mother. Until late in his life there was no thought of publication, as is witnessed by the fact that the private diary contains intimate personal details about himself and his family, together with material on his Intelligence work which was omitted from the published versions. As he observed, 'The main function of my diaries has been a personal one, for reference of thought, deed and event.'[16]

The diary performed these functions admirably and is replete with the Colonel's often colourful views, strong opinions, triumphs, errors and contradictions. Its other function was to serve as 'a wonderful safety valve'.[17] So sensitive was the diary that Meinertzhagen's children were strictly warned that although they could look at parts of it, they were *never* to disclose its content on pain of being forbidden to touch it again.[18] Its role as a safety valve is borne out by the sometimes vehement and almost violent views expressed – views which have clearly alienated some readers who are, perhaps, unaware of this function of the diary.

It is the use of the diary as a safety valve that explains the inclusion of the Russian episode – and one other particularly dramatic event, the Ronda incident in 1930 – when more mundane aspects of his 'other work', as Meinertzhagen called his Intelligence activity, do not merit a mention. Both episodes were on a plane above the rest: the intensity of the experiences made their mark on Meinertzhagen and he needed to tell his diary about them, though he was careful to omit them from the published versions. It is reminiscent of the story of King Midas and his barber; in this case the diary served the purpose that the bulrushes did for the barber.

Meinertzhagen did not normally confide his Intelligence activities to his diary – one of the most noteworthy features of which are the sporadic gaps, sometimes quite lengthy, which appear when he was engaged on sensitive work. The most significant of these gaps for the purpose of this research is that covering the period 17 March to 3 August 1918 when, working at the highest levels of British strategy, he deliberately left the pages of his diary blank.

This pattern was followed on other occasions. Lieutenant-Colonel Nigel Watson, who served under Meinertzhagen in Intelligence in the inter-war years, has confirmed that Meinertzhagen directed the raid by British Intelligence on ARCOS, the Soviet Trade Delegation, in London in 1923. Most people are familiar with the formal police raid on ARCOS in 1927, but there are few who know of the earlier operation by Intelligence. British Intelligence Officers surreptitiously entered the offices of the delegation by night with the object of examining anything of value to Intelligence, since it was firmly believed that ARCOS was being used as a cover by Russian Intelligence. Colonel Watson told me that Meinertzhagen visited the scene briefly to supervise the operation, but nothing is said in the diary about it.

Likewise Meinertzhagen refrains from discussing details of his secret work for Anthony Eden when the latter was Foreign Secretary in the 1930s. The diary tells us that he dealt with Eden alone and always orally, so there would be no record of the various enterprises he embarked upon. These activities he deemed 'dirty work involving methods of which I thoroughly disapprove; but in most cases the results have justified the means'.[19]

The fact that Meinertzhagen was engaged in this work and the evidence of Colonel Watson both combine to suggest that his fight against the Bolsheviks was far-reaching and not a figment of his imagination, as some have suggested. His attitude towards using distasteful methods to achieve his ends reflects Lawrence's insight that 'Meinertzhagen knew no half-measures. He was logical, an idealist of the deepest, and so possessed by his convictions that he was willing to harness evil to the chariot of good.'

The apparent contradiction in keeping much secret while recording the more momentous events was typical of the man. He was a mass of contradictions, combining cold-blooded ruthlessness with gentle sensitivity, and wildly unconventional behaviour with being a solidly conservative member of the establishment.

What does this enable us to say about the remarkable diary entry of 18 August 1918? Can it be trusted? From what we know about the man and his diary a strong case can be made for accepting it. The diary was considered reliable enough to be consulted by many scholars, including the official historians of both the East African and Palestine campaigns. Such was Meinertzhagen's reputation that he was persuaded to publish (albeit modified) versions of the diary: questions about its veracity only crept in after Meinertzhagen was safely dead – perhaps inspired, as the Official Historian of Canadian Military Intelligence suggested to me, by jealousy over his rich and vital life or even his social position with its substantial private means and numerous useful contacts.[20]

Be that as it may, Meinertzhagen clearly rendered some very substantial service at one point in his career – or so we may deduce from the fact that he could refuse a knighthood in 1951 but still be offered a CBE, which he accepted, in 1957. It is a staple of the British honours system that someone who refuses to accept an honour – and thus insults the Crown – is not given a second chance. Meinertzhagen must have rendered some service of a very high order for this rule to be waived in his favour.

Yet such is the import of this particular entry in the diary that we would have to be cautious about accepting it even had Meinertzhagen been whiter than white – and that he was not. Whether he made mistakes, exaggerated or even manipulated the record in parts of his diary are beside the point in this case. Either an attempt to rescue the Romanovs was made or it was not, and its broad outlines stand or fall irrespective of any later revision or contemporary errors. Why should Meinertzhagen have put something like this into his diary if the event never took place? He delighted in practical jokes which depended upon deceiving their victims. Was this one of them? The general content of the diary is supported by a mass of evidence from other historical sources, but it seems reasonable to expect that support for this particular entry would be hard to find. On its own the diary cannot be accepted as conclusive evidence: what other sources, if any, shed light on the matter?

12

THE PRIEST'S TESTIMONY

Colonel Richard Meinertzhagen's diary is apparently contradicted by the testimony of a priest, Father Storozhev, who told Judge Sergeyev that he had celebrated Mass for the Romanovs in Ekaterinburg on 14 July 1918, and that the whole family had been present. If his account is accepted at face value, then either Meinertzhagen is wrong – he was writing about these events over a month after they were supposed to have happened – or Storozhev cannot be accepted as reliable.

There are curious elements in the priest's testimony which suggest that he was, in fact, an unreliable witness. Religious services at the Ipatiev House, the House of Special Purpose, were normally conducted by another priest, Father Meledin, and Storozhev had only celebrated Mass once before, on 2 June, six weeks previously. On the morning of 14 July he was surprised to hear someone knocking at the door of his apartment, and when he opened it he found a Red Guard standing outside. The guard told him that he had come from the Ipatiev House and that the priest was 'required' to say Mass for the Romanovs that day. Taken aback, Storozhev said that Meledin was due to take the service but was brusquely told that 'Meledin is replaced. They want you.' There was little choice in the matter, so at 10 a.m.

Storozhev duly reported to Ipatiev House accompanied by a deacon, Father Buimirov.

Meledin, who must have been familiar with the appearance of the Romanovs, was due to take the service but is suddenly replaced at short notice by a priest who had only seen them once, and that six weeks before, and whom the Bolsheviks specifically insisted on. This cannot but arouse suspicion. There is no reasonable explanation for this, and none was ever offered to either Storozhev or Buimirov.

Storozhev told Sergeyev that he had noticed some changes in the appearances of the prisoners. On his first visit, he recalled, Nicholas's beard had been longer and wider than on the second, 'When, it seemed to me, Nicholas Alexandrovitch had shaved around his beard'. The hair of the Grand Duchesses was also different: on 2 June it was 'cut fairly short at the back', yet a mere six weeks later it 'had grown and now came to the level of their shoulders at the back'.[1]

This is peculiar because among the debris discovered in the house after the Whites had occupied Ekaterinburg were part of the Tsar's beard in the stove and hair cuttings from his four daughters in the bathroom and in a box in the vestibule outside the rooms occupied by the family. Some of those who doubt the official version of events have suggested that these cuttings are evidence of an attempt to disguise the family before the Bolsheviks removed them from Ekaterinburg. They might equally represent the hair cut in early June before Storozhev saw the family for the first time. While these are intriguing theories, we lack the evidence necessary to establish their real significance – in particular, the date on which the Tsar's beard and his daughters' hair was cut. Be that as it may, it is highly unlikely that the girls' hair could have grown to shoulder length in the space of only six weeks.

During the final service, according to Storozhev, something unusual took place: instead of reading the prayer 'Who Resteth with the Saints', Buimirov began to sing it, at which the Romanovs all fell to their knees. Why this should have occurred is not clear; all we can deduce is that, for some reason, this particular prayer had a special significance for the family on that

Chaya Goloschekin, Ekaterinburg's
Regional Commissar for War.

Alexander Beloborodov –
accessory to murder or
framed by the Whites?

The four daughters of Tsar Nicholas II
(from left to right):
Marie, Tatiana, Anastasia and Olga.

Yakob Yurovksy – commander of
the Tsar's executioners.

Georgi Biron – one of the
Tsar's executioners?

Major Stephen Alley, SIS officer, who maintained that two of the Romanovs had escaped.

Colonel Richard Meinertzhagen, whose diary refers to an attempt to rescue the Romanovs.

Arthur Thomas *(fifth from left)*, Consul Preston's deputy, pictured in Siberia in spring 1919.

A photograph from the *Harrogate Herald,* 4 September 1918. The Grand Duchess George and the exiled King Manoel of Portugal are fifth and sixth from left. Peering out second from right is an unidentified young woman bearing a strong resemblance to the Grand Duchess Tatiana.

Detail from the photograph in the *Harrogate Herald.* Is the young woman in the centre, peering from behind a companion, the Grand Duchess Tatiana?

Owen Tudor and his second wife, pictured in the late 1920s.

The grave of 'Larissa Feodorovna', tucked into corner of a cemetery in Lydd in Kent.

TO
MY VERY BELOVED
LARISSA FEODOROVNA
WHO DIED JULY 18TH 1926
AGED 28 YEARS
THE WIFE OF
OWEN TUDOR
3RD THE KING'S OWN HUSSARS

occasion. Both priests were puzzled by the morning's unusual turn, and Storozhev left an equally puzzling account of their reactions to it:

> Father Deacon and I walked in silence to the art school building, where he suddenly said to me: 'Do you know, Father Archpresbyter, something has happened to them there.' Since the Father Deacon's words somewhat confirmed my own impression, I stopped and asked him why he thought so. 'Yes precisely,' the Deacon said: 'They are all some other people, truly. Why no one even sang.' And it must be said that actually, for the first time, not one of the Romanov family sang with us during the service of 14 July.

Only Vasili Buimirov could have explained what he meant by these ambiguous words, yet neither he nor Father Meledin were consulted by the Whites. It is a curious omission, the reason for which remains unknown. It could be that neither man was in Ekaterinburg during the inquiry or that both had been killed. Nor can we exclude the possibility that the Whites ensured that they were not interviewed. Should Buimirov's words be taken literally – as some doubters have suggested – as indicating that substitutes had been found for the family? It seems highly unlikely. If he was speaking figuratively, what was he trying to say?

Why should the family have fallen to their knees at that particular moment? Again, there is no explanation, and guesswork is not going to provide a satisfactory answer. We can only agree with Buimirov that something had happened within the House of Special Purpose which had had an effect on the imperial family.

Storozhev did not tell Sergeyev what that something was – if indeed he knew. What is interesting is that Court Investigator Sokolov used the priest's testimony in his book, although in 1919 he had suggested that Storozhev was less than trustworthy because he had been carrying messages to the family from the Germans. We know this from a telegram sent by the British High Commissioner in Siberia, Sir Charles Eliot, on 14 July 1919, exactly one year after the service. Eliot reported that the 'Officer conducting investigation also thought it possible that imperial family received communications from the German government through the priests who attended them but this point is very obscure'.[2] Had Buimirov's singing been some sort of signal and the family falling to their knees a reply? There is no answer to the riddle.

The idea came from Sokolov, and we do not know what inspired it. Like so much else, he does not mention it in his book. As Eliot found the point obscure, we are entitled to assume that Sokolov did not see fit to share his evidence with the High Commissioner. The idea that Russian Orthodox priests were implicating the Tsar in negotiations with the hated Germans would not have been welcomed by the intensely patriotic Sokolov, and its omission or a disinclination to follow it up would be understandable, even if not forgivable. The idea was perfectly feasible. With the Germans looking for ways to restore the monarchy under circumstances which would benefit them, and the initiatives to liberate the family which we have already described, some means of communication with the imperial family would have been highly desirable. There was also a German mission in Ekaterinburg, the officers of which occupied a train in one of the stations. The priests would have been an obvious means of approach, especially as Dr Derevenko, the Tsarevich's physician who remained at liberty, was ideally placed to act as a go-between. This may be significant in the light of the fact that the Whites never saw fit to record any testimony the doctor could have offered.

Storozhev's testimony needs to be treated initially with caution in that it is uncorroborated by any primary source; none of those who might have confirmed or denied his story was consulted. The possibility of his having acted as a bridge for the Germans is the biggest single source of doubt so far as his evidence is concerned; if this was indeed the case, his words are fatally compromised. There are too many loose ends raised by his testimony which for some reason went unchecked. On these grounds alone it does not represent conclusive evidence.

How do Storozhev's claims square with Meinertzhagen's diary? Doubts can be cast on both men, but there is circumstantial evidence which lends support to Meinertzhagen. There was the matter of the aeroplane flying over the Ipatiev House in mid-July as reported by Sir Charles Eliot, who wrote that 'There is some evidence that they [the Bolsheviks] were much alarmed by an aeroplane flying over the garden of the house and I fear it is comprehensible that in a fit of rage and panic they made away with his Imperial Majesty'.[3]

Why should a solitary aeroplane, which dropped no bombs, did no damage and may even belong to the Red army, excite the guards to 'rage and panic'? There was nothing to connect this unknown machine with the Romanovs other than the aerial rescue attempt referred to by Meinertzhagen in his diary. If a rescue had been attempted using an aeroplane, then we would expect the Bolsheviks to be looking out for a possible repetition – which might explain their heightened reactions.

Was it possible that Meinertzhagen had made a mistake with the date he gave for the rescue? We have noted that he was writing this entry in his diary over a month later – and he made two mistakes in the same entry when he says that the Romanovs were taken to Ekaterinburg in November 1917 and again when he wrote that the rescue took place on 1 August, though he corrected this date. So a mistake could have been made, but that is not to say that it was.

We should also remember that the original guard on the Ipatiev House was replaced on 4 July and Avdiev and his deputy were arrested. Sokolov suggests that the Bolsheviks were concerned that the original guard were becoming too close to their prisoners, but there is nothing in any of the evidence we have about conditions in the house to sustain that argument. The deliveries of dairy produce by the nuns is hardly convincing evidence, and it is anyhow entirely isolated. All other reports indicate that conditions were harsh, with drunkenness and theft widespread. We are, admittedly, dealing in conjectures, where one version is as hard to prove as another, but in the context of known events, it seems more than possible that Avdiev and Moshkin were arrested and the guard replaced because of a rescue mission.

The Bolshevik communiqué announcing the death of the Tsar referred to unambiguously to the fact that 'a new plot of counter-revolutionaries was exposed, which aimed at tearing the crowned executioner from the hands of the Soviet government'. We might well ask not what *new* plot had been exposed but what previous plot or plots had there been[4] – and the communiqué implies that there had been at least one. Meinertzhagen's words are the only concrete evidence we have of a previous attempt.

There is also the fact that Chaya Goloschekin, the Regional Commissar for War, raced to Moscow from Ekaterinburg on 4 July and discussed the Romanovs with the Bolshevik leadership. Bolshevik rule was shaky at the time, but von Mirbach, the German ambassador, had yet to be assassinated and the real crisis still lay in the future. What provoked Goloschekin to go all that way to discuss the issue if nothing had happened?

There are no easy answers, and Storozhev's evidence does not fill the gap. Yet he was not the only witness to supply material to the Whites – and a Red Guard who was arguably the most intriguing witness of all gave the Whites evidence which contradicted Storozhev and is much closer to Meinertzhagen.

13

THE WHITE CROW

William James, the American philosopher and psychic re-
searcher, once remarked that 'If you wish to upset the law that
all crows are black, you must not seek to show that no crows are,
it is enough if you prove the single crow to be white'.

All the 'crows' in the shape of the Red Guards who testified to
the murder of the imperial family have been black, to the extent
that they maintain that every member of the family was murdered. There is, however, one white crow whose testimony was
not simply suppressed but mutilated beyond recognition. It was
this testimony that Judge Ivan Sergeyev had begun to investigate
when he was summarily dismissed in January 1919 – which inevitably raises the question of whether this was the real reason
for his dismissal.

This Red Guard was Georgi Nikolaevitch Biron, who was
assistant to the Chief Military Communications Officer of the
Bolshevik Third Army at Perm in November 1918. The first
news of the part he played in the murder took the form of an
account given in an official report by Général Janin, the
head of the French Military Mission in Siberia. Drawing on
information supplied by White headquarters in Omsk, Janin
wrote:

Nicholas II was killed with revolver and rifle shots by several men directed by a man called Biron who fired first. The Tsarevich was sick and hardly conscious of what was going on around him, according to certain descriptions. On top of this he was stupefied to see his mother and sisters killed before his very eyes. The Empress and her daughters, whose attitude in their last moments was very dignified, were killed after having been raped over several days, on several occasions and in various different ways. ... The Lett, on rushing out, is supposed to have said to several witnesses: 'Now I can die, I have had the Empress ....'[1]

This account, like the other stories emanating from Omsk in the winter of 1918–19, is a fabrication. However, Biron's story is given in full in Nikolai Ross's *Gibel Tsarskoye sem'i*,[2] and is worth studying in the light of Meinertzhagen's account.

Biron's version was given on 13 January 1919 to an inspector from Section 1 of the Criminal Investigating Division by Samson Ilich Matikov, a twenty-two-year-old student from Georgia who had been studying at the Petrograd Polytechnic Institute. From 5 November 1918 he had been living in Perm, having travelled from Petrograd disguised as a soldier returning from the front in Persia. He shared a flat in Perm, at 20 Okanskaya Street, with his brother Yosef and his family, and Colonel Georgi Osipovich Klerzhe, who had been on the General Staff of the old imperial army. Living in the same building were Biron and his wife, in the company of one Shpilevsky, who was also serving with the Third Army's Chief Military Communications Officer. It was through talking to Shpilevsky that Matikov and his flatmates discovered that Biron had been involved in the murder of the Tsar, and they deliberately steered the conversation round to the subject in Biron's presence so they could hear it from his own lips.

According to Matikov, Biron told his story boastfully, telling the company that 'about three days' before the Czechs took Ekaterinburg, the Military Council of the Third Army decided to shoot the family because of 'various transportation difficulties' in the event of an attack by the Czechs and White Guards. Biron was among the executioners.

The day before the occupation of Ekaterinburg by the Czechs, the Romanovs' servants were seized and taken to the city prison. That evening, a group of eight men arrived at the Ipatiev House. Lots had been drawn to determine which of them were to kill particular members of the family, though the Tsar himself was exempted from these proceedings, since a Latvian sailor called 'Pashka Berzin' had already demanded that he should be allowed to kill Nicholas.

When the murderers entered the house, Nicholas was sitting at the table alone, drinking tea. He said, 'It's hot and stuffy. I could do with a drink.' Then he caught sight of the revolvers in the hands of the murder squad and fell silent as he realized what was about to happen. He began to tremble, as a result of which Berzin jeered and laughed at him, telling him that his time was up. Nicholas fell to his knees and begged for mercy, pleading and grovelling. Berzin answered him with taunts, kicks and laughter, finally shooting him in the forehead at point-blank range.

Alexandra was then brought into the room, naked. Matikov thought she had been either raped or grossly insulted, but it is important to recognize that this was purely his interpretation, and that Biron had said nothing to him on the subject of rape. Biron's only comment was that 'she was naked and her body was very beautiful'. She carried herself with dignity and was killed with two shots, falling across the body of her husband.

One at a time the Tsar's daughters were brought into the room and shot. In Biron's view their spirits were broken and they looked 'totally stunned'. The Tsarevich was shot last of all, but Biron could not remember whether he had been shot in the bedroom or been taken to the room in which the rest of the family had been murdered.

The corpses, with the exception of the Tsar's, were then loaded onto a lorry and driven out of town, where they were buried in an unknown, unmarked spot. The Tsar's body was put into a car, driven rapidly for a quarter of an hour and then thrown into a marsh with two-pood (72-lb) weights attached to his head and feet.

Biron's story had a significant twist in the tale. According to

Matikov, 'Regarding Princess Tatiana Nikolayevna, Biron said that she had run away or disappeared with a Red army officer, a commander of the guard, long before this, i.e. before the murder of the Tsar, perhaps even from Tobolsk.'

Although this testimony is strictly hearsay, it is stronger than most evidence of that kind. Not only was Biron a first-hand eyewitness, but Matikov informed the inspector that his brother and Colonel Klerzhe were then in Omsk, and that the Colonel had actually noted down what Biron had said. If this was hearsay evidence, it was evidence of a very high order since it was possible for investigators to cross-reference it with the records of the other witnesses, one of whom had a contemporary written record.

The account that the Whites fed Général Janin bore no relation to what had actually been said. Nowhere does Biron claim to have shot the Tsar. On the contrary, he specifically names Pashka Berzin. He does not even say that he fired first. Rape is not mentioned. Nor is there any record of Biron rushing out and telling anybody that he had 'had' the Empress and could now die. If concrete evidence were ever needed of the Whites' penchant for twisting the evidence to suit themselves, this provides an indisputable example. It also lends Biron's account a plausibility that it might otherwise lack.

This credibility grows still greater when we examine what happened to the testimony afterwards. Judge Sergeyev received the account on or shortly before 20 January 1919, the day on which he issued 'urgent and secret' directions to the Court Investigator of the Omsk District Court to pursue the evidence in accordance with Article 292 of the Criminal Court Regulations. He requested the Court Investigator to examine Yosef Matikov and Colonel Klerzhe: 'as well as the usual questions', they were to be asked ten further questions about particular aspects of Biron's statement.

These questions were comprehensive and professional, contradicting General Dietrichs's later assertions that Sergeyev was lazy and incompetent. They included details of when, where and in what circumstances the two witnesses had met Biron, whether Biron had told them about the murder, and what he said about it.

They were asked to relate, in detail, the facts as reported by Biron, with particular reference to the time, place and circumstances of the crime, the individuals involved, their behaviour and that of the victims. Sergeyev also asked for more information about which Bolshevik organization had decided on the killings, when they passed their resolution, how it was worded and exactly who had taken part in the deliberations. They were to be asked what Biron had said about the disposal of the bodies and for more information about Pashka Berzin – what Biron had said about him, and whether he had given any clues that could help to establish his identity. Sergeyev also needed to know whether the witnesses had met Shpilevsky: if they had, they were to be asked to relate everything they had heard from him in detail. Further questions were left to the discretion of the Court Investigator.

Sergeyev specifically asked, 'Did Biron say anything about the fate of the ex-Grand Duchess Tatiana Nikolayevna? What exactly did he say?' His questions reveal a detailed and sensible attempt to follow up the evidence in his possession. He can be seen trying to cross-reference his sources and to test the accuracy of the report while obtaining as much detail as possible. There is no suggestion that he rushed into accepting it at face value. As he explained to the Court Investigator,

These facts are extremely important in helping us to determine the weight and significance of Biron's information, by comparing them with other information we have on this matter. It is also desirable to make clear whether the witnesses talked with Biron by chance, or whether they got the information out of him according to a premeditated plan and with a definite purpose. For this reason it would be useful to have information from the witnesses regarding the circumstances which took them to Perm, and the conditions of their residence there.

Sergeyev was adopting a cautious line and wanted to check the details and assess the evidence in the context of other information in his hands; it is a pity we do not have all the information that he had, since it might well suggest that he had good reasons for taking Biron's words seriously; but, alas, there is every reason to assume that his material was traduced once it fell into the hands of the White army. What we do know is that as late as 20 January 1919 Sergeyev did not hold the opinion attributed to him in Report No. 106 of 1 February, in which he is supposed to have written that he had no doubt that all of the imperial family had been massacred in the Ipatiev House. But between those two dates, of course, he had been abruptly dismissed and replaced by Court Investigator Sokolov.

Sergeyev had asked the Omsk Court Investigator to 'Please comply with my request with all speed, since the urgent verification of any information that can be obtained from questioning these witnesses is vital'. 'Urgent' and 'vital'; the emphasis given to these words is clear. Yet if any moves were made to follow up the evidence, they were short-lived, and any information gained was lost for good. Nikolai Ross follows Sergeyev's request with Document 75, signed by the Court Investigator of the Omsk Regional Court and sent to Sokolov on 31 March 1919. It reads: 'This request, in accordance with your spoken announcement, is hereby returned unacted upon.'[3]

To curtail this line of inquiry so abruptly and with a verbal command suggests that the White authorities had already made up their minds about the results of the inquiry before Sokolov had even had time to settle into his new task. A verbal suppression only makes sense if they were trying to conceal something: given Sokolov's links with the British through Robert Wilton, and the fact that Sergeyev's dismissal followed directly upon his discovery of this evidence, it looks as if they knew about a British rescue attempt and its outcome. Since Sergeyev had sent his instructions to follow this inquiry to Omsk, it makes perfect sense that White headquarters learnt of it and decided to dismiss him before his inquiries led him to establish anything solid.

Is Biron's evidence reliable? This is the key question, and there can be no certain answers without the evidence of the other witnesses whom the Whites stopped Sergeyev from reaching. Question marks must be placed alongside some of the words attributed to Biron. Either he or Matikov might be confused over dates. As it stands, the testimony says that the decision to shoot the Romanovs was taken 'about' three days before the city fell to the Czechs, that the murders were committed the day before the city fell, and that the servants were arrested and taken to the prison. All of this is at odds with the known facts. The massacre was in the early hours of 17 July, but the city did not fall to the Czechs until 25 July. Most of the family's remaining servants were removed to the city prison at various times over the three months that passed between the arrival of the Tsar, the Tsarina and Marie in April and the murder of the family. Four retainers were still with the Romanovs at the very end and suffered the same fate.

Biron's account of the death of Nicholas may well be regarded with scepticism. From all that we know about him, Nicholas was no coward and on more than one occasion he had expressed his wish to die for Russia. It is inconceivable that he would have grovelled in the manner related here. What Biron's words actually reflect is that Bolshevik propaganda depicted Nicholas as a coward. There was a story in circulation at this time, spread by the Reds, that the family had been forbidden to look out of the windows of the house. Nicholas chose to do so, and one of the guards fired a warning shot into the window frame which frightened the Tsar so much that he hid under a bed. It was nonsense, of course, but it illustrates what was in fact a Bolshevik ploy to denigrate the Tsar and his family.

Much depends on how sound Biron's memory was four months after the event, as was the case in Perm when he spoke to Matikov; and on how accurately Matikov was able to recall all that was said during what must have been a fraught evening two months previously. Mistakes could have been made by both parties, so we need to beware of treating every detail too literally.

Nevertheless, there are solid grounds for crediting the major part of Biron's version. In November 1918, the Bolsheviks were still maintaining that only Nicholas had been shot; yet here Biron is departing from the party line and maintaining that the family had been massacred. This counts heavily in his favour, as does the fact there was no question of him speaking under duress or needing to hide anything, as was the case with Red Guards in White hands.

Nor is it the case that Biron was small fry, whose words could be treated with contempt. He occupied a responsible position in the Red army which involved handling highly sensitive material. As an assistant to the Chief Military Communications Officer, he had the enormous advantage of being in a position to know how news of the fate of the Romanovs was transmitted to Moscow. He tells us that a courier was used – which makes sense, given that telegraph wires in a war zone could be, and frequently were, tapped or broken.

One man who might have been expected to know something of the truth was Biron's colleague Shpilevsky. He was not only Biron's friend, he worked in the same sensitive section of the staff of the Bolshevik Third Army. It is clear that he accepted Biron's testimony, for he had informed Matikov and his companions about it. It is significant because he was in a position to have known about the Bolsheviks' last days in Ekaterinburg, to have known his friend and colleague well enough to be able to dis-cern whether he was lying, to have had some idea of where he was and what he was doing on the day in question, and to have had some idea of the messages passed between the Third Army and Moscow.

Still more significant, perhaps, was the official message bearing the grim tidings of the murder of the family from the Intelligence Section of General Poole's force in Archangel in North Russia to London. Sent to the Director of Military In-telligence, it was based on information received from an un-identified officer eyewitness. It identified the persons responsible for the imprisonment and murder of the family, and mentioned 'Commissary Goloshchokin [*sic*] who ordered the Czar to be shot, sentence being carried out by a sailor whose name is as yet unknown'.[4]

The telegram was sent on 28 August, when Sergeyev had been in charge of the case for three weeks. It indicates that at that early date he knew that a sailor had killed the Tsar, so his interest in Pashka Berzin can be traced back to those early days, when the trail was still relatively fresh. Unfortunately we do not know what else, if anything, he had discovered in this respect between then and January 1919.

Although Biron's evidence was twisted and suppressed by the

Whites, Sokolov appears to have made an extraordinary mistake in sending his photograph to London. It is included in the Foreign Office file containing the official documents on the murder and is accompanied by photographs of five other assumed murderers. There is no explanation in the text Sokolov sent with the photographs of why these people should have been included or what their significance was. However, it would now appear that Sokolov knew a good deal more than he was prepared to publish.

There is also the question of the Grand Duchess Tatiana running off with an officer from the Red Guard. Biron's reference to this is rather vague, but it does give us a plausible explanation of how a rescue was effected without creating a major upheaval in the city, while restricting knowledge of it to a few people. It also supplies us with a far more convincing reason for the replacement of the guard on the Ipatiev House than that assumed by Sokolov. If an officer of the guard had been subverted – and it is worth remembering that subversion was a powerful tool in the hands of the British in the First World War, and one which they had learnt to use with some success by 1918 – this would have compromised the rest of the detachment, whose loose behaviour and want of discipline were notorious.

The German Foreign Ministry's files provide a measure of support for Biron. The files closed showing that the Germans had no certain knowledge about the fate of the imperial family. One document in the collection takes on a new importance in the light of Biron's testimony. It was provided by a Herr Pollmann who had been in White-occupied Siberia and who returned from Ekaterinburg and Omsk in August 1919 via the River Ob, by courtesy of the Swedish expedition to the river estuary. He stated:

> The Tsar's family with the exception of the Grand Duchess Tatiana really was murdered. The only survivors of the company were Miss von Buxhoeveden and the teachers. The elderly Dr Botkin and the Prince Dolgorouki were likewise killed. The inquiry that Kolchak had formed yielded that the corpses were burnt. The place of cremation is well-known.

They had also found there among other things a jaw of the Tsar, distinguishable from gold fillings of the teeth. The Grand Duchess Elizabeth with others in Alapaevsk was thrown down a shaft. The corpse was later buried. The Grand Duke Michael was also found in safety with Kolchak.[5]

Pollmann's evidence is important in a number of respects and he was clearly well informed. It corroborates Biron's evidence about the Grand Duchess Tatiana. It informs the Germans of the atrocity at Alapaevsk, which had not been referred to in the files previous to this. It confirms what is already known about the Grand Duke Michael. It anticipates the version of the destruction of the bodies of the family by fire. There is also the intriguing reference to the Tsar's jawbone being found at the site of the pyre. This has never come to light before and Sokolov does not mention such a crucial find. The Whites may have felt the nature of the find demanded a considerable degree of sensitivity, but that argument is not convincing. What we do not know is what or who Pollmann's source or sources of information were. Gossip and rumour can be ruled out since the rest of the material is too well informed to be sustained from such sources. Moreover, Pollmann's words carry the weight of one who was on the spot and who had no axe to grind.

Biron's evidence could be dismissed as fantasy if it stood alone, and if it is considered independently of what is now a considerable weight of corroborating evidence. There is the entry in Meinertzhagen's diary; there is the fact that Biron's testimony was not merely suppressed but twisted beyond recognition by the Whites; there is the report from British Intelligence at Archangel, according to which a sailor had shot the Tsar; there were other witnesses to Biron's testimony; there is the sudden sacking of Sergeyev; there is the confusion among the Bolsheviks surrounding the replacement of the guard on the Ipatiev House by Yurovsky and his Chekists at the critical time; there is the unexplained appearance of Biron's photograph among the documentary evidence on the Public Record Office: all point to the feasibility of a rescue under what were otherwise impossible conditions. It is unlikely that so much evidence, drawn from so many different and independent sources, coincides simply by chance. While this evidence does not as yet provide a full picture, attempts can now be made in that direction.

14

CORROBORATION

Meinertzhagen was not the only British Intelligence Officer to refer to efforts to rescue the Romanovs. Two other Intelligence Officers, Major Stephen Alley and Major William Peer Groves, both provide evidence that an operation was mounted and met with some degree of success.

Alley enjoyed the reputation of being one of the best SIS officers of his generation. Like Steven Gordon-Smith, he had been born in Russia – on the family estate near Moscow, in 1876 – and he could speak Russian as readily as English. His father was an engineer, who had been largely responsible for the development of the railways in the Russian empire – the Alleys even boasted a private station on their estate.

Commissioned into the Surrey Yeomanry in the Territorial Army, Alley returned to Russia in 1912; according to his wife, he had something to do with oil wells in the Ukraine. During the war he served in MI1(c), the Secret Intelligence Service, in Petrograd as station deputy to Colonel C. J. M. Thornhill and later to (Sir) Samuel Hoare. Between February 1917 and the spring of 1918 he was station chief there. After the war he was prominent in the Bolo Club – or Bolo Liquidation Club, as it was sometimes known – the members of which were SIS officers who had been engaged in the struggle against the Bolsheviks. 'Sally', as he was nicknamed, enjoyed playing the buffoon in this company, but such behaviour covered one of the sharpest minds to serve in Intelligence.

Until his retirement in 1957, Alley worked for the counter-espionage service, MI5; he combined this with service as a King's Messenger, responsible for carrying diplomatic bags. Growing tobacco in the Balkans was a cover for undisclosed activities during the inter-war years.

His charm and good humour, and the social position bestowed by his family, brought him into contact with many of the aristocracy of Russia and Eastern Europe, and with two royal families. He knew the Tsarina and reputedly warned her against the influence of Rasputin shortly before the monk was murdered. The Romanian royal family also fell under his spell, and he was a particular favourite of Queen Marie.

Alley died in 1967, the same year as Meinertzhagen, but his widow, Mrs Beatrice Alley, was interviewed by Clare Selerie-Grey on behalf of Anthony Summers. Among the papers in Anthony Summers' collection are letters which enlarge on points raised during the interview. Mrs Alley's most categoric statements reads: 'Early in the war he was made head of our secret service out there, and he thoroughly believed that Anastasia was alive. He thoroughly believed it, and he thought he recognized the photograph, *because he knew someone had been saved of that family*.'[1]

As an Intelligence Officer, Stephen Alley had been taught to be cautious, yet his statement clearly implies that one member of the family had been saved – in other words, whoever it was had been extricated by somebody from outside, rather than escaping through luck or his or her ingenuity. This is explicit. More importantly, Alley 'knew'; the words here do not imply gossip or hearsay. And finally, there is the reference to Anastasia, the youngest of the Tsar's daughters. The conversation had been prompted by a photograph of Anna Anderson, the Anastasia claimant, in a newspaper at the time when her story was beginning to emerge. Mrs Alley related how she had asked her husband if, with his background in Intelligence in Russia at that point, he thought there was any truth in the story. His reply was that it 'could easily be true, as two of the sisters were known to have escaped'.[2]

He declined to say any more since, according to Mrs Alley, 'He was a real clam and anyway I couldn't keep secrets'.[3]

This off-the-cuff remark was the furthest he was prepared to go, but the fact remains that he volunteered the information. Mrs Alley was not making it up – indeed, she confirmed it on other occasions – but can her memory of a conversation fifty years earlier be entirely reliable?

Mrs Alley died before I could speak to her, so there was no practical alternative other than to speak to Claire Selerie-Grey to obtain her impressions at first-hand. In the notes she had made at the time she recorded that Mrs Alley was completely coherent and her memory good. She confirmed that Mrs Alley had said that her husband had told her that he knew one of the Tsar's daughters had been saved, and that there was no question of it having been a case of escaping. And yet Alley, let us remember, had also said that *two* of the Tsar's daughters had survived the massacre at Ekaterinburg.

William Peer Groves told his daughter and one of his sons a very different story – that the whole family had been rescued. Born in 1878, the son of a brewer, Groves swiftly proved himself to be adventurous, ingenious, enterprising and precocious. On leaving school in 1897 he voyaged round the world, but nowhere left as deep and abiding an impression on him as Japan. In modern parlance he 'went native', becoming a lifelong follower of the Mahayana School of Buddhism, wearing the kimono, eating with chopsticks and bathing naked in communal baths. He built a collection of Japanese pottery and porcelain that was almost unrivalled in the West.

He took the science tripos at Cambridge, married in 1902 and was made a director of the family brewery in 1908. On the outbreak of war in 1914, he followed up an early interest in flight by joining the Royal Naval Air Service as an observer for 12-inch naval guns, winning the Légion d'honneur and being decorated by Général Pétain in person. He was also one of the crew of the submarine scout airship SS40, which the Admiralty lent to the army in order to study the feasibility of dropping agents from it by parachute. In it he made three flights behind enemy lines by night.

The last months of the war saw him working as a liaison officer, acting on behalf of the Admiralty's portion of the newly formed Air Ministry with the Japanese Navy. His fluent Japanese and his appreciation of Japanese culture made him ideal for this post, and he was awarded the Order of the Rising Sun, Fourth Class. Groves's Japanese link has a bearing on the Romanov case. According to Groves, the imperial family was indeed taken to the notorious ground-floor room in the Ipatiev House – not to be murdered, but as part of a rescue plan by 'loyal guards and British Intelligence'.[4] Shots were fired to deceive the other guards, who were not party to the plan, but in the darkness and confusion one of the bullets hit the Tsarevich, who bled profusely and later died from his wound. The family were then smuggled out into the hands of British Intelligence, who took them to Japan and then on to Canada, where they assumed new identities.

Groves's story was told 'on *strictest secrecy*'. His daughter, Mrs Ariel Clarke, wrote that her father told her the same story 'on various occasions', a fact worth noting since most fantasists are unable to resist the temptation to embroider and enlarge their tales with each new telling.[5]

Groves only told the story to one of his two sons, the late Commander Michael Peer Groves, who served in Naval Intelligence and might have been expected to spot a humbug when he saw one. Commander Groves told Summers and Mangold that he was reading an account of the murder of the Romanovs, and asked his father for his views on the subject. He was told that the family had not been murdered at Ekaterinburg.

Commander Groves went on to volunteer further information in a letter to Anthony Summers. His father had been with one of two groups of British servicemen who travelled north from Odessa on the Black Sea. One party went to Kiev, and the other set off for Siberia. Groves went with the party to Kiev, but at some stage separated from them and returned to Odessa alone and 'considerably later' than the others. Both groups returned to the port 'escorting various royalty', who remain unidentified. The Commander added that his father was 'more than reticent' about his journeys in Russia and about his reasons for going there at all. He confirmed that his father always maintained that the murder story was untrue and that he went to visit the Anastasia claimant in Germany several times, though he would never disclose what passed at these meetings.[6]

We can discount the idea that Major Groves was a fantasist straight away. His account never altered, and he remained deliberately reticent about sensitive details. The information he gave his son was in response to a direct question. What possible motive could he have for misleading his children?

The aspect of the story which excites suspicion concerns the movement of the parties from Odessa. In the story he told his daughter, he indicated that the escape took place on the night of the murder – in the early hours of 17 July 1918. No British mission could have travelled from Odessa at that time, since the port was in the hands of the Central Powers; besides which there was no way of reaching the port while Turkey barred the Dardanelles, the only sea route from the Mediterranean to the Black Sea. However, Groves had been in southern Russia in 1919, reporting on the condition of the White army there and on relations between the Whites and the French and Greeks.[7] It is hard to believe that this mission had anything to do with the Romanovs: the family would have had to be hidden in the interior of war-ravaged Russia for at least five months, which seems improbable.

Nevertheless, that is apparently what the Tsar's mother, the Dowager Empress Marie, believed. At a luncheon in Malta on her way into exile in 1919, she sat next to a lieutenant in the British army, Robert Ingham, and she began to talk about her son. She claimed to know where he was and was convinced that he and his family had escaped; she assured Ingham that they were hiding in a place which she refused to disclose. According to Ingham, she said she was careful not to let others know.[8] Why she should tell this to a young lieutenant in the British army is unclear. Were they the fond imaginings of an eccentric old lady who refused to face the truth?

All eyewitnesses are at one in reporting that the Dowager Empress betrayed no sign of abnormality during her voyage or when she was in Malta; on the contrary, she and her party appeared cheerful and carefree. Major Groves visited the Dowager Empress at the San Antonio Palace in Malta, and it appears that he was able to confirm to her that the family were alive and safe, giving her a piece of jewellery as evidence. We do not know what Groves said to the Dowager Empress, but it left her more than ever convinced of her son's survival.

The Dowager Empress later told the Marchioness of Milford Haven, the Tsarina's sister, that the Romanovs were hidden in a monastery in the far north of Russia, which could only be reached in the summer months. Their guardians were reputed to be 'Old Believers', a sect of the Orthodox Church that had resisted the seventeenth-century transformation of relations between Church and State.[9] However, this appears to contradict Groves's statement that they had been taken to Canada.

From Malta the Dowager Empress went to live in Britain with her sister, Queen Alexandra, the Queen Mother. News of any British involvement might have reached her there. She persisted in her belief that all her son's family were still alive. Queen Alexandra knew at least some of the truth, but we will never know how much since all her papers were destroyed when she died in 1925. That she knew something was made clear by her Maid of Honour, the Hon. Violet Mary Vivian, the sister-in-law of Field Marshal Lord Haig. After the publication of *Armour Against Fate*, where I had originally raised the prospect of a rescue, the Earl Haig, the Field Marshal's son, wrote to me and remarked that his aunt 'always said there was truth in the Anastasia claim'.[10]

This is the nearest we have ever had to an admission by a member of the British establishment that not all the Romanovs died in Ekaterinburg, coming as it does from a source which was intimately connected with the royal family and its innermost secrets. There can be little reasonable doubt that this information originated with Queen Alexandra, whose correspondence[11] reveals that she was active in the Romanovs' interest and had to be cautioned against sending any more letters or telegrams to the Dowager Empress.[12]

The nature of the source, a private conversation with a young nephew, suggests that the information was not intended for public consumption. Taken in the context of the background outlined above, there can be small reason for distrusting it. Unfortunately Miss Vivian never left any papers and, in her nephew's recollection, she was not the sort of person who would have kept any.

The biggest single weakness in Groves's version is that he had no personal connection with these events, whatever they were. He acquired his information either while serving with the Japanese, a possibility we shall need to look at more closely in due course, or after he had returned to Odessa, where he may have picked up a garbled version of the facts. Without knowing the circumstances in which he heard the story, nor who his informant was, it is difficult to put the information into perspective; there would, for example, be a considerable difference between what was gleaned at an Intelligence debriefing and what was said after half a dozen drinks in the Officers' mess.

Nevertheless, there are various reasons why we cannot altogether discard his words. That he only told two of his three children, on strictest secrecy, part of what he knew about events in Ekaterinburg in 1918 counts strongly in his favour. He was in Russia in 1919. He brought tidings of some sort to the Dowager Empress, which she was evidently glad to get. Even if Groves did pick up a garbled version of events, it remains that three good Intelligence Officers all confirm that an operation of some sort was attempted by the British. Criticism can be levelled against each one of these accounts in isolation, but when they are considered together and in the light of the background evidence, such an operation looks increasingly probable. If the Romanovs who were left in the hands of the Bolsheviks were murdered as a result of this operation, then it lays a heavy and unwelcome burden at the door of the House of Windsor, and may go far to explain the increasingly ridiculous secrecy that still surrounds the British records.

15

HIS BRITANNIC MAJESTY'S CONSUL

There was one British official who was unequivocally present in Ekaterinburg in July 1918, and who could have thrown much needed light on the murk which smothers the events of that month. This was Thomas Preston, the British Consul, whose residence was only a few doors away from the Ipatiev House. Throughout his life he publicly maintained that the whole family had been murdered, and on 22 July 1960, he swore an affidavit denying the Anastasia claimant's story.[1]

As we shall see, Preston was rather more than a mere Consul; and his evidence is contradictory. He argued that 'a dispute arose between Moscow and the Ural Regional Soviet over the fate of the Tsar and his family, the former being anxious for their transfer to Moscow, the latter insisting that they should be brought to Ekaterinburg. In this it would seem that Sverdlov was playing a double game.'[2] In fact, there is no evidence of any dispute between Moscow and Ekaterinburg over the complicated railway manoeuvres carried out by Yakovlev. As we have seen, the whole charade was almost certainly organized by Moscow with the aim of keeping the Romanovs out of German hands. It is difficult to see how Preston could reconcile his claim that there was a quarrel with his view that it was all the result of a ploy by

Sverdlov. Had that been the case, then there would be no grounds for any genuine friction.

It may be that Preston was unconvinced by his own case, for he quickly switched his argument, insisting that the cause of the quarrel was money. The Ekaterinburg Soviet, he claimed, 'began to use the Royal Family as a means of extorting money from the Central Government by means of threatening to kill them, whilst the Central Government were anxious to deliver the royal family over to the Germans at Moscow.'[3]

Three observations need to be made about this. We have established that the Bolsheviks were not anxious to surrender the Romanovs to the Germans, realizing that they would be asking for trouble if they did. Secondly, there is not the slightest shred of evidence which indicates that the family were used as a tool for blackmail in this way. Had they been, there would surely have been a telegraphic exchange on the subject. And if the Bolshevik Central Executive Committee were genuinely so anxious to surrender the Romanovs to the Germans, would they not have paid what was asked and got the prisoners out of the hands of the Ekaterinburg Soviet?

Nor is it unreasonable to ask why the local soviet needed to bargain for money in this way. The Bolsheviks had been busily evacuating the city for weeks, and Preston had sent a telegram on 12 June to Francis Lindley, Counsellor to the remains of the British diplomatic legation at Vologda, which actually itemized the considerable quantities of both cash and bullion they were moving from Ekaterinburg: 'Bolsheviks evacuated town transporting 36,000,000 roubles cash, 200 poods gold, 1,000 poods platinum at railway direction Perm.'[4] This great wealth was still at Perm, within comfortable reach of the Ekaterinburg Soviet, as late as 26 June.

There is a further curious aspect to Preston's account, which suggests that he was absent-mindedly compromising his own words about the Ekaterinburg Soviet's robust independence from Moscow. Twice he states that they asked Moscow what they should do with the Tsar when it became clear that the city could not be held for much longer, and he gives two versions of the reply they received. In his book, this reads 'Act as you consider necessary', yet his version in the official file at the Public Record Office says 'Do whatever you think fit'.[5]

The discrepancy in the wording might be explained by a faulty memory, writing years later without the original document in front of him. Yet that is a minor quibble beside the question that must be answered – how did Preston know, or claim to know, the contents of the cables exchanged between Moscow and Ekaterinburg, bearing in mind that the Bolsheviks were so sensitive about the messages travelling the wires that they interrupted foreign diplomatic communications and insisted that those dispatched by foreign diplomats were sent *en clair*?

No such telegram was ever discovered at the post office in Ekaterinburg. Preston was probably aware of this flaw in his argument, and he tried to counter it by claiming that his information came from the subsequent account of Chaya Goloschekin, the local Commissar for War.[6] Yet Goloschekin's only account of these events took the form of a statement he made in the city theatre on 20 July: it does not contain any reference to these telegrams, quite apart from which it was highly unlikely that he would have cited the texts of official communications in such circumstances. One can only wonder where Preston gained his information – or whether he invented it for the official record.

Substance might be lent to his version by the official papers of the British consulate, but they have never been released by the authorities. All that the Public Record Office can boast are a small number of documents in the political files that deal specifically with the murders, and a small number of telegrams Preston is supposed to have sent to Lindley and others reporting events after the city had been taken by the Whites.

What makes Preston's claims still more suspect is that the Ekaterinburg consulate does not seem to have functioned as a normal consulate at all. An insight into the consulate's real activities can be gleaned from Preston's request for British propaganda from the Foreign Office in March 1918. This was supposedly for the 'benefit of Allied subjects', who would appreciate the news in the light of the fact that the Bolsheviks were suppressing foreign news reports and spreading false information.[7] Just who these Allied subjects were and how many they numbered is a matter for conjecture. What is not a matter of conjecture is that none of the Britons among this community ever had their births, marriages or deaths registered at the Ekaterinburg consulate, although it is one of the duties of a consul to register such events among the compatriots in his area. There are no discernible records covering the normal day-to-day activities which should have occupied consular time during a period of great tension – citizens who wanted to get away, who had lost their passports or who had suffered the unwarranted attentions of the local authorities. It may well be that the Ekaterinburg consulate was chiefly concerned with more exacting tasks.

Certainly the consulate was heavily involved in anti-Bolshevik operations. Most of the propaganda material Preston requested was aimed at a Russian audience, and was designed to subvert the Bolsheviks in the Urals. The official record shows that Preston was seeking to mount a major counter-revolutionary campaign using the good offices of two Britons named Humphreys and Wallace. In July he asked for 30,000 roubles with which to fund this, so it was obviously no small venture.[8] On 10 July, the Central Telegraph Agency reported that a large number of counter-revolutionary pamphlets had been found inside Bolshevik newspapers awaiting delivery from the Ekaterinburg post office. The suspicion must be that this was the work of the British consulate.

More than this, the consulate was earnestly engaged in assisting the advancing Czechs and Whites. The interruption of the Czechs' eastward march to Vladivostok coincided with the Allies beginning to abandon hope of the Bolsheviks turning against the Germans and their growing belief, not altogether unfounded, that they were actively co-operating with the Germans. It was decided to back the counter-revolutionary forces, which offered the prospect not only of overthrowing the Bolsheviks but of reopening the fight against the Germans. The Allies rallied to the Czechs, who represented the strongest and best organized anti-German forces in the territory of the old Russian empire.

Preston himself confirmed the new orientation when he wrote of receiving 'a secret message, brought by a special messenger through the Red lines from Archangel, officially confirming the fact [that] the Czech movement was to be given Allied support as an anti-Bolshevik army'.[9] He also tells us that he and his colleagues among the Allied consuls in Ekaterinburg were in secret contact with the advancing Czechs, and that the Czechs fed their agents into the city where they co-operated with the Allied consuls, warning them to hoist their national flags so their consulates would not be targeted by Czech artillery. It also meant that there was now a route whereby messages could reach Vladivostok and London through the Czech lines.

A British officer, Captain C. S. Digby Jones, was stationed in the consulate to act as courier between the Czechs, the Consul and the British forces in North Russia under Major-General Poole. He was also connected with the propaganda campaign, and it was with this in mind that he had originally sought to go to Russia.[10] He had set out from Murmansk for Ekaterinburg accompanied by a civilian, a Mr Reed.[11] We can only guess Reed's precise business in Ekaterinburg, but when I mentioned him to Sir Ronald Preston, Sir Thomas's son, he recalled being taken to see 'old Reed' in his childhood, and understood him to have been an officer from the Secret Intelligence Service.

Whether Digby Jones or Reed had any connection with the Romanov case is difficult to ascertain. The name Jones appears scrawled in the margin of Sir Charles Eliot's report alongside the passage describing the sounds of uproar and shooting that were heard in the Ipatiev House in the early hours of 17 July. We know from a statement given to Arthur Thomas, the Acting Consul in Ekaterinburg on the occasion of Digby Jones's death on 25 September 1918, that Lieutenant-Captain Theodore Arthur Meise of the White Russian army stated that he and Digby Jones left Vologda together on 8 July and arrived in Ekaterinburg on 17 July, perhaps in time to hear and see what was happening.[12]

Although Digby Jones's name and death appear in the Foreign Office card-index in the Public Record Office under reference WS7/163706, the documents themselves have disappeared and nobody can shed any light on their whereabouts. Further traces of this clumsy weeding are to be found in the War Office file, WO 106/1233, the contents list of which has two references to Digby Jones but no documents. The process is repeated in file WO 106/1237, where there should be documents on a Captain Pablenco and another on the murder of the imperial family.

Staff at the Public Record Office were unable to explain the absence of these documents and suggested that I ask the Ministry of Defence. The Ministry sent a reply from Common Services (Records) saying that they could not shed any light on the missing documents and advised me that no formal, authorized extraction had been made and the papers must have been removed without authority.

There can be no question that the consulate in Ekaterinburg was being used as a centre for anti-Bolshevik activity on a considerable scale. It seems reasonable to conclude that the Consul had a lot to hide and that this extended to the Romanovs, since the consulate was being used to watch the Ipatiev House. Was Preston's subsequent reticence prompted by something other than his having nothing more to say? It seems likely that it was.

The first clue that the robe was not as seamless as the authorities might have hoped comes in the shape of Preston's report on the murder of the Tsar. It reads: 'According official statement Maximalist leaders Nicolai Romanoff after trial was sentenced capital punishment and shot night of sixteenth.'[13] This seems clear enough, except for one fact: it is dated 11 July 1918. This was unlikely to have been a mistake on Preston's part, or on that of a filing clerk at the Foreign Office since the telegram is in order of date in a well-catalogued correspondence. Moreover, it is superseded by a later telegram of 22 July, sent to Lindley at Vologda, which reads: 'According to official Bolshevik statement late Emperor after trial was sentenced to death and shot on night of sixteenth.'[14]

Taken with the other facts we have noted, this suggests that the correspondence was no more than a blind, calculated to mislead. I do not base that view solely on the content of the file, nor even on the fact that another, more secure means of communication led eastwards through the Czech lines to Vladivostok, where there was not only a British consulate, but an SIS station.

Thomas Preston knew that the imperial family had been shot.

He also knew that two of the Tsar's daughters were not among the dead – and he knew because he had seen the bodies of the victims.

That information comes from Preston's wife and his sister-in-law. In 1987 a production team was working on a programme for Channel Four television about life in Russia during the Revolution sixty years before. They interviewed a great many people from all walks of life who had lived through that experience. Most had been children at the time, but they were surprised and delighted to find that there were two elderly ladies in Norfolk who had been adults. Initially, the team had no idea that they were connected with the Romanov case, in which they were not interested anyway. For the purpose of the interview, both ladies spoke in their native Russian, which meant that an interpreter was needed: both were of advanced years, Lady Preston being ninety-one, and her sister, Madame Bibikov, eighty-seven.

The two women had been in the consulate in July 1918: Mrs Preston had been with her husband, while her sister had sought refuge there after her husband, a White officer, had been killed by the Reds. Lady Preston and Madame Bibikov told the Channel Four team that Thomas Preston had been a mining engineer in Russia when he was asked to become a temporary and acting consul in Ekaterinburg. The real impact of their testimony, however, came when the ladies spoke eagerly about the Romanovs. They confirmed that everybody in the consulate was expecting something to happen to the imperial family, so when shots were heard at about 2.15 a.m. on the morning of 17 July, they did not come as a surprise. However, the two ladies insisted that there were not enough shots to account for all the prisoners held in the house. This version of events would seem to be closer to Biron's account than to those which report a general fusillade of shots.

The uncertainty continued until the early hours of the morning, when someone knocked at the door of the consulate. Preston answered the door to find a Red Guard there, who asked him to follow him. He was taken to the Ipatiev House where he was shown the bodies and was informed that he was there as official foreign eyewitness to the fact that the Romanovs had been shot. On his return he told his anxious wife and sister-in-law the sad news, but said that two of the Tsar's daughters were not among the slain. Anastasia was one, and he thought the other was Tatiana.

Dare we believe it? It does coincide with other facts which have come to light, not least of which is that the remains of *all* the Romanovs have yet to be accounted for. It would go a long way towards explaining how the Hon. Violet Mary Vivian could be so sure of her facts, and it would also explain much about the attitude adopted by the British royal family. It could also account for the persistent and highly suspicious suppression of historical documents in this country and, perhaps, the British royal family's steadfast opposition to the Anastasia claimant – either they knew she was who she said she was and were not prepared to admit it, or they knew the real Anastasia was elsewhere and that the claimant could not be the Tsar's daughter.

The ladies also introduced another factor into the conversation, which in the light of what we have noted about communications from Ekaterinburg speaks highly for the veracity of their account. They said that communications with Britain ran through what they called 'long channels', which went east to Vladivostok. The ladies stated that the Japanese wanted to help the Romanovs, but began their effort too late. Instead, they were immensely helpful to the British. More will be said about the Japanese connection in the next chapter.

According to the Channel Four team, both ladies argued vehemently over the minor details, but both told the same overall story. Both struck the television team as being extremely eager to tell it, which suggests, perhaps, that they had seized what might well be their last chance to make the truth known. It is the nearest we are ever likely to come to a deathbed confession so far as this particular story is concerned.

In the event the Channel Four television programme was never screened. However, Sir Ronald Preston confirmed to me that the interview had indeed taken place. For the time being the programme recordings and, more importantly for the historians, the transcripts – both of which were witnessed – are in storage in the United States. Their release would put the matter beyond all reasonable doubt.[15]

That is by no means the end of the evidence to come from the Ekaterinburg consulate. Preston's deputy, Arthur Thomas, has already been mentioned. He was a Cornish mining engineer, who became acting consul in Preston's stead when the latter went to Vladivostok in the autumn of 1918. Like Preston, he was to maintain publicly that the whole family had been murdered, repeating the standard version again and again in lectures he gave on the evils of communism in the 1920s and 1930s.

Not only did Arthur Thomas give lectures, but he provided his local newspaper with an exclusive account of his experiences in Russia. In an interview with the *Cornishman and Cornish Telegraph*, which was also reprinted in its sister paper, the *Cornish News and Redruth Effective Advertiser*, he listed the victims in the Ipatiev House: 'Those who were considered to be murdered were the Czar and Czarina, their three daughters and son.'[16] A slip had been made. Nicholas and Alexandra had four daughters, not three. Given Preston's role as official foreign eyewitness, this is unlikely to have been a journalistic error. Moreover, Herbert Thomas, who took down the story, was one of the best provincial journalists of his day, widely respected and hardly the sort of man to make a clumsy slip like that. Had one daughter been rescued by British Military Intelligence the slip would have been a perfectly natural one, since the Consular staff were clearly not ignorant of Intelligence activities in Ekaterinburg.

There is another fact of arguably greater significance where this story is concerned. As a British official, even of a temporary and acting kind, Arthur Thomas would have been subject to the full weight of the Official Secrets Act, which was strongly enforced in 1920 in the aftermath of the war, given the very real fears of German resurgence and communist subversion. It was one thing to be pressed for an interview, but quite another for Thomas to walk into a newspaper office and offer the information. Yet that is what he did, according to the centenary edition of the newspaper, which recorded that he went to see Herbert Thomas and said, 'Herbert, would you like the story of the murder of the Czar and Czarina of Russia? I was there in Ekaterinburg when it happened and I can give you the only story that is known of what happened'.[17]

Thomas emphasized the murder rather than his own experiences. It was a story that the King did not want the public to know about, yet he was never prosecuted under the Official Secrets Act. Nor did he ever correct the error in the number of daughters who had been killed. A deliberate leak seems unlikely, as the *Cornishman* was hardly the ideal medium in which to make the story known to the world at large. Perhaps he simply wanted to get the story off his chest, but his papers are silent about his motives.

What we can be certain of is that the British consulate in Ekaterinburg knew a great deal more about the fate of the Romanovs than we have been led to believe. Taken together with what else has been unearthed, and especially that the remains of *all* the Romanovs have yet to be accounted for, we can state with reasonable confidence that two of the Tsar's daughters were not killed at Ekaterinburg, and that British Intelligence had a hand in the fate of one of them.

16

SIBERIAN FLIGHT

Colonel Richard Meinertzhagen's diary tells us that the rescued Grand Duchess was in Britain by 18 August 1918. How had she got there? None of the sources that comment on this case sheds any light on this. Certainly, secrecy would have been a paramount consideration because of the risk to the life of the girl and because of the political problems the King would have faced had the news leaked out. Meinertzhagen was certainly aware of the risks, confiding to his diary that 'Even now I feel it a bit dangerous to disclose detail' on the grounds that 'I am sure that if her identity were known she would be tracked down and murdered as the heir to the Russian throne'.[1]

This legitimate extra layer of secrecy means that tracing the details of events after the rescue is an almost impossible task, but some slight straws of evidence exist which may be worth following. The first of these is Meinertzhagen's claim in his diary on 18 August 1918 that an aeroplane was used. Where did it come from and where would it have flown? General Poole's forces in North Russia were far beyond the range of any of the aeroplanes available in 1918, and the small British Military Mission in South Russia had neither the machines nor the support facilities to handle such a task.

The testimony of Lady Preston and her sister point us eastwards, towards Vladivostok, as does Major Groves's connection with the Japanese. A flight across Siberia, though not without hazard, was the only practical route open. It had the advantage of flying over friendly territory, with opportunities to rest, recuperate and refuel. Moreover, the Japanese army was in Siberia, and was the most powerful Allied force there. It was, perhaps, this support which Lady Preston and Madame Bibikov had in mind when they spoke about Japanese help for the British. And since the Trans-Siberian railway was in White hands, another means of transport was available should the flight be deemed too perilous.

British Intelligence had men on the spot who could supervise arrangements and security. Omsk, the White capital, seems to have been a centre of British activity, with SIS agent ST12 reporting that the 'names of two first-rate men at Omsk' would shortly be sent to London.[2] British Intelligence certainly had a station in Vladivostok. In the spring of 1918 it was run by a Major Bell, who was replaced because he proved quite unable to efface himself and vanish into the background like a good SIS officer should. He was superseded by a man called Shaw from Hong Kong, acting in conjunction with a Major Carvel. By September, the station was commanded by Colonel MacDonald, with Major C. A. Cameron on his way from the Western front to take control of executive operations. Vladivostok was also playing host to the cruiser HMS *Suffolk*, which could provide secure communications; secret telegrams were sent by her commander, Captain Payne, but their contents remain undisclosed.[3]

Since a rescue by air lies at the heart of the issue, it follows that one of the rescue team needed to be a pilot. Records of RAF operations in North Russia in 1918 are still closed: the file reference is AIR1/?/204/157/1, and the collection has still not been released to the Public Record Office.[4] The question mark in the reference takes the place of a number in the sequence of Air Force documents, normally 180 or 181, which has not been allocated to this file and will not be allocated until it is ready to be transferred to the Public Record Office.

However, one officer who was serving in North Russia in 1918 caught my eye because of a blatant attempt to disguise the nature of his duties. His name appears in the *Nominal Roll* which listed the officers serving with the force in North Russia.[5] Captain John Sanderson Poole, DSO, was entered as an Infantry Officer with the 60th Foot, the King's Royal Rifle Corps. Checking his name against the *Army List* for July 1918, we find the initials *f.c.* beside it, indicating that he had been transferred to the air service with effect from 17 February 1917 and was now commissioned in the RAF. Most of the British officers in North Russia were elderly and had been brought out of retirement to train the Russian levies it was hoped to raise to fight the Germans. Poole was, by comparison, a mere stripling of twenty-one and the only one of this gallant band who could be expected to face the rigours of genuinely active service.

Born on 16 September 1896, Poole was the son of a stockbroker. He was educated at Rugby where, not excelling as a scholar, he joined the Army Class. Natural progression took him to the Royal Military Academy, Sandhurst, but the outbreak of war saw him in the front line more quickly than he could ever have anticipated. He faced the German gas attack at Second Ypres in April 1915, but his service on the Western front was brought to an abrupt halt when he was blown up and taken prisoner the following month.

While in captivity he had the first real opportunity to display his mettle, making three escape attempts in the course of as many months. The last of these succeeded and he reached Britain via the Netherlands, becoming a hero in the process. Forbidden to return to the Western front, as he was wanted by the Germans, he was interviewed by the Director of Naval Intelligence, Sir Reginald 'Blinker' Hall, regarding his future employment. According to his own record, the choices ranged from propaganda work in the USA 'to a trip in a submarine in a less pleasant role'.[6]

Poole also had a half-hour audience with the King. It seems that Poole created quite an impression, for 'Leo Battenburg', later Lord Leopold Mountbatten, told him a week later that he had dined with the King and had been treated to Poole's story by him. Poole met the King again some six months later when he was presented with his DSO at Buckingham Palace. Evidently he had remained in the King's mind: he was asked about his activities since they had last met, and the King 'smiled understandingly when I explained that my absence had been due to flying instruction in the RFC'.[7]

Poole's autobiography shows him to have been modest with a self-effacing humour and a reluctance to discuss particular aspects of his military career. The facts that he had made a strong impression on the King and that he had been considered for what are euphemistically termed 'special duties' may well help to explain his silence about one part at least of his activities in Russia.

His presence there came about, he tells us, as a result of meeting a friend while he was engaged in training recruits for overseas service at Sheerness, where he had been sent after being injured when he crashed his Sopwith Camel fighter. He heard of the Russian expedition entirely by chance, he says, from this unnamed friend 'who was organizing the party' and persuaded him to apply for a posting with the force.[8] He did and was accepted. It sounds an unconvincing story.

Once in Russia, he seems to have been seized by an amazing – and very convenient – loss of memory. At the very time when the rescue operation would have been in progress, the only excuse he can offer is that 'My memory of this phase has faded, and I can only assume that I travelled on the seaplane-carrier *Nairana*'.[9]

With his subsequent appointment as staff captain to the Dwina River Column, a small British force which advanced up the River Dwina, his memory returns with startling clarity.

It has, alas, proved impossible to trace any of Poole's papers. A close friend of his, Mrs Pamela Mayor, told me that it was very probable that he was involved in a secret mission in Russia as it would have been entirely in keeping with his character.

Vladivostok was not, of course, the end of the journey. There were still several thousand miles of ocean to cover before any Romanov who had been rescued could reach Britain. The solution to this problem may well lie in the voyage of Prince Arthur of Connaught to Japan and Canada.

Prince Arthur was a grandson of Queen Victoria, his father being Field Marshal Prince Arthur William Patrick Albert,

Duke of Connaught and Strathearn. Prince Arthur was George V's only male contemporary in his immediate family, and from the time when the future King was still the Prince of Wales, Prince Arthur often shared some of his royal duties. In the summer of 1918 he was to lead a mission to Japan, the avowed aim of which was to present the Emperor Yoshihito with the baton of a British field marshal in order to counter Japanese concern over Britain's ability to see the war through to a victorious conclusion. Prince Arthur had not originally been intended to lead the mission, but it was felt that a senior member of the royal family would create a better impression. When the mission was planned, in April 1918, there could have been no connection between the Prince's mission to Japan and the Romanovs: the imperial family were still at Tobolsk, and the King's hopes were based on proposed rescue attempts like those of Lied and Gordon-Smith.

These hopes were brought to naught when the Romanovs were moved to Ekaterinburg. Something had to be arranged rapidly while still maintaining secrecy. Might Prince Arthur's visit have fitted the bill? The mission arrived at Yokohama on 18 June and its official duties were soon completed. On 29 June the party began a holiday in Nagoya and Kyoto, surrounded by a wall of secrecy contrived by their hosts. The secrecy was unusually heavy, even for a royal visit in wartime, and resulted in critical voices being raised in Japan. After the visit, a correspondent from the newspaper *Jiji* gained an interview with Viscount Hatano, the Minister of the Imperial Household Department who had been largely responsible for the domestic arrangements for the visit. Hatano told the correspondent that

the secrecy observed as to his Royal Highness's programme of travel was objected to, but this secrecy was in accordance with a strict request emanating from a certain quarter where extreme anxiety was felt. The programme of the royal journey was marked secret, and with the exception of the Reception Committee no one, not even himself, could get an advance view of it.[10]

147

Such secrecy was not only inspired by fears for the Prince's safety: a telegram from the British ambassador, Sir Conyngham Greene, reporting a conversation between the Prince and the Japanese Prime Minister, included the statement that, 'His Excellency added that it was evident in dispatching Prince Arthur to Japan the King had something more in mind than ceremonial of handing of Field Marshal's Baton.'[11]

The level of secrecy even affected the British ambassador, who lamented that

I have had to depend on the brief official programme and on the meagre records of the press for the following brief account of the Prince's movements after his departure from Tokyo. The silence of the press is of course the result of instructions to keep His Royal Highness's movements secret and not due to any lack of interest in them.[12]

Their holiday in Kyoto and Nagoya over, the Prince and his companions left Japan for Canada aboard the Japanese battle-cruiser *Kirishima* on 10 July, and after a two-day delay in the Inland Sea caused by bad weather arrived at Victoria Island off Vancouver on the evening of 24 July. They stayed on the island for another short holiday until 27 July.

There would have been no shortage of opportunities to transfer the rescued Grand Duchess into the care of the Prince's party during this period – and given the cloak of secrecy organized by the Japanese, there would have been little chance of any information leaking out. The transfer could have been effected while the Prince was on holiday in Japan, or when the *Kirishima* was delayed in the Inland Sea; alternatively, a Japanese destroyer could have carried her direct to Victoria Island to join the mission there – the log of HMS *Suffolk* at Vladivostok reports the arrival and departure of a number of Japanese warships during this period, any one of which could have been used to take her to whichever destination they had in mind.

That something was happening during this period seems clear from the nature of the gaps in the records. In the folder covering the Prince's mission at Windsor Castle, document No. 81 has vanished and been replaced with a piece of paper stating that Colonel Clive Wigram, understudy to Lord Stamfordham, had removed a document from the file on 10 July 1918. The date fits the timetable of events perfectly, since it would have taken over a week to get the rescued Grand Duchess across Siberia, and several days more for the information to filter through. The same applies to the *Canada Register* when it comes to the holiday on Victoria Island; the fact of the holiday is briefly recorded, but the reference number, 36524S, is written in red ink, indicating that the material was secret. The *Register* refers to copies of the papers relating to the arrangements in the Foreign Office and Admiralty files, yet the documents which correspond to this entry have all disappeared.[14]

Even private papers have not escaped. Lieutenant-General Sir William Pulteney was one of the members of the mission. On 1 August 1918, he wrote from Canada to his friend Lady Desborough, a close friend of the royal family, praising the fresh and delicious smell of the trees on the island. He began his letter with the words 'You will have got my letter from the Pacific'.[15] The letter is not in the collection and is the only one missing from a complete and meticulously catalogued correspondence. Had Pulteney been less than totally discreet? If he had, then somebody had taken the trouble to ensure his indiscretion never became public.

There is a good case for asking why a brief private holiday was subject to such a cloying degree of secrecy. And why was another holiday needed so soon after the one at Kyoto? The intervening period had been occupied by nothing more strenuous than an uneventful sea voyage: what convincing reason was there for spending several more days on a sparsely populated island off the Canadian coast?

The escape route from Russia to Canada via Japan was well established by this time. Its foundations were laid in April 1918, when the commanding officer of the Royal Navy's China Station, Admiral Sir Frederick Tudor, informed the Admiralty that 'I approved the action of the Naval Attaché at Tokyo who accommodated British refugees from Russian territory, women and children at the Royal Navy Sick Quarters at Yokohama pending arrangements for their passage'.[16] Further correspondence shows that this route to safety via Japan was continuously developed and was fully operational by July.

If we accept that this route was used to get the Grand Duchess to safety – always subject to the proviso that it is a probability rather than an established fact – the question remains of how the Prince's mission managed to get her across Canada without attracting unwelcome attention. Canada was playing host to another visitor from the mother country at this time – Amorel Meinertzhagen, the wife of Colonel Richard Meinertzhagen. She returned to Britain aboard the Canadian Pacific Ocean Service Ltd's vessel *Corsican*, occupying Cabin 14. In the adjoining Cabin 13 was Miss Marguerite Lindsay, aged twenty-two and whose profession was listed as a masseuse. Also travelling on the same ship was Henrietta Crawford, a War Office matron. The age attributed to Miss Lindsay would have enabled one of the Tsar's two eldest daughters to pass for her, while the presence of a War Office matron could have been a contingency measure to provide against any injury suffered during the rescue.

The *Corsican* docked in London on 8 August, time enough for her arrival to coincide with the reference in Meinertzhagen's diary on 18 August to a Grand Duchess being in Britain. At this stage Miss Lindsay vanishes. Her address, listed in the return that the ship's master was required to furnish under the Aliens Act of 1905 and the Merchant Shipping Act of 1906, was clearly non-residential – the Bank of Montreal, 9 Waterloo Place, London, a few doors away from the offices of General Poole's Mission at 6 Waterloo Place. The Bank does not keep customer records from so long ago, and there appears to be no further trace of Marguerite Lindsay. Nor do the Registers of Births in England, Scotland, the Isle of Man or any of the Dominions disclose any record of her birth.

Again, the evidence is more intriguing than conclusive, and there are the usual unanswered questions. Why should Amorel Meinertzhagen have needed to sail from Canada across an ocean made perilous by U-Boats and mines little more than a month after the sinking of the hospital ship *Llandovery Castle*, with all the outrage that her sinking had provoked? Who was Marguerite

Lindsay? Was it her real name? What happened to her, and why does all trace of her vanish? Amorel Meinertzhagen's papers might have thrown some light on these matters, but those papers relating to her marriage with Meinertzhagen have been destroyed.

The Siberian and Japanese links tally too closely with the evidence of Lady Preston and her sister, Meinertzhagen and Major Groves to be easily dismissed. The constant suggestion of concealment indicates that there was more to Prince Arthur's mission than the presentation of a baton to the Emperor of Japan. There is sufficient to suggest that the Siberian route was overwhelmingly probable, even if it did not exactly follow the course I have charted.

17

A GRAVE IN LYDD

Lydd is an unremarkable market town in Romney Marsh, Kent. Its parish church, known as the 'Cathedral of the Marshes', its army camp and the proximity of Dungeness nuclear power station make an uneasy combination. The east winds which sweep across the flat landscape can make life unpleasant; as the diarist of the 3rd Battalion, the Royal Tank Corps, had occasion to note in 1923 shortly after his unit had moved there, 'I wish to reiterate the fact that Lydd is an extremely cold place in winter.'[1] It makes an unlikely last resting-place for the body of a Russian Grand Duchess, but there is a strong possibility that a survivor of the massacre at Ekaterinburg is buried here.

After the publication of *Armour Against Fate*, in which I had first raised the possibility that Tatiana had escaped, two ladies from Lydd contacted me on the grounds that they might have information of interest. Mrs Eva Bowler and Mrs June Daniels live in a house which stands opposite a corner of a cemetery in Lydd. Both had been intrigued by an isolated grave in that corner of the cemetery; they were driven to it for reasons neither could explain. Their interest was excited by the legend on the head-stone, which read:

A GRAVE IN LYDD

TO
MY VERY BELOVED
LARISSA FEODOROVNA
WHO DIED JULY 18th 1926
AGED 28 YEARS
THE WIFE OF
OWEN TUDOR
3rd THE KING'S OWN HUSSARS

It is difficult to say what first excited the ladies' interest. It might have been the unusual name of the woman, or that she had died so young, or that for many years someone had placed flowers on the grave every 10 June, or that the Owen Tudor mentioned was in the Hussars when, so far as anybody knew, Lydd had no connection with that particular regiment.

Simply to satisfy their own interest, they tried to find out something about the couple whose marriage had ended so tragically early. They discovered that they had been married in London at the now defunct Register Office of St George's, Hanover Square, and that the wedding was a very private affair with none of the publicity or celebration which normally accompanies such a joyful occasion. There were two witnesses to the marriage, K. M. Huntington and D. Swinburne. Since Owen Tudor was an army officer, they searched the *Army List* for 1923. There was no sign of Huntington, but a Denis Swinburne was a lieutenant in the Royal Ulster Rifles.

The information on the marriage certificate was irregular; certainly some of it was untrue. Both partners to the marriage had given their address as the York Hotel, Mayfair, which was clearly not a home address. Where the certificate asked for the rank or profession of the parties, Owen Tudor had answered 'Of Independent Means' and had entered his father's rank or profession as being of independent means as well. In fact both these statements were false. Owen Tudor was an officer in the 3rd Hussars and he did not have independent means – he was an impoverished subaltern who had to live on his pay. His father, Henry Morton Tudor, was a retired admiral of some standing.

Owen Tudor's wife had given her name as Larissa Haouk. The

153

patronym on the headstone strongly suggested she was Russian, and this was confirmed by what little was known about her among Lydd's more elderly residents. Yet Haouk was not a Russian name. Her father was named as Adolph Haouk, deceased, who had also been gifted with independent means. After stumbling upon what appeared to be clear attempts to mislead, the ladies were more than ever determined to get to the bottom of this increasingly mystifying affair.

They managed to trace the surname Haouk by dint of contacting foreign embassies in London. Only one laid claim to the name and it was the Moroccan Embassy, which told the ladies that the name was as common in Morocco as Smith was in England. So could Larissa have been Moroccan? It seemed unlikely. Larissa is an East European name and Feodorovna is a Russian patronymic. Morocco at the time had been influenced by France and Spain rather than by Russia, though it might have been possible for a Russian family to have settled there. That seemed unlikely too, since Larissa's father's Christian name was Adolph, spelt in the German style – and in any case, if there was Russian blood in the family the patronym would have been taken from her father's name, which bore no resemblance to Feodor, the Russian for Frederick. It is possible that Larissa had adopted the patronym as a convert to the Russian Orthodox Church; but if that were so, when had she become a convert? The patronym does not appear on the marriage certificate and the records of the Russian Orthodox Church in the Public Record Office at Chancery Lane contain no reference to her having joined their communion.

Then there was the question of Larissa's age. The marriage certificate gave it as twenty-seven in 1923, which meant that she was probably born in 1896. The headstone over her grave gave it as twenty-eight in 1926, which would make her year of birth 1898. Her death certificate stated that she was twenty-nine, as did the register in St John's Church, Lydd – which meant that she had probably been born in 1897. The more the two ladies probed, the more mysterious it all became. The only certainty seemed to be that somebody had had good reason to hide the truth and had gone to considerable lengths to do so. But for what reason?

Larissa's death certificate recorded that she died on 18 July 1926 from heart exhaustion resulting from spinal caries and pulmonary tuberculosis. The latter was one of the great killers of the time, as feared as cancer, heart disease or AIDS today. Spinal caries is a form of osteoporosis or crumbling of the spinal column; the vertebrae progressively disintegrate, leading to curvature of the spine and death. Mrs Bowler and Mrs Daniels were fortunate enough to find an eyewitness in Lydd, a Mrs Lamb, who told them that Larissa had indeed been seriously ill, spending her time in an elongated bath chair and unable to sit up straight. In those days, the ailment was more often than not the result of a severe physical jolt, such as might be suffered in a fall from a horse.

It was on the death certificate that the patronym Feodorovna first appeared. The entry in the Register of Deaths in St Catherine's House, however, reads 'Larissa T. Tudor' rather than 'Larissa F. Tudor'. Some sort of mistake had been made, but by whom? Perhaps it was simply a typing error or a mistake at the time of death – or had the initial 'T' been in Owen Tudor's mind for quite another reason?

Mrs Lamb also revealed that Owen Tudor was devastated by his wife's death and cut a very sorry figure at her funeral, having to be supported at the graveside. She told the two ladies that there had been just one other person present at the funeral, an unknown male whom she assumed to have been Tudor's best man. She was certain that he was not from his regiment, but whoever he was it proved impossible to trace him.

The ladies then telephoned Army Records to try to find out more. They were told, quite properly, that papers on former officers were held in confidence, but the official to whom they spoke volunteered the information that while Owen Tudor was listed as having served at Lydd between 1923 and 1926, there was no record of his having been married.

Each new obstacle only served to whet the ladies' appetite the more. They tried to trace Owen Tudor's brother officers from the 3rd Hussars by examining the entries in the *Army List*, in order to discover whether any of those officers were still alive. They then had the good fortune to find the one officer who was in a position to tell them more about Owen Tudor's first marriage – for he turned out to be the very officer who, he claimed, had tried to prevent the marriage from taking place at all.

The officer was Lieutenant-Colonel Nigel Watson. He had joined the British Army in 1918 but transferred to the Indian Army in September that year when he joined the 3rd Hussars who were then serving in India. His officer training was thus at Quetta instead of Sandhurst, and while at Quetta he studied Russian and became a first-class interpreter. His knowledge of Russian, and the tension between the British and the new Bolshevik regime in the Soviet Union, led to his being frequently employed on extra-regimental duties which involved confidential Intelligence work that sometimes meant considerable activity – and this work brought him into contact with Richard Meinertzhagen.

Lieutenant-Colonel Watson told me that this was during the period when Richard Meinertzhagen was serving with the General Staff at the War Office and, later, with the Foreign Office.[2] Officially, Meinertzhagen was serving with the Colonial Office during this period, but there has always been the suspicion that he also worked for Intelligence, and the Foreign Office was the Department of State responsible for Secret Intelligence. Beyond that, the Colonel could tell me no more than that he had pleasant memories of his association with Meinertzhagen.

Nigel Watson and his brother officer Owen Tudor had been posted to Constantinople with the 3rd Hussars in 1921, and they were to remain there until 1923. Watson's work, however, had been outside the normal, run-of-the-mill regimental duties. He was responsible for screening the numerous would-be applicants for immigration into Britain, a large number of whom were White Russians. This was a necessary task at the time, since fear of Bolshevism spreading to Britain was very real – in 1919 the British Military Mission in Rome had warned Count de Salis that 'the regulations regarding Russians are now so strict in Great Britain that difficulty was made a short time ago about certain members of the Imperial household!'[3] This wariness was also extended to former enemy aliens, notably Turks because of the imminent danger of war in what was known as the Chanak

Crisis, when Britain found herself alone in resisting the efforts of Mustafa Kemal's resurgent Turkey to reoccupy Constantinople and the Ottoman Empire's old European lands.

Mrs Bowler and Mrs Daniels had found that Nigel Watson's recollections of Owen Tudor had been ready enough, even after the passage of more than sixty years. The Colonel, they said, had told them that he had been ordered to go to the York Hotel in Mayfair, where Owen Tudor and his fiancée were staying, to teach Tudor some Russian the evening before his wedding. Larissa, Watson had told them, was a belly-dancer in a night-club in Constantinople, the daughter of a pork-butcher. Owen Tudor was smitten by her, and in defiance of warnings and his Colonel's order had married her and been forced to leave the regiment.

On a second occasion, they said, he had told them that she had come from a very good family in St Petersburg, the tsarist capital, and he had in fact been sent to the York Hotel to try to dissuade Owen Tudor from going ahead with the marriage. When Mrs Daniels asked him who had sent him to stop the marriage, she said that he replied 'It's a military secret . . . .'[4] The ladies also claimed that he had agreed with them when they said they had discovered that Larissa's real name had been Tatiana, and they also told me that he had – strictly off the record – confirmed their suspicion that she was the second daughter of Nicholas II. When I put this to the Colonel, he denied that he had ever confirmed either of the two statements.

When I went to see him, the door was not opened by the Colonel but by a friend of his. During our conversation, the friend observed that he thought that Peter Wright was as much a traitor as Burgess and Maclean, since he had 'signed on the dotted line' as had he and the Colonel, which I took to imply that both of them had worked in Intelligence circles at some stage in their careers. I knew from colleagues who had spoken to Intelligence Officers that an Intelligence Officer is invariably accompanied by a minder whose job it is to monitor the conversation. I was told that the two men had served together in Yugoslavia during the Second World War, which struck me as odd since the Colonel's friend did not look old enough to have served then – but perhaps he simply carried his years well.

The Colonel was courteous and charming, and in spite of carrying more than ninety years his mind was razor-sharp. He discussed his early military career with me, and since I knew from Mrs Daniels that he had taken part in the ARCOS raid of 1923, I raised the subject to check that her account was reliable. He readily confirmed that he had been one of the officers involved under Meinertzhagen's direction. Meinertzhagen, however, had paid only a brief personal visit to the site to see how affairs were progressing, but it was all to no avail as the Russians had left nothing there of any use to Intelligence. Meinertzhagen, he recalled, struck him as a stern, single-minded character, a man with a mission who would let nothing stand in his way. In fact, while we were discussing Nigel Watson's work for Intelligence, he said that he had worked for both MI5 and MI6 and he knew all the ropes.

The Colonel told me that Owen Tudor had met Larissa in a night-club in Constantinople, where she was a dancing girl, and fallen for her. When Owen Tudor and Larissa had gone to London to marry, he had been sent to try to stop the marriage and point out to Tudor that if he persisted, he would have to leave the Hussars.

In this, Nigel Watson was confirming what he had told me in an exchange of correspondence before we met, namely that the only marriage his 3rd Hussars Colonel – or anybody else[5] – had sent him to stop was that of a brother officer, Owen Tudor, to a lady who was employed at one of the night-clubs in Constantinople. Bearing in mind that he had told Mrs Daniels that the identity of the person who sent him on his mission was 'a military secret', I again asked Nigel Watson whether he was certain who had sent him. He reminded me of what he had said in his letter to me. He had told me in his letter that Larissa had very good manners, and Mrs Daniels had told me that he had said that Larissa was beautiful. But when I asked him to describe Larissa to me, he said that he had never met her.

One fact that did make me wonder, however, was how Nigel Watson knew where to find Owen Tudor if he had been sent after him by his 3rd Hussars Colonel. Had Tudor eloped in the manner described, either with a Turkish pork-butcher's daughter or with a well-bred refugee from St Petersburg who had been supporting herself in Constantinople in the only way she could, and leaving aside how he managed to get his fiancée to England – then he would surely have seen to it that his whereabouts were unknown to the regiment until after the marriage had taken place. Yet Nigel Watson knew precisely where to find him.

The Colonel had been as kind and helpful as he could have been, he had been invariably civil and a gentleman, but it was clear that he could only tell me so much. It remained to be seen what further research would yield in the matter of Owen Tudor's first wife.

18

THE HOUSE OF TUDOR

Tudor was not the original family name. The family had been blessed with the more prosaic name of Jones until 26 December 1890 when, according to the *Executive Officers Services Book*[1], their surname was changed to Tudor. They were a naval family, and both Owen Tudor's father and uncle reached the rank of admiral. Young Owen was intended to follow the same path, for after attending junior school at St Lawrence College, Ramsgate, he joined the Royal Navy in 1915 and served as a midshipman aboard HMS *Repulse*. An accident in 1917 caused an injury to one of his eyes, forcing him to leave the navy that December.

The next year is the only one in a career spent in the armed services which is not accounted for by the official record. The reason for this was simple; the navy was barred to Owen Tudor because of the injury to his eye, and he was not yet old enough to join the army. He spent 1918 back at St Lawrence College, which had moved to Chester for the duration of the war. It was there, in the senior school, that he met Denis Swinburne, who taught him to ride, and ride well – which was to stand him in good stead later. The present headmaster of the College very helpfully consulted the school records for me: they revealed that while neither Tudor nor Swinburne shone academically, both were good and keen sportsmen, heavily engaged in many of the school's sports.

From St Lawrence, the two friends both entered RMA Sandhurst. Here Swinburne's riding lessons paid handsome dividends; Owen Tudor won the Saddle, so becoming a prize catch for the army's cavalry regiments. The 20th Hussars were lucky enough to land the catch, but they did not keep him long and he transferred to the prestigious 3rd The King's Own Hussars in 1921.

His new regiment proceeded to Constantinople that year, where they formed part of the post-war army of occupation. They remained there until 1923. This makes the story about his elopement with a lady of dubious reputation perfectly feasible, but it does not necessarily mean that is what happened. From 1923 to 1926, Owen Tudor's life is an enigma.

As we know, after his wedding in 1923 he transferred to the 3rd Battalion, the Royal Tank Corps, based at Lydd in Kent. Records of his life there are strangely scarce, and those concerning his wife are even scarcer. There is nothing about them in the local archives, either in Lydd or at the County Record Office in Maidstone; we have already noted that Army Records contain a reference to his service in Lydd but say nothing about his being married. The disappearance of all records and photographs is a matter for concern. Is it intentional?

Most of the information I have been able to find comes from a small number of elderly residents of Lydd. So far as the army is concerned, Owen Tudor's prowess as a sportsman was the only indication that he had been there. A former sergeant of the 3rd RTC, Mr Bingham of Whitstable, commented on his glowing reputation as a sportsman, but he only joined the unit when Owen Tudor was about to leave it, so he never got the chance to learn anything about him except by reputation. Another former sergeant, Mr Willis, who still lives in Lydd, wrote that 'After we had settled down as a complete unit we had a very good sports team and it seemed to arrive [sic] around from [sic] his leadership. He was a very good athlete and was liked by all ranks of the Regiment.'[2]

Tudor's prowess on the sports field is the only aspect of his service that is deemed worthy of notice in *The Tank Corps Journal*.[3] One would expect some note of an officer's service to be kept by his regiment, even if it only acknowledged his existence, yet the successor to the 3rd RTC, the 3rd Royal Tank Regiment, has nothing about Owen Tudor and neither does the Royal Tank Corps Museum at Bovington.

The Royal Tank Corps had a system of temporary ranks until 21 August 1923, when a permanent list of officers was instituted. Officers were attached to the Corps from their parent regiments, often on a short-term basis, and it is possible that this was the case with Owen Tudor. What is unusual, however, is that whereas the arrivals and departures of all the other temporary officers are faithfully recorded in the *Journal*, those of Owen Tudor are not mentioned.

The first time Tudor is mentioned is in the edition for April 1924, when he was playing for the battalion's rugby and hockey teams.[4] He continued to do so for the next two years, combining those games with athletic prowess. His crowning achievement was to be picked to represent England in the 120 yards hurdles in June 1926: at a time when sporting achievement was highly esteemed and provided a route to fame, this could only reflect glory on the unit.

I managed to trace a first cousin of Owen Tudor; she was also Denis Swinburne's wife. However, she did not know him very well: as she explained, 'we were first cousins and I knew him from childhood – but not well as he was eight years older than me'.[5] She described him as being 'very good-looking with natural wavy hair',[6] and he seems to have been regarded as attractive by women of all ages.

Money was a big problem for Owen Tudor in those early years in the army: Mrs Swinburne remarked that 'he had no private income, so was dependent on others' generosity'. Her mother, his aunt, gave him a small private allowance, but with his army pay these were slender means for a young officer in a prestigious cavalry regiment where expenses were high and officers were still expected to have some form of private income. Living on one's pay was not the done thing. Life might have been easier in the less prestigious RTC, but he now had a sick wife to care for, and before the creation of the National Health Service medical treatment had to be paid for. Mrs Swinburne painted a grim picture of their life together at Lydd:

> After marrying Larissa, Owen was transferred to [the] newly formed Royal Tank Corps and posted to Lydd in Kent – a cold, bleak area near Dungeness – with little money and an ailing wife and feeling ostracized by everyone; it must have been a terrible time for them. Larissa got progressively worse, with spinal TB or cancer and needed much care and attention.[7]

Unfortunately, Mrs Swinburne never met Larissa, nor did she visit the Tudors in Lydd. Tudor never spoke to her or his family about his first wife. She did not know who K. M. Huntington, the other witness to the wedding, was. When asked for the source of her information about her cousin's first marriage, she had to concede that it was based on gossip by family and friends. Nor did she know the man who was with Owen Tudor at his wife's funeral.

Unfortunately she is the nearest source we have to Owen Tudor's immediate family. She was familiar with the Constantinople story, writing to say that 'He joined them [i.e., the 3rd Hussars] in the Eastern Mediterranean area (Greece? Turkey?) where he met Larissa, who had escaped from Russia and was earning her living in the only way she could'.[8]

The story had clearly done the rounds, though it was rumoured in the RTC that Larissa was Belgian – a good cover in the aftermath of the First World War, during which many Belgian refugees had been living in Kent. Mr Willis, for example, wrote to say that 'She was a Belgium [sic] woman, we all knew she was and all the unit was very sorry for them both'.[9]

There were, fortunately, still some people in Lydd who remembered the Tudors. Mrs Bowler spoke to Mrs Lamb, who was a young girl at the time and had been smitten by Owen Tudor in the way that young girls are by handsome men. She told Mrs Bowler that she used to watch out for him as he walked across the Rype – a large green behind the church – on his way home, but she rarely had an opportunity to speak to him. She often used to wait for him near Ferndale, the house where the Tudors were living, and so came to speak to Larissa quite frequently. She described her as being tall, amazingly thin and very beautiful, having brown hair with an auburn tinge to it. This sounds remarkably similar to Gibbes's description of the Grand Duchess Tatiana. She was able to recall one particular conversation with her that may have a particular significance. Larissa told her that the happiest time she had spent in this country was spent in Yorkshire. The Constantinople story makes no reference to Yorkshire: when was Larissa there, and why? Unfortunately Mrs Lamb died before I could speak to her, so it was impossible to get her to enlarge on this recollection.

However, I was able to trace other residents of Lydd in that period. Mrs Esther Terry and Mrs P. Winkfield both confirmed that Larissa was tall, thin, dark and beautiful. They and another resident, Mrs Alice Clayphon, remarked on how happy the couple were.

Mrs Clayphon said that 'They used to go out in the garden at the back of the house and they would laugh. They did an awful lot of laughing, they were very, very happy, they laughed a lot.'[10]

Mrs Terry had been a domestic servant in one of the houses next to Ferndale and used to see Larissa, out in her bathchair in the garden, from one of the upstairs windows of the house in which she was working. She recalled: 'They were so happy together. Awfully happy they were. And I used to like to get down my father's garden path to listen to them laugh, though I never heard them talking, naturally.'[11]

Mrs Terry also recalled how she watched Larissa talk to the little girl, Ruth Goball, whom she used to look after: 'Unbeknown to the little girl, she dressed a doll while she was laying there. She took her time, I suppose several days at it. She gave it to the little girl called Ruth and she kept that doll for a long time. She was ever so pleased with it.'[12]

Even more helpful than the verbal descriptions was positive identification from a photograph. This photograph was shown to those who remembered Larissa, together with photographs of other people from the period who were in no way connected with the case. It was the clearest and most detailed one I could find, and shows Tatiana when she was a young woman. Mrs Terry said,

> That could be her, the features are very much like her. I didn't see her hair really, because [she was] lying down you know, but her features .... .[13]

Mrs Winkfield had known her best and had actually spoken to her. A farm backed onto Ferndale, and Mrs Winkfield and two young friends used to play in the farmyard and lean over the fence and talk to Mrs Tudor. When she saw the photograph, she exclaimed, 'Yes, that's her, definitely, that's her!' Her reaction was so strong, unequivocal and spontaneous that it must be taken seriously.

I gave Mrs Winkfield two further opportunities to reconsider her opinion. When I asked, 'So you would say without a shadow of a doubt?', I was cut short by her reply: 'Oh I would say so, yes!'

Towards the end of the interview I asked her if she thought the photograph was a very good likeness, to which she said, 'Well, it is as I remember her anyway.'[14]

The third resident of Lydd who provided positive identification was Mr Herbert Prebble, who lived in Manor Road, the same road in which Ferndale stands. He used a magnifying glass to examine the photographs, and on coming to that of Tatiana he paused and asked, 'Was this her? I think that's her – she was a Russian princess or something, wasn't she?'[15]

Mr Prebble was in fact the third person who said that Larissa had been a Russian princess. Mrs Clayphon used to tell her mother, 'Oh, I've seen the princess!' A Mrs Collins, who does not live in Lydd but knew Owen Tudor after his second marriage, always understood that his first wife had been a Russian princess. Is all this to be dismissed as mere coincidence?

All of the witnesses agreed that the Tudors lived very privately – indeed, Mrs Winkfield said that their way of life was almost secretive. There seems to have been little social contact with Tudor's brother officers or in the town. None of the witnesses ever noticed any visitors, though Mrs Terry thought Larissa might have had a nurse. Such a very private existence cannot be explained by the need to cover a past as a 'dancing girl' from Constantinople.

Isolation was not complete, however. A Mr and Mrs Bishop also lived in Ferndale with their son John. Mr Bishop was an inspector for the Prudential Insurance Company, but the Bishops were not natives of Lydd. So far as Mrs Terry could remember, they arrived shortly before the Tudors moved in and left shortly after Larissa died. One incident involving their son tied in with something Mrs Lamb had told Mrs Bowler – that she had heard Larissa shout at the boy in Russian one day. It looks as if young John had done – or was about to do – something which either alarmed or exasperated her, and that she shouted at him in her native tongue.

Mr Prebble said that Owen Tudor devoted all his money to looking after Larissa. While medical bills would have figured prominently in the family budget, as might a nurse, the Tudors still had money to spare: both Mr Prebble and Mrs Terry stated that Owen Tudor kept a horse, a beautiful, well-groomed beast that was stabled on a nearby farm, where Mrs Terry's brother was employed to look after it. Keeping a horse is an expensive hobby, and it is unlikely that he could have afforded such a horse without some extra income. Where had this come from? At the very least it seems to contradict Mrs Swinburne's account of their impoverished existence in Lydd.

In this connection, we need to note that when Larissa died she left £227 4s 5d. While not great riches, it represents a tidy sum for the time, more than a year's pay for much of the population. To put matters into perspective, a tank driver in the 3rd RTC earned three shillings a day, or £54 15s a year. Where did she acquire this wealth? It did not come from her husband. Larissa was unable to work, and there is little likelihood of her having managed to save such a sum from her alleged employment in Constantinople after three supposedly difficult years in Britain.

The fact that Larissa made no will is also curious. Of course, she might not have bothered, as is the case with so many people, or she might have refused to face the inevitable. But with such a tidy sum to dispose of and with death both near and inevitable, the lack of a will suggests that another reason was uppermost in her mind. Making a will would, of course, have meant signing a legal document, which would eventually be open to public scrutiny. Was the lack of a will under these circumstances a deliberate measure to ensure that the secret of her identity was kept?

What happened to Owen Tudor after his wife's death? Surely an officer who had disgraced the regiment by running off with a lady with the reputation Larissa supposedly had would have eked out a lonely and miserable existence in the Royal Tank Corps? But no: the Hussars immediately asked for his return. Mrs Swinburne tells us that 'Everyone in my family was astonished at the 3rd Hussars *asking* Owen to return. They must have thought very highly of him as an asset on the polo field and socially to ask him to come back! His mother, my aunt, was so pleased.'[16]

It is an improbable outcome for a man who had defied his Colonel's orders a mere three years before. Perhaps the regiment was anxious to regain the services of the man who had won the Saddle at Sandhurst, but that seems a little tendentious when set against his wilful disobedience, which had threatened the regiment with disgrace. It suggests that somebody was taking the trouble to watch over Owen Tudor and knew exactly when the time was ripe for his return to the Hussars.

After his return to the regiment, no further hindrance was placed in his way. He was gazetted captain in October 1927, less than a year after his return, and as one of his contemporaries from this second period in the regiment told me, 'he was given more than a fair crack of the whip'.[17]

Before the outbreak of the Second World War Owen Tudor was selected for special duties, which remain unspecified, and he even enjoyed a brief period as commander of the regiment in the field in 1941. He retired from the army in 1950 with the rank of lieutenant-colonel; curiously, the Hussars' museum in Warwick contains no reference to him at all, not even an obituary.

During his second spell with the Hussars he remained firmly in the background, acquiring a reputation as a loner. He did not socialize and he and his second wife, a daughter of Lord

Hothfield whom he married in 1928, did not entertain to dinner and were not invited in return. Those brother officers with whom I have corresponded all commented on how odd this appeared in an extremely sociable regiment. This tendency towards isolation continued after Owen Tudor retired; he never attended an old comrades' or officers' dinner and appears to have dropped out of sight altogether. As one of his brother officers put it, he was 'a loner to the last'.[18] It may be significant that, in the years before his death, letters to Owen Tudor from local historians in Lydd asking for information about his first wife were never answered.

The slender evidence that is available about the Tudors' life in Lydd does not enable us to draw many firm conclusions – but that, perhaps, is what was intended. What is noteworthy is that Larissa Tudor's appearance was indistinguishable from that of the Grand Duchess Tatiana, and that she was reputed to be a Russian princess. This carries weight because although many Russian princesses fled abroad after the civil war, few had reason to hide their true identities; indeed, most traded on them as heavily as they could. By itself that does not mean that Owen Tudor's wife was a Romanov, but there are other aspects that need to be considered alongside it.

There is too much evidence which contradicts the official line that Larissa was a whore from Constantinople; it is likely that the story was engineered to provide a plausible reason for Owen Tudor leaving the Hussars and being marooned in Lydd for three years. The fact that the Hussars asked him to return suggests that it was invented as a cover.

There is also every indication that somebody somewhere was looking after them. Money was made available by some means, and Owen Tudor's career was being followed, so that when the time was ripe he could be asked to rejoin the Hussars. Neither of these would have been possible without official sanction. Beyond that we can only observe that they were very much in love, which adds poignancy to their story. Be that as it may, there were other factors involved in the case quite apart from their mutual love.

19

THE TATTERED SEAM

The story that Larissa 'Haouk' was a whore from Constantinople already looks threadbare – and became still more so when in 1941 Owen Tudor was promoted to command the 3rd Hussars, the regiment he allegedly had to leave in disgrace. The officer who had the final say in that decision was the Regimental Colonel, Brigadier Philip James Vandeleur Kelly. Owen Tudor was serving in York when the regiment's able commanding officer, 'Billy' Petherick, was transferred elsewhere. Kelly exercised the ultimate authority on promotion within 'his' regiment, but was undecided on who to appoint. He consulted one of his officers, Sir Douglas Scott, Bt., who was at the Staff College, Camberley. Scott recommended Owen Tudor, whose second spell in the Hussars coincided with Scott's joining the regiment. Kelly accepted this advice without demur, and Owen Tudor got his promotion.

There is, of course, nothing irregular in such a procedure, but in the context of Owen Tudor's past and his first marriage it is highly significant for one very good reason. Kelly had been Colonel of the regiment in Constantinople in 1923, and according to the official story it was he who had sent Nigel Watson to the York Hotel in London to try to prevent the marriage. Kelly took an immense pride in the regiment and was renowned for his devotion to it. He was not the man to overlook the fact, if fact it was, that a junior officer had defied his own orders and contracted a marriage which would reflect badly on the regiment.

In 1923 he had – apparently – regarded the matter as serious enough to send one of his most capable officers, who was engaged on important and sensitive work, chasing off to thwart a renegade's marriage plans. And yet less than twenty years later he appoints this same renegade to command his beloved regiment!

When I visited Nigel Watson, as I have described in a previous chapter, I noticed a farewell letter from his Kalmuks which the Colonel keeps framed and hanging in his flat. The Kalmuks were tribesmen of the Russian Empire who proved themselves worthy soldiers in the Tsars' service, and many of them fought valiantly with the Whites. Those who escaped the defeat of the White armies fled abroad, like many other Russians. Some became drivers, for the transport of the British units around Constantinople. Apart from the fact that his Kalmuks clearly had a very high opinion of Watson, I could not help noticing that the date on the letter was August 1923. Owen Tudor married Larissa on 16 August that year. The fact that this is a farewell letter suggests that the Kalmuks did not expect to see Nigel Watson again. Shortly after this, as we have seen, Watson's military career turned to Intelligence duties, which suggests that, whatever orders concerning Owen Tudor he may have been given by Colonel Kelly, Watson was not in London in August 1923 purely to track down a love-sick brother officer.

There is another aspect to all this. At the time it was a standing rule that no officer under the age of twenty-eight could marry. There were no exceptions. For some reason this rule was not enforced in Owen Tudor's case. Had it been, he would have had to leave not merely the Hussars but the army altogether. The Royal Tank Corps was a new formation, and it would in no case have been prepared to jeopardize its still tenuous existence by flouting this or any other rule. And yet not only was Owen Tudor not required to resign his commission, but he was accepted by the Royal Tank Corps; unless somebody in a powerful position had been looking after his interests, he could never have got away with it.

We have noted, too, that *The Tank Corps Journal* recorded the arrivals and departures of the officers serving with the Corps – except for Owen Tudor. It also recorded all births, marriages and deaths within the Corps – except Larissa's. Bearing in mind that Army Records told Mrs Daniels that Owen Tudor's marriage was not recorded while he was stationed at Lydd, we can see the same clandestine hand at work here. What was so important about this young woman that made her of particular interest to Intelligence and required the removal of all traces of her connection with the army?

One indication can be found in the immigration records – largely because, not surprisingly, there is no record of Larissa ever having set foot in Britain. To understand the significance of this we need to look briefly at the contemporary background to immigration into Britain.

The British government was alarmed by the possible spread of communism and the attendant danger of revolution. During the war, socialism and other forms of radicalism had made great strides, and the authorities lived in fear of this movement boiling over into revolution. Would-be immigrants from Russia and the former enemy countries were seriously regarded as being a potential source of revolutionary ferment.

As a Russian arriving from Turkey, Larissa Haouk would have been doubly suspect, and there would have been close and detailed scrutiny of her case before she set sail and before she was allowed to land. Under the Aliens Order of 1920, no alien could land without the express permission of an Immigration Officer. To ensure that no one could escape their vigilance, entry into the country was restricted to sixteen specific ports. A Traffic Index was used, requiring each person who had been given permission to land to complete a form identifying them and informing the Home Office of their planned movements and residence in Britain. A 'Registered Certificate' would then be issued to those who had satisfied the legal requirements for entry and had convinced the Immigration Officer of their right to land. This document was needed if the immigrant wished to stay in a hotel or obtain work and when reporting to the local police. Aliens were obliged to register with the local police and show the certificate to hoteliers, who had to keep a list of all aliens residing on their premises.

The Home Office assures me that there is no record of anybody called Larissa Haouk having entered the country between 1918 and 1923.

The law specifically excluded certain classes of people from landing at all, including persons convicted of crimes in a foreign country covered by the Extradition Act; those likely to be a burden on public funds; those with no visible means of support; those of notoriously bad character; prostitutes and those living on their earnings.[1] Larissa's nationality, her alleged profession and her poor health which would have meant that she would have been a burden on public funds – all combined to ensure that she would have been refused permission to land.

Under the rigorous procedures outlined above, there was not the slightest chance of Larissa Haouk evading the attentions of the authorities at some stage in the proceedings, certainly not when she was staying at the York Hotel in Mayfair. We can only conclude that she was in the country before 1920 or that somebody influential was pulling strings for her – and Owen Tudor was not in a position to do so.

The possibility that she was already resident in Britain is a real one. Mrs Lamb told Mrs Bowler about how Larissa had said that the time she spent in Yorkshire was the happiest she had spent in this country. I raised the possibility that the rescued Grand Duchess may have stayed in Yorkshire in *Armour Against Fate*. The idea was founded initially upon a curt, one-line note from General Pulteney to his friend, Lady Desborough. The note read, 'What was the name of the doctor at Harrogate please?'[2] Neither Pulteney nor his wife were ill at the time. Yet if a rescued Grand Duchess was ill or possibly injured, a doctor who was used to treating sensitive cases with discretion, such as could be found in an aristocratic spa-town, would have been required.

A stronger influence was the presence in Harrogate of the Grand Duchess George, a great aunt to the Tsar's children. She lived on the outskirts of the town and during the war she had founded four hospitals in the area for the wounded. A hospital would provide comfort and treatment, not to mention privacy, for a young lady who had been thrown bruised into an aeroplane and then endured a gruelling flight across Siberia before making her way to Britain via Japan and Canada. Nearby was the famous sanatorium at Knaresborough where TB cases were treated.

In June 1989 I was contacted by Bill Booth, a former employee of the BBC who lived in Yorkshire. He drew my attention to a photograph that had appeared in the *Harrogate Herald* on 4 September 1918. The photograph shows a group of local dignitaries in the company of the Grand Duchess George and the exiled King Manoel of Portugal. The caption provides names for everybody present except for one person – a young lady who peers out from behind Lady Radcliffe, the wife of Sir Joseph Radcliffe, Bt. The photograph is not clear enough to permit any certainty of identification, but the unnamed young lady bears an uncanny resemblance to the Grand Duchess Tatiana.[3]

The newspaper destroyed all its old negatives on the grounds of shortage of space in the early 1970s, so it was not possible to develop a clearer photograph from the original negative. Newspaper photographs are composed of numerous black and white dots; enlargement merely separates those dots without adding to the clarity of the picture.

There is no clue to the identity of the young lady who looks so like Tatiana, and it is impossible to draw any hard and fast conclusions on the basis of this photograph – but we can justifiably ask why the young lady's name was not published along with the rest of the group.

The name Haouk on Larissa's marriage certificate is not Russian and is, quite obviously, fictitious. Few people other than students of royal genealogy would think of connecting this surname with that of the Countess Julia von Hauke, the daughter of General Count Maurice von Hauke, the wife of Prince Alexander of Hesse and by Rhine and thus an ancestor of the House of Battenberg, better known to the British public when they adopted the Anglicized name of Mountbatten. I suggest that, since she was unable to use her own name, the rescued

Grand Duchess used a name which was closely linked to her family. As the Romanov girls spoke English well but were not accomplished in German, the spelling mistake is readily understandable.

Nor would anybody but the most dedicated student of the British royal family realize that the church of St George's, Hanover Square, was the scene of two other royal marriages which had been undertaken without the sovereign's permission or approval – those of Augustus, Duke of Sussex and sixth son of King George III. Both his marriages, to Lady Augusta Murray and Lady Cecilia Buggin in 1793 and 1830 respectively, were solemnized there. It seems certain that the wedding of 16 August 1923 did not carry royal approval; it is unlikely that the King would have consented to the Grand Duchess marrying a junior officer in his service due to the security risk involved. The risk would have existed on two counts: the danger to the Grand Duchess's life if it were known that she was alive in Britain; and the possibility of news of the King's intervention leaking out. The official line was that all of the Romanovs had been murdered; the King would have been gravely embarrassed had it become known that an already restless and critical public had been deceived over the affair.

The Royal Marriage Act – which the Duke of Sussex had treated with such indifference – could not apply to this later wedding, but royal approval could make the difference between marrying in a church and in a registry office. A church wedding would have entailed a greater expense than either Owen Tudor or his bride could have borne by themselves, while the King could not have spent such a sum without attracting the attention he was so anxious to avoid.

Larissa's patronym – which does not fit any of the normal derivatives for Feodorovna – also calls for comment. The correct patronym for the daughters of the Tsar was Nicolayevna, but its use in this case would have been a definite pointer to her real identity. However, Feodorovna was the patronym of the Tsarina, her sister the Grand Duchess Elizabeth and the Dowager Empress. All three women had selected this patronym when they converted to the Orthodox Church, and intriguingly

Larissa's grave in Lydd is positioned in accordance with the dictates of that faith – but, as has already been observed, there is no trace of anyone by the name of Haouk having been converted while in Britain.

The appearance of the patronym at her death suggests that Owen Tudor chose to acknowledge her true identity as closely as he dared, something which mirrors the use of Haouk as a surname.

The illnesses which eventually led to her death fit this picture. It has been noted that spinal caries was often the result of a severe physical jolt such as might be suffered in a severe fall from a horse. It normally takes eight to ten years to prove fatal. Being thrown, bruised, into the back of an aeroplane could have provided the severe physical jolt; eight years from 1918 takes us to 1926, the year of her death.

We have already touched on the link between Yorkshire and the sanatorium there. Larissa certainly had tuberculosis and it had already touched the Romanovs. Nicholas's brother George was dying from the disease when he went to Abbas Tuman in the foothills of the Caucasus Mountains in the vain hope that the fresh mountain air would ward off the disease. He was killed there in an accident on his motorbike in 1899. Moreover, the conditions under which the family were imprisoned were ideal for such a disease to have taken hold. The coincidences – if coincidences they are – in these illnesses are nothing short of uncanny if Larissa was not a daughter of the Tsar.

On the other hand, spinal caries is often the result of tuberculosis, yet if the death certificate is examined, it states that she had suffered from tuberculosis for two years and spinal caries for four years; on top of which such timing is entirely wrong for an accident which took place in 1918. How did her doctor in Lydd, Dr John Procter, know how long she had suffered from spinal caries? Were there any medical records and where did they come from? It is unlikely that they could have come from Turkey, where she is supposed to have been four years before her death. One of the problems with spinal caries is that it does not always develop immediately after an accident, nor is it always immediately noticeable. We do not know on what information the doctor based his opinion, or whether it was just surmise.

That said, we must also note that if Larissa had suffered from spinal caries for four years, she would have had the ailment in 1922. When the newly wed Tudors arrived in Lydd in 1923, Larissa was already confined to her bathchair. How was she supposed to have been able to earn a living as a 'dancing girl' in Constantinople under such circumstances?

In the end, however, the Intelligence connection overshadows all others. We have seen that Owen Tudor's father and uncle were both admirals. The uncle was Sir Frederick Tudor who, it will be remembered, was the Commander of the China Station in 1918 and organized the passage of refugees from Siberia to Japan and then Canada. His station was one of the quietest of the theatres of war, involving little more action than the hunting of a few mines. Yet he left the command laden with decorations – the Japanese Orders of the Sacred Treasure and the Striped Tiger, both first class, and from Britain the KCB and the KCMG. It might be significant that while he was at Britannia Royal Navy College, Dartmouth, he made the acquaintance of the Duke of Clarence and the Duke of York, later King George V. Afterwards he was warmly regarded by the King, who perhaps found him a man he could rely on to carry out a sensitive duty and remain discreet about it. Another curious coincidence?

While on the subject of Admiral Tudor, it is interesting to speculate on what Owen Tudor did with his leave from Turkey – he was there for two years, and it is unlikely that he would have served for that length of time without some leave. Did he see his uncle and perhaps meet the rescued Grand Duchess or learn about her existence and decide to flirt with her? We do not know, but Mrs Swinburne suggested a possible meeting-place in this country which depended upon Sir Frederick Tudor. He became President of the Royal Navy College at Greenwich after his return from the Far East. She thought it possible that they could have met while visiting the Admiral there.[4] It is an interesting speculation, but for want of definite evidence speculation it must remain.

There remains the identity of the unknown man who

supported Owen Tudor at his wife's funeral. Might it have been Richard Meinertzhagen? There is no entry in his diary for the week in which she died and the funeral took place. While that does not prove anything, it is surely of more than passing interest that his diary is also silent during the week in which she and Owen Tudor married – and still more so when we remember that Meinertzhagen often left the pages of his diary blank when engaged on sensitive Intelligence work. Again, we are faced with evidence of the direct involvement of Military Intelligence in the affair – or yet another extraordinary coincidence.

It was noted earlier that Owen Tudor used to place flowers on his wife's grave most years on 10 June. It was also noted that there was some confusion over the year of Larissa's birth, with such records as exist presenting three possibilities – 1896, 1897 and 1898. Had the Grand Duchess Tatiana died on 18 July 1926, she would have been twenty-nine years old. Her birthday was 10 June.

The last time Owen Tudor visited the grave was a few years before his own death in 1987; the flowers he placed there were plastic, and they are still there today.

20

A CASE TO ANSWER

There is a powerful array of evidence to suggest that King George V did not abandon his Russian cousins in the way that the official papers that have been released ask us to believe. British records seek to hide the fact that rescue attempts were made. Evidence of concealment is reflected in the dissembling over the fate of the original proposal to grant refuge to the Romanovs in Britain. Evidence that later attempts were made to rectify the situation thus created are provided in the Vatican Papers, which show that Queen Mary was still seeking to help any Romanov survivors as late as August 1918. In addition, the Grand Duke Vladimir stated that plans were being made to rescue the Romanovs from Tobolsk, and there are the questions raised by the rather more tendentious evidence of the Lied Mission and Steven Gordon-Smith's venture.

The suppression of these efforts might be understood, even accepted, were it not that we have been consistently assured for decades that nothing was or could be done to help the Romanovs. It inevitably begs the question: what else was done besides?

From the material set forth here, the conclusion that some sort of effort was mounted by the British is inescapable. No less than three Intelligence Officers commented on it, two of them senior officers. It would seem that it met with some degree of success. Is their evidence reliable? To argue that all three were liars or fantasists is unpersuasive, not least in view of the ways in which their testimonies were recorded – a private diary not intended for publication, and conversations within their families. Moreover, while none of them knew all the details, the salient points in their evidence are confirmed from other sources.

Those in the T. E. Lawrence camp who would decry Meinertzhagen as a fantasist ignore that much of the content of the original diary – as opposed to the published extracts – is substantiated from other sources. By its very nature it is far more difficult to find supporting evidence for the attempt to rescue the Romanovs, though we might note in passing that John Buchan, the celebrated novelist and one-time Governor-General of Canada, worked in Intelligence during the First World War and was heavily involved in its propaganda efforts in Russia. He moved in the same circles as Meinertzhagen, and one of his characters, Sandy Arbuthnot, is widely reckoned to be based on him. Two of Buchan's novels, *The House of Four Winds* and *Hunting Towers*, are centred around the rescue of a female member of East European royal families from local revolutionaries. Did these owe something to what he knew about Meinertzhagen – or is it just one more casual but remarkable coincidence?

The testimony of both Stephen Alley and the Preston ladies was to the effect that two of the Romanov girls were not murdered. In this context it is worth noting that not only have British Military Intelligence files not been released, but the files of the Ekaterinburg consulate are similarly withheld, notably those covering communications to Vladivostok when the Czechs were approaching Ekaterinburg. It is astonishing that such attempts to cover up what happened persist.

What of Anastasia? Did she escape, or was she the daughter who was rescued? We learnt in 1992 that her body might be missing from the remains found in the forest near Ekaterinburg, and the Hon. Violet Mary Vivian's words indicating that she did get away suggest that she might have been rescued. The solution to this is inextricably woven into the whole vexed and highly complicated issue of the identity of Anna Anderson, the late Anastasia claimant in the United States. I am in no position to offer a definitive opinion on the validity of Anna Anderson's claims which are as well supported as they are denied. What makes me doubt her claim is a recent book by James Blair Lovell, *Anastasia: The Lost Princess*, in which Mr Lovell was fed three different versions of what happened at Ekaterinburg – though it has to be said that one of them was invented by the claimant with the intention of wrong-footing Summers and Mangold. On the other hand, if she was capable of inventing one story, where does that leave her other two versions, both of which are mutually exclusive?

It may be that the real Anastasia was hidden elsewhere with the knowledge of the British royal family – or that they knew the claimant was genuine and ruthlessly turned their backs on her, perhaps because of what she might reveal.

My own view is that there is a stronger likelihood of her elder sister, Tatiana, having been rescued. Meinertzhagen, for reasons of security, does not reveal the identity of the girl he claims to have rescued. However, Biron's testimony – the only independent testimony from any of the Ekaterinburg Bolsheviks – says that Tatiana had gone missing, albeit with a Red Guard. She was the most adventurous of the Tsar's daughters and their natural leader, so this would have been in keeping with her character. There are also the questions raised by the evidence surrounding the Lydd connection, and that irritatingly blurred photograph from Yorkshire.

It is curious that some of those implicated in the Romanov case seem to have developed an unexplained fascination for the name 'Tatiana'. There is Thomas Preston's error in reporting that on 1 May 1918 the 'ex-Emperor of Russia with Grand Duchess Tatiana was brought to Ekaterinburg by Bolsheviks from Tobolsk', when he was summarizing the events of that year. There are several errors in that brief statement – the Tsar had arrived there on 30 April and was accompanied by the Tsarina and the Grand Duchess Marie. An innocuous mistake, perhaps, given that Preston was writing years later. What suggests that it was not so innocuous is that he named his only daughter – born in Vladivostok – Tatiana.

Lieutenant-General Sir William Pulteney, of the missing letter from the Pacific fame, married into the prosperous Arnott family of Ireland. One of the Arnott sons, until recently heir to the family property, chose to call his only daughter Tatiana. We cannot read too much into this, but it is odd that two individuals closely connected with the Romanov case should have this same point of focus – Tatiana is not the best known or most common name in the English-speaking world.

The Lydd scenario cannot be offered as conclusive evidence since it is far from complete. However, we can establish beyond any reasonable doubt that 'Larissa', whoever she was, aroused more than a little interest on the part of British Military Intelligence. There are also a host of coincidences which can only be described as unlikely and extraordinary if she was not the Grand Duchess Tatiana. She was reputedly both Russian and a princess, the names she used, her uncanny resemblance to Tatiana, the causes of her death, the fact that she shared the same birthday – all combine with the Intelligence background to build up a case that is otherwise difficult to explain.

My suspicion that the British were more than idle spectators of the Romanov affair was reinforced by an interview on 16 October 1990 with a former Minister of State for Foreign and Commonwealth Affairs, who is alleged to have seen documents which the Foreign Office continues to hold,[1] although Parliament has been assured by others that all available documents dealing with the case have been released.

He refused formally to confirm that documents were still being withheld, but in the course of the conversation I formed the conviction that they were and that he had examined them. When I asked him what degree of co-operation he had found between the British, the Czechs and the Whites when he examined the documents, he replied, 'Not much, I don't think there was very much.' Foreign Office documents could hardly be expected to say very much about the Czechs and White Russians; there was only the slimmest of diplomatic links between the parties in those early days and most of the contact that existed ran through military channels. The true significance of the reply lies in the clear indication that he had looked at documents which are being withheld. He also told me that a colleague of his had examined the surviving papers of today's SIS on the subject, but there were so few of them that they could shed little light on the question. I understand that SIS files are subject to a twenty-five-year clear-out when most of them are destroyed.

What was more important than this, however, was that he fielded all my questions very competently until I came to the question of Sir Thomas Preston's evidence. He looked away from me and muttered that he knew nothing about that.

It seems unlikely that Foreign Office documents would help very much even if all those being held were released. The former minister told me that he would have loved to have discovered that a member of the imperial family had escaped, but he had found no indication that any had done. Here, again, we are faced with the problem that Foreign Office documents only show part of the picture. They do not normally comment on matters concerning Military Intelligence – indeed, the Foreign Office deliberately distances itself from that sphere.

However, the evidence suggests that Military Intelligence was the agency through which efforts were made, and it could be added that in 1918 it was the only body which could have achieved anything. It should also be added that Military Intelligence files dealing with covert operations are, when kept, never released and would not therefore be 'available' to be published or withheld.

Asked why there had to be so much secrecy about the Romanov case, the former minister emphasized that the affair was close to the royal family. It is acknowledged by the Public Record Office that matters which are close to the royal family, or concern Intelligence operations, are closed to the public. Most people are content to accept a degree of secrecy – but it is reasonable to question how far that secrecy ought to go, and whether it should cover events which occurred over seventy years ago. The present system treats the tax-paying public like children and allows them to be fobbed off with all sorts of myth paraded as history. While we can accept that the royal family had a particularly personal interest in the matter, it can equally well be argued that the public have a real personal interest as well – after all, many of their relatives were killed or wounded, and many lives wrecked, in the carnage of the First World War. Such secrecy also raises questions about the power exerted by the Crown. We are told that these powers are limited and can be exercised only on the advice of government ministers.

In *Armour Against Fate* I suggested that the main reason for so much secrecy would have been the possibility that a rescue operation was unconstitutional. This view was founded on a statement by the late Lord Mountbatten: 'I do not say it would have been inconceivable. But in the light of the government's attitude, and the fact that King George V was a constitutional monarch, it would have been virtually impossible.'[2] Jonas Lied's view was that Lloyd George vetoed any effort. However, I am less certain than I was about the unconstitutional argument. If there was a cover-up then it involved civil servants, the army and government ministers – which suggests that it went beyond being merely a royal secret.

That the British army had its hand in this is evident because those documents which have been released into the Public Record Office were passed to the Foreign Office by Intelligence. This is established by the preamble to the main file on the murder of the Romanovs:

Confidential to Foreign Office from Director of Intelligence

I have got together such evidence as is available about the murder of the Russian Imperial Family and sent copies to you and the Public Record Office, where the documents can be available to historical students in the future. There is sure to be a crop of claimants and there was a danger that sources of evidence might die, leaving no record behind them.[3]

The preamble notes that 'such evidence as is available' is being sent: I suggest that 'available' is one of those words that mean something different to officials than to the rest of us – namely those papers that the authorities feel they can safely release without divulging a full and accurate account of what happened. They do not contain anything which might differ from the scenario the authorities want us to accept. I have found with monotonous regularity that documents which would enable us to trace the course of events have either not been sent to the Public Record Office or have been removed from the files.

This leads on to the role of the Intelligence services in government. If it did nothing else, Peter Wright's *Spycatcher* showed that these services are by no means as even-handed and impartial as we have been led to expect. That their role goes far beyond supplying Intelligence to the executive is illustrated by a conversation that Malcolm Turnbull, counsel for the defence in the Wright case, had with his client:

> After court that Thursday evening, we asked Peter whether he thought Thatcher knew she was telling a lie.
> 'Oh, heavens no,' he chuckled. 'She has just said what MI5 told her. They don't argue the toss with politicians. We just tell them what to say and the poor beggars have to say it.'
> 'But the politicians get the blame if it turns out to be false,' I protested.
> 'Well, of course, that's their job isn't it?' Peter replied as though it was the most obvious thing in the world.[4]

Peter Wright was not trying to be cynical, but this conversation illustrates an alarming aspect of our national life. If ministers make decisions on such a basis then the public are being manipulated for whatever ends these unelected officials have in mind. It is an entirely unsatisfactory situation.

After it was announced on 10 May 1992 that a grave alleged to contain the remains of at least some of the Romanovs had been found off the old forest road near Ekaterinburg,[5] Prince Nicholas Romanov, the present head of the family, told readers of *The Times* that the family did not want a Russian state funeral for the remains, believing that this would be a mistake.[6] He was, he said, sceptical about the validity of the find, and he attributed the constant searching and discoveries to a strong desire in Russia to exorcize the crime.

We do know that Yurovsky, supposedly head of the execution

squad at the Ipatiev House, was not telling the whole truth about the events of 1918. His account or protocol relating to the murder of the family contains a number of serious discrepancies, as we have seen. The fact that Yurovsky was writing after a lapse of two years may have something to do with this, but it is more likely that his discrepancies can be explained by his having written at the request of the Soviet authorities. While this does not necessarily invalidate the whole account, it does mean that Yurovsky has to be studied with some caution.

The reason for these discrepancies is discussed by Edvard Radzinsky. On the basis of discussions with a former member of 'a certain "serious institution"', Radzinsky suggests that Yurovsky remained discreet even when confronted by the contradictory claims of Peter Zakharovich Ermakov, the Upper Isetsk Military Commissar who was supposed to be responsible for the disposal of the bodies, that in fact he had shot the Tsar, because Yurovsky knew that two of the Romanovs were still alive. Neither he nor Ermakov could risk an open breach without that dangerous fact becoming public.[7] The accounts of the disposal of the bodies of the Romanovs written by these two eyewitnesses are at complete variance. We have seen what Yurovsky had to say, but according to Ermakov there was no second burial in the common grave beside the old forest road – instead he and two trusted colleagues burnt the bodies in the forest on the night of 17–18 July 1918.

The question that needs to be faced is: when did the two children escape? Radzinsky's informant believed they were removed from the lorry carrying the bodies when it got stuck in mud near railway booth 184. The evidence of the Preston ladies suggests that two daughters had already gone before the lorry left the house. Only Yurovsky and Ermakov could have told us when their deception began, but both of them tried to ensure that the secret would die with them.

In the light of John Major's recent statements about blowing away 'the cobwebs of secrecy', which are an insult to the intelligence of a free people, dare we hope that the cobwebs which lie so heavily over the British involvement in the Romanov case will be included? If the Prime Minister is sincere about blowing away these cobwebs, he could find the events of seventy-four years ago a good place to start. The alternative will otherwise remain what it is now – that posterity is denied, and history will consist of half-truths fed to the public for propaganda purposes.

APPENDIX

T. E. Lawrence once wrote to Lionel Curtis that

> One of the ominous signs of the time is that the public can no longer read history. The historian is retired into a shell to study the whole truth; which means that he learns to attach insensate importance to documents. The documents are liars.

In the case of the Russian imperial family the last sentence is certainly true. The official documents that have been released are simply those which point to a desired conclusion. In the course of this study there have been several occasions where the suppression of documentary evidence has been only too clear. This is useful on two counts. It shows that somebody has something to hide and that they are prepared to go to some lengths to hide it. Secondly, it prevents the study degenerating into a rehearsal of a convenient fiction.

The following list represents those documents that are known to exist and to have been suppressed. Its true significance lies in that it is not merely a list of documents where relevant material might be found, but where the individual items form the next step in the pursuit of specific leads. The fact that so many crucial documents have been either removed or withheld excites alarm – it would be normal for some documents to be lost or withheld for good reasons, but when this is the fate of so many and so consistently, then questions need to be asked.

I have not mentioned the lack of documentation from the Foreign Office or Military Intelligence files. The lack of material in the Foreign Office files about the plight of the family is too well known for me to need to dwell on the point. Documents dealing with the covert operations of Military Intelligence are, when kept, never released.

Official Papers

Siberia 4: Irkutsk prisoners of war and Ex-Czar: Ref. WO 106/1218

Siberia 5: *Never given to the Public Record Office*

Canada Register 1918–1919 [IND 18846] Vol. 29, No. 36524S: Ref. CO335

Air Force element in North Russia, 1918: Ref. AIR 1/?/204/157/1

The Vatican initiative: Ref. FO 380/20–28

Log Book of HMS *Glory*: Ref. ADM 53. *The available logs run to May 1917 only*

Papers relating to the death of Captain C. S. Digby Jones: Ref. WO 106/1233, Nos. 142 and 181. *Although a reference to his death is to be found in the card index to Foreign Office papers for 1918 (No. 67157), there is no trace of the relevant documents*

Re murder of Royal Family: Ref. WO 106/1237, No. 799

Records of the Ekaterinburg Consulate: *Apart from a small collection containing telegrams sent to Vologda and Moscow, there is nothing else from what must have been a very busy consulate prior to the Bolshevik evacuation of Ekaterinburg*

Telegrams Russia to Admiralty, January–July 1918: Ref. ADM 137

APPENDIX

Papers in Private Possession

Letter from General Sir William Pulteney to Lady Grenfell: In *Grenfell Papers, D/ERv C2130*, Herts County Record Office

Papers of HRH Prince Arthur of Connaught: *Disappeared without trace*

Papers of the Grand Duke Mikhail Mikhailovitch: *Disappeared without trace*

Papers of HM Queen Alexandra: *Destroyed after her death*

Letter from the Tsarina via Mr Gibbes: *Disappeared without trace*

A NOTE ON SOURCES

British files, which one might have expected to be particularly fruitful when dealing with the murder of an Allied sovereign who was the King's cousin, are remarkably threadbare. Once the British offer of refuge had been withdrawn in the spring of 1917, there are only two Foreign Office documents which deal directly with the Romanovs until they were reported murdered. These two documents were from August 1917, when the King asked the Foreign Office whether it was true that the family had been moved to Tobolsk, and May 1918 when the King is concerned about their treatment.

The military files, held mainly in the collection Military Operations and Intelligence, WO106, are equally noteworthy for their many gaps. These gaps inevitably occur at points where the documents concerned would be of inestimable value in verifying whether there ever was a British rescue mission, and also at points where they would allow the course of that mission to be traced. This is not accidental, nor is it simply a case of believing these documents are where the answers might lie. The weeding has been too thorough and too consistent for either of these arguments to apply.

In the former Soviet Union, where I went to examine the

available material in February 1991, there was little prospect of anything being revealed by the Soviet regime. There was the correspondence of King George V with the Tsar, but beyond that the most startling evidence lay in what was supposed to be the Tsarina's diary for 1918. This is almost certainly a forgery. The headings on each page change markedly on 4 July 1918, the date when the original guards at the Ipatiev House were replaced. This is odd when according to Edvard Radzinsky, who rediscovered the diary, these headings were all written into the diary by the Grand Duchess Tatiana. Moreover, the style and the spelling are not the Tsarina's. What this means is that the Soviet state was determined to hide just what did go on from the prying eyes of posterity and this is mirrored in both the official Soviet records and the testimonies of Bolshevik witnesses. As products of a regime whose founding father introduced the concept of 'the necessary lie' this is, perhaps, to be expected.

Regrettably, I have not been able to return to the new Russia, where access to documents is supposed to have been transformed. Future researchers there might like to consider the observation that their research should not be confined to the records of the Cheka and the KGB, but should also embrace those of Sovnarkom, the Bolshevik equivalent of the Foreign Ministry, and the files of the Red army.

Arguably the most noteworthy discovery has been the official German files on the Romanovs. These yielded remarkable results in unexpected directions. I had not been expecting to find very much on Nicholas II's brother, the Grand Duke Mikhail Alexandrovitch. It is one of the greatest pleasures of research to find something which is genuinely new and which cannot reasonably be disputed. More work remains to be done on associated files and this is already in hand. The documents are on microfilm and those wishing to study them should be warned that they are not in the best condition. Partly because of the type of microfilm readers which one has to use to read these documents – the machines have inflicted scarring on a number of pieces – and partly because of the quality of some of the photography, the documents are not easy to read and all too often words are either entirely or partially obscured. Researchers might find it helpful to take a magnifying glass.

While my research has concentrated on primary sources, there have been occasions when these have not been available, either because of the deliberate suppression noted above, or because they have mysteriously disappeared. This means that the treatment of some aspects of the case has had to rely more heavily on secondary, published sources than would have been ideal. The treatment of Judge Sokolov's material illustrates this. I have had to rely on the 1926 edition of his *Enquête Judiciaire sur l'Assassinat de la Famille Impériale Russe*, published in Paris.

I am aware that some academics affect to despise the work of Summers and Mangold in their *File on the Tsar*, but theirs is not a view I find convincing. They by no means represent the whole body of academic opinion and their view all too often boils down to a dislike of the fact that Summers and Mangold are journalists who do not write in the pompous prose so beloved of some academics. I have felt that the content of a work is far more important than the writer's background or style, and have acted accordingly.

NOTES

1. DECLARATION OF INTEREST

1. Siberia 4. Correspondence and Telegrams. PRO WO106/1218.
2. M. E. Occleshaw, *Armour Against Fate*, 1989. See pp. 251–87.

2. THE END OF TSARDOM

1. Reported by Leopold Trepper in *The Great Game*, p. 379.
2. The character sketches are mainly drawn from J. C. Trewin, *Tutor to the Tsarevich: An Intimate Portrait of the Last Days of the Russian Imperial Family Compiled from the Papers of Charles Sydney Gibbes*, and N. A. Sokolov, *Enquête Judiciaire sur l'Assassinat de la Famille Impériale Russe*.

3. MURDER MOST FOUL?

1. G. Botkin, *The Real Romanovs*, pp. 194–5.
2. A. Summers and T. Mangold, *The File on the Tsar*, pp. 263–4.
3. E. Radzinsky, *The Last Tsar: The Life and Death of Nicholas II*, pp. 248–56.
4. Ibid, pp. 257–9.
5. The sketch of conditions inside the house is drawn from Sokolov, op. cit., pp. 165–71.
6. PRO FO 371/3335, No. 107, 2 October 1918 from Ekaterinburg, 10 October from Vladivostok.

4. THE SMOKING GUNS

1. Lockhart Moscow to Foreign Office about 17 July 1918, No. 339 PRO FO 371/3335.
2. G. Botkin, op. cit., pp. 222–5.
3. *The Times*, 26 July 1918.
4. Sir R. Paget (British Ambassador at Copenhagen) to Foreign Office, PRO FO 371/3335, No. 131067, 29 July 1918.

5. THE ORTHODOX VIEW

1. PRO FO 371/3335, No. 107, 2 October 1918 from Ekaterinburg, 10 October from Vladivostok.
2. Summers and Mangold, op. cit., pp. 88–9.
3. Sokolov, op. cit., p. 190.
4. Eliot to Foreign Office, PRO WO 106/1231, *Siberia Inter: Pol: November 1918*, No. 285, 29 November 1918.

6. THE HERETICS

1. Sokolov, op. cit., facing p. 16.
2. Summers and Mangold, op. cit., p. 98.
3. Ibid., p. 125.
4. Ibid., p. 126.
5. See Captain P. Bulygin, *The Murder of the Romanovs*, p. 239, and R. Wilton, *The Last Days of the Romanovs*, p. 97.
6. Summers and Mangold, op. cit., p. 146.
7. Ibid., p. 102.
8. *Report of Mr N. A. Sokoloff, Examining Magistrate, into the Circumstances of the Murder of the Russian Imperial Family*, British Library, Cup.24.aa.19.
9. Summers and Mangold, op. cit., pp. 157–61.
10. J. F. O'Conor, *The Sokolov Investigation*, p. 215.
11. Summers and Mangold, op. cit., p. 332.
12. *Sunday Times*, 10 May 1992.

7. THE KAISER'S WILL

1. Prince Philipp zu Eulenburg-Hertefeld to Professor Kurt Breysig, 22 September 1919, from J. C. G. Rohl, *1914: Delusion or Design*, p. 131.
2. I. Vorres, *The Last Grand Duchess*, pp. 160–1.
3. Wilton, op. cit., p. 70.
4. *Alleged Secret Clauses Appended to the Treaty of Peace between the Bolshevik Government and the Quadruplice*, in *1918 January–October Military and Political*, PRO WO106/1152, No. C.X.027166, Petrograd, 12 April 1918.
5. Sokolov, op. cit., p.139.

6. Von Mirbach to German Foreign Ministry, 11 May 1918, A19964, PRO GFM 6/139. The collection on the Romanovs in the German Foreign Ministry files is drawn mainly from two other collections: *Weltkrieg* and *Russland Nr 82 Nr 1 Secreta*. It is rarely possible to tell from which collection documents in the Romanov files stem.

7. Ibid., 26 June 1918, A27476.

8. E. Mawdsley, *The Russian Civil War*, p. 41.

9. K. D. Erdmann (ed.), *Kurt Riezler Tagebücher–Aufsätze–Dokumente*, p. 111.

10. Ibid., p. 118.

11. PRO GFM 6/139, von Lersner at Gross Hauptquartier to Foreign Ministry, 13 July 1918, A29982.

12. G. Freund, *Unholy Alliance: Russian–German Relations from the Treaty of Brest-Litovsk to the Treaty of Berlin*, pp. 252–3.

13. PRO GFM 6/139, Riezler to Foreign Ministry, 20 July 1918, A30727.

14. PRO GFM 6/140, Riezler to Foreign Ministry, 24–5 July 1918, A31329.

15. Ibid., A31365 and A31742, 24 and 27 July 1918 respectively.

16. Ibid., Helfferich to Foreign Ministry, A32240, 31 July 1918.

17. Ibid., Kaiserin Augusta to Exellenz von Mohl, A34158, 8 August 1918.

18. Ibid., Under Secretary of State to Exellenz von Mohl, A34158, 15 August 1918.

19. Ibid., Hauschild to Foreign Ministry, A36399, 29 August 1918.

20. Ibid., A37912, 10 September 1918.

21. Ibid., Hauschild to Foreign Ministry, A38734, 15 September 1918.

22. Ibid., Nadolny, Berlin, A37972, 10(?) September 1918. The date on this document is not clear.

23. Ibid., Ratibor to Foreign Ministry, A33231, 3 August 1918.

24. Ibid., Spanish ambassador in Berlin to Foreign Ministry, A32984, 4 August 1918.

25. Ibid., Ratibor to Foreign Ministry, A34027, 8 August 1918.

26. Ibid., A34202, 12 August 1918.

27. Ibid., von Lersner to Moscow Legation, A34075, 12 August 1918.

28. Ibid., Consulate-General Petersburg to Foreign Ministry, A38790, 26 August 1918.

29. Ibid., von Hintze, Berlin, Abschrift A.37912.Ang.20815, 17 September 1918.

30. *Rumänien No. 1*, PRO GFM 6/86.

8. THE VATICAN INTERVENES

1. *Embassy and Consular Archives*, PRO FO 380/20, No. 46, 257/18.
2. Ibid.

3. Ibid., PRO FO 380/18, 352/18.
4. *Archivio Degli Affari Ecclesiastici Straordinari. Liberazione dell Imperatrice Madre e delle Granduchesse di Russia*, Jean Greméla to Pope Benedict XV, 3 August 1918, in *Russia–Polonia, Periodo 1872–1921*, 80368. Copies in author's possession.
5. See Gordon Brook-Shepherd, *The Last Habsburg*, London 1968.
6. *1919 Correspondence Sent*, PRO FO 380/24 280/19, Gaisford to Lord Curzon, Telegram 69, 31 May 1919, and PRO FO 380/25 310/19, Gaisford to Lord Curzon, Telegram 60, 26 June 1919.
7. *Archivio*, loc. cit.
8. Ibid., Cardinal Secretary of State to Mons. Valprè and Mons. Pacelli, Nos. 191 and 192 respectively.
9. Ibid., Valprè to Cardinal Secretary of State, No. 319, 13 August 1918.
10. PRO GFM 6/140, Cardinal Pacelli, Apostlic Nuncio in Bavaria, to Chancellor von Hertling, 12 August 1918 and von dem Bussche to Pacelli, 27 August 1918, both A35098.
11. Ibid., Treutler to Hertling, 3 October 1918, and ? to Pacelli, 4 October 1918, both A41233.
12. *Archivio*, loc. cit., Auswartiges Amt, No. A39044/139112 to Cardinal von Hartmann, 21 September 1918, and Apostolic Nunciature in Bavaria to Cardinal Secretary of State, No. 9481, 27 September 1918.
13. Summers and Mangold, op. cit., p. 363.

9. TSAR IN WAITING

1. Radzinsky, op. cit., pp. 281–7.
2. Ibid., pp. 282–3.
3. PRO GFM 6/139 Armin von Reyher to HRH Prince Henry of Prussia, A29471, 15 June 1918. Rybinsk lies on the River Volga north of Yaroslavl. It was renamed Andropov in honour of the late Soviet leader in the 1980s. Under present conditions it has probably reverted to its original name.
4. Ibid., von Mirbach to Foreign Ministry, A28438, 3 July 1918.
5. Ibid., A248 No. 138, 3 July 1918.
6. Ibid., Riezler to Foreign Ministry, A30727, 20 July 1918.
7. Ibid., Berckheim in Kiev to Foreign Ministry, A30977, 22 July 1918.
8. Ibid., von Reyher to HRH Prince Henry of Prussia, A31145, 23 July 1918.
9. Ibid., Riezler to Foreign Ministry, A31268, 22 July 1918.
10. Ibid., Riezler to Foreign Ministry, A31283, n.d. but probably 23 July 1918.
11. PRO GFM 6/140 Breiter in St Petersburg to Foreign Ministry, A35833, 25 July 1918, and von Lersner to Hertling and the Kaiser,

8 July 1918, enclosing letter from von Reyher, A37696, 24 July 1918.

12. PRO WO 106/1219, No. 815, Political/Secret CX046610 P.C.437, Stockholm, 26 August 1918.

13. PRO WO 106/1220, 721D, Japan/Military, 8 July 1918.

14. PRO ADM 137/883, Telegram No. 551, Naval Attaché, Petrograd, to Admiralty, 29 June 1918.

15. PRO GFM 6/140, Oberleutnant Bauermeister, Headquarters in the Field, to Foreign Ministry, A39669, No. 4366, 21 September 1918. A *Sawod*, or *Savod*, is a local government district.

16. Ibid., Kemnitz in Riga to Foreign Ministry, A40813, No. 61, 29 September 1918.

17. Max Hoffmann, *War Diaries and Other Papers*, Vol. II, p.658.

18. PRO GFM 6/140, Berchem in Kiev to Foreign Ministry, A44463, 21 October 1918.

19. Ibid., Comment on newspaper report, illegible signature, A24675, 15 September 1919.

10. HM PREFERS ...

1. 'HM prefers that nothing should be published' is the comment added by Lord Stamfordham, the King's private secretary, to the cover page of the Foreign Office file *Murder of Ex-Czar*, PRO FO 371/3977 Part I, No. 98898. It could be regarded as the theme of all British records relating to the Romanovs.

2. Field Marshal Sir William Robertson, *Soldiers and Statesmen*, Vol. I, p.313.

3. Lord Stamfordham to A. J. Balfour, 6 April 1918, PRO FO 800/205.

4. Ibid., Folio 88.

5. Summers and Mangold, op. cit., p.246, and Meriel Buchanan, *The Dissolution of an Empire*.

6. D. Lloyd George, *War Memoirs* (2 vols), Vol. I, p.971.

7. Ibid., p.976. The italics are Lloyd George's.

8. A. Kerensky, *La Vérité sur le Massacre des Romanovs*, p.116.

9. Summers and Mangold, op. cit., p.254.

10. Details are in J. C. Trewin, *Tutor to the Tsarevich*, p.90.

11. Summers and Mangold, op. cit., pp.251–2.

12. Recorded interview with Mrs. P. Eykyn, 3 October 1990.

13. Ibid.

14. PRO FO 371/3350.

11. A DIARY IN OXFORD

1. See *Armour Against Fate*, p.256, quoting Meinertzhagen's *Diary*, Vol. 20, pp. 169–70, Rhodes House Library, Oxford.

2. Ibid.
3. R. Meinertzhagen, *Army Diary* 1899–1926, p. v.
4. Ibid., p. 296.
5. Interview with Lieutenant-Colonel Nigel Watson, 4 June 1990.
6. Meinertzhagen, op. cit., p. v.
7. Private information.
8. See M. Cocker, *Richard Meinertzhagen – Soldier, Scientist and Spy*, p. 237, and *Richard The Lion-Heart* in the *Observer*, 28 March 1971.
9. See J. E. Mack, *A Prince of Our Disorder*, D. Stewart, *T. E. Lawrence*, and M. Yardley, *Backing into the Limelight*
10. Meinertzhagen, loc. cit., Vol. 71, p. 60, 9 March 1960.
11. Cocker, op. cit., p. 197.
12. Meinertzhagen, op. cit., p. v.
13. Letter from Mrs T. Searight, 17 January 1983.
14. Meinertzhagen, op. cit., p. 40.
15. Ibid., p. v.
16. Ibid.
17. See *Armour Against Fate*, p. 284, citing Meinertzhagen, loc. cit., Vol. 67, p. 88, 3 February 1957.
18. Information from R. R. Meinertzhagen, Esq., the Colonel's surviving son.
19. Meinertzhagen, loc. cit., Vol. 67, p. 6, 8 October 1956.
20. Conversation with Major S. R. Elliot, 20 March 1990.

12. THE PRIEST'S TESTIMONY

1. All quotations attributed to Storozhev are drawn from his testimony to Sergeyev, 8–10 October 1918, and cited by Sokolov.
2. Sir C. Eliot to Foreign Office, PRO FO 371/3977 Part I, No. 616, 14 July 1919 from Vladivostok, and FO 538/1, no. 266, 10 July 1919.
3. Sir C. Eliot to Mr Balfour, PRO FO 371/3977 Part I, 5 October 1918.
4. We can discount the forged letter signed 'Officer' which the Cheka compiled and the Tsar was supposed to have received as entirely unconvincing.

13. THE WHITE CROW

1. Summers and Mangold, op. cit., p. 195, drawing on Janin's report of 29 January 1919 – by which time Sergeyev was no longer present to contradict it – in French Foreign Ministry document no. 500-507.
2. N. G. Ross, *Gibel Tsarskoye Sem'i*, pp. 128–30. I would like to record my thanks to Mr Alexander Anderson for drawing my attention to this.

3. Ross, op. cit., pp. 129–30.
4. Forsint Archangel to DMI, PRO FO 800/205, No. 358, 28 August 1918.
5. PRO GFM 6/140, Note to A28351, Berlin 6 November 1919.

14. CORROBORATION

1. Transcript in *Summers Collection*.
2. Record of meeting between Claire Selerie-Grey and Mrs Beatrice Alley, 17 August 1974, *Summers Collection*.
3. Ibid.
4. Letter from Mrs Ariel Clark to Anthony Summers, 7 February 1972, *Summers Collection*.
5. Ibid.
6. Letter from Commander Michael Peer Groves to Anthony Summers, 24 January 1972, *Summers Collection*.
7. PRO AIR2/125, *Extracts from Diary of Visit to Odessa*.
8. R. Ingham, *What Happened to the Empress*; G. Richards, *The Rescue of the Romanovs*; Summers and Mangold, op. cit., p. 370, f/n to p. 92 and f/n 2; PRO ADM 137/952.
9. Copy of a letter from the Marchioness of Milford Haven to Mrs R. Chrichton, her lady-in-waiting, *Summers Collection*.
10. Letter to the author from the Earl Haig of Bemersyde, OBE, 6 June 1989, confirmed 25 May 1990.
11. Official Correspondence in PRO FO 800/205.
12. Balfour to Sir Arthur Davidson, 6 April 1917, PRO FO 800/205, Folio 77ff.

15. HIS BRITANNIC MAJESTY'S CONSUL

1. Printed in Vorres, op. cit., pp. 241–5.
2. T. Preston, *Before the Curtain*, p. 95. See also PRO FO 371/3342, letter from Preston 28 September 1918, F. 73; and FO 371/3977 Part I.
3. Preston to Foreign Office, 28 September 1918, PRO FO 371/3342, *Political Russia*. Files 156756–164836 1918, F. 73.
4. Ibid.
5. Contrast Preston, op. cit., p. 101 and PRO FO 371/3342.
6. Preston, op. cit. p. 101.
7. PRO FO 395/184, Nos. 82146–105055, 9 May to 16 July 1918.
8. Ibid.
9. Preston, op. cit., p. 81.
10. See correspondence in PRO FO 395/184 and *Copies of Telegrams sent from British Consulate, Ekaterinburg, to the British Representatives at Moscow and Vologda*, PRO FO 371/3342.
11. War Office to General Knox, PRO WO106/1234, no. 325.

12. *Declaration made by Lieutenant-Captain of the Russian Army, Theodor Arthur Meise*, courtesy of the family of Captain Digby Jones.
13. PRO FO 371/3342, No. 12, 11 July 1918, F. 84.
14. Ibid., 22 July 1918, F. 85.
15. Conversations with a Channel Four producer, by telephone 14 October 1991, in person 2 April 1992. I am prepared to reveal the identity of this informant to *bona fide* researchers only.
16. 'Camborne Engineer in Russia', in the *Cornishman and Cornish Telegraph*, 21 January 1920, p. 2, and the *Cornish News and Redruth Effective Advertiser*, 17 January 1920, National Newspaper Library, Colindale.
17. The *Cornishman*, 20 July 1978, p. 29.

16. SIBERIAN FLIGHT

 1. See *Armour Against Fate*, p. 282, quoting Meinertzhagen, loc. cit., 18 August 1918.
 2. *MIO(a). North Russia. Box 23, File 18. General Poole's Mission Personnel. 1918 January–May.* PRO WO106/1150, 30 April 1918.
 3. See PRO ADM 137/766, *China Station Telegrams*, No. 329, 28 June 1918.
 4. Private information.
 5. *Nominal Roll of Officers 'Syren' and 'Elope' June–July 1918*, PRO WO 106/1151.
 6. J. S. Poole, *Undiscovered Ends*, p. 32.
 7. Ibid.
 8. Ibid., p. 42.
 9. Ibid., p. 45.
10. PRO FO 371/3234, *Political. Japan. Files 6083–9874*, No. 276 140777, 15 August 1918.
11. Ibid., No. 198/99 115461, 1 July 1918.
12. Ibid., No. 162924, 26 September 1918.
13. See f/n 3.
14. *Canada Register 1918 to 1919*, PRO CO 335 [IND 18846], Vol. 29, No. 36524S, 29 July 1918, and *West and South East Coasts of America General Operation Telegrams 1918*, No. 138, 25 July 1918, PRO ADM 137/960.
15. See *Armour Against Fate*, p. 279, quoting General Pulteney to Lady Desborough, 1 August 1918, *Grenfell Papers*, Herts. Record Office, D/ERv C2130/164.
16. *China Station Records. General Letters.* PRO ADM 137/718, General Letter No. 126.

17. A GRAVE IN LYDD

1. *The Tank Corps Journal*, Vol. V, No. 55, November 1923.
2. Letter to the author, 10 November 1989.
3. Vatican Correspondence, PRO FO 380/21, No. 132/19, 21 February 1919.
4. There is an independent witness to this statement and I am prepared to share this testimony with *bona fide* scholars, subject to an undertaking that the privacy of the witness is not disturbed.
5. Letter to the author, 1 December 1989.

18. THE HOUSE OF TUDOR

1. *Executive Officers Services Book 3 L–Z*, PRO ADM 196/41 and 196/20.
2. Letter from Sergeant W. Willis, 7 March 1990.
3. *The Tank Corps Journal*.
4. Ibid., Vol. V, No. 60, April 1924.
5. Mrs Hilary Swinburne in questionnaire, December 1990.
6. Ibid.
7. Ibid.
8. Ibid.
9. Sergeant Willis, loc. cit.
10. Interview with Mrs A. Clayphon, 21 November 1991.
11. Interview with Mrs E. Terry, 30 November 1991.
12. Ibid.
13. Ibid.
14. Interview with Mrs P. Winkfield, 21 November 1991.
15. Interview with Mr H. Prebble, 7 June 1992.
16. Mrs H. Swinburne, loc. cit.
17. Interview with Colonel Peel, 14 July 1990.
18. Response from a former officer of the 3rd Hussars who prefers to remain anonymous.

19. THE TATTERED SEAM

1. Information on the control of immigrants is drawn from Holdsworth, *History of English Law*; Roche, *The Key in the Lock: Immigration Control in England from 1066 to the Present Day*; Bevan, *The Development of British Immigration Law*.
2. See *Armour Against Fate*, p. 285, quoting *Grenfell Papers*, loc. cit., Pulteney to Lady Desborough, 11 March 1919, D/ERv C2130/164.
3. *Harrogate Herald*, 4 September 1918.
4. Letter from Mrs Swinburne, 5 May 1991.

20. A CASE TO ANSWER

1. See G. Richards, *The Rescue of the Romanovs.*
2. Summers and Mangold, op. cit., p. 254.
3. PRO FO 371/3977 Part I.
4. M. Turnbull, *The Spycatcher Trial*, p. 114.
5. *Sunday Times*, 10 May 1992.
6. *The Times*, 13 May 1992.
7. See E. Radzinsky, op. cit., pp. 360 ff.

SELECT BIBLIOGRAPHY

I. Primary Sources

INTERVIEWS
Mrs A. Clayphon
Mr F. Batt
Mr and Mrs W. Bingham
Mrs P. Eykyn
The Lord Fanshawe
Colonel C. Peel
Mr H. Prebble
Mrs E. Terry
Colonel N. Watson
Mrs P. Winkfield

PEOPLE AND ORGANIZATIONS WHICH SUPPLIED GENERAL INFORMATION
Mrs E. Bowler
Mrs J. Daniels
Mr R. Karel
Mrs P. Mayor
Sir R. Preston, Bt.
Mrs H. Swinburne
A retired officer of the 3rd, the King's Own Hussars, who prefers to
  remain unidentified
The Earl of Bemersyde, OBE

Mr I. Lilburn
National Meteorological Office
Soviet Embassy Press Department

PAPERS IN PRIVATE POSSESSION
Papers of Charles Clarke, valet to the Grand Duke Mikhail Mikhailovitch
Papers relating to Captain C. S. Digby Jones
Diary of the Duke of Devonshire
Papers relating to the Grand Duke Mikhail Mikhailovitch, the Iveagh Bequest, Kenwood
The Summers Collection, courtesy of Mr A. Summers
Papers of Arthur Thomas, courtesy of Mr R. G. Thomas

NATIONAL NEWSPAPER LIBRARY, COLINDALE
Cornishman and Cornish Telegraph
Cornishman
Cornish Post and Mining News and Redruth Effective Advertiser
Dunfermline Journal and Advertiser for the West of Fife
Evening News
Evening Standard
Harrogate Herald
Luton News and Bedfordshire Advertiser
Morning Post
New York Times
Sunday Times
The Times

SOTHEBY'S (AUCTIONEERS)
The Sokolov Archive

QUEEN'S OWN HUSSARS MUSEUM, WARWICK

3RD THE KING'S OWN HUSSARS JOURNAL AND ASSOCIATED MATERIAL

LYDD MUSEUM

ROYAL TANK CORPS MUSEUM, BOVINGTON

THE TANK CORPS JOURNAL

RECORD REPOSITORIES

The British Library
N. A. Sokoloff – The Murder of the Russian Imperial Family. Report of Mr N. A. Sokoloff, Examining Magistrate, into the Circum-

stances of The Murder of the Russian Imperial Family, Cup.
24.aa.19.

Hertfordshire County Record Office
Letters of Lieutenant-General Sir William Pulteney to Lady Desborough (Mrs Grenfell) D/ERv C 2129, C2130/1–170

Imperial War Museum
Department of Sound Records – Lieutenant E. J. Furlong, 015/08/04

Kent County Archives, Maidstone
Report on the Survey of the Kent Estates of Sir Richard Tufton, Bart.
Kent Estate Cash Books 1914–1938
Lydd Council Minutes 1867–1938
Rate Book 1733–1970
Churchwardens' Accounts
Church accounts and treasurers' accounts

Rhodes House Library, Oxford
Diary of Colonel Richard Meinertzhagen, CBE, DSO

Royal Free Hospital, Hampstead
Council Minutes 1908–1922
Agenda Books 1916–1920
Hampstead General Hospital House Committee 1909–1922
Annual Reports 1911–1923

Windsor Castle
Prince Arthur of Connaught's Mission, 1918, RA GV PS 24190

Central State Archive of the October Revolution, Moscow
Diary of Alexandra Feodorovna
Correspondence from King George V to Tsar Nicholas II

Segreteria Di Stato, Sezione II, Rapporti con gli Stati
Archivio Degli Affari Ecclesiastici Straordinari – 1918 – Liberazione
dell Imperatrice Madre e delle Granduchesse di Russia – Russia 544

Public Record Office
Air Historical Branch Records
AIR1/462/15/312/122–124. Syren Force 1919
AIR2/125/9793. Extracts from diary of visit to Odessa

Admiralty Records
ADM53. Ships' Logs
ADM125/66. China Station Records
ADM137. Operational Records, Royal Navy
ADM186/611 A History of the White Sea Station, 1914–1919
ADM196. Executive Officers' Services

Colonial Office
CO42
CO335. Canada Register 1918 to 1919
CO714. Index

Board of Trade
BT26/648. In-Coming Passengers. August 1918
BT32/7. Ships Inward. July and August 1918

Foreign Office
FO175
FO187
FO262. Japan: Correspondence
FO263. Consular Correspondence Register
FO371. General Correspondence after 1906: Political
FO380. Embassy and Consular Archives
FO538/1. Vladivostok Consulate 1918
FO800

German Foreign Ministry
GFM6/139 and 140
Rumänien No. 1, GRM6/86

War Office
WO95. War Diaries
WO106. – Directorate of Military Operations and Intelligence: 60; 61;
    679; 680; 682; 683; 684; 1098; 1147; 1149–1152; 1164; 1166; 1190;
    1218–1323

Records of the Russian Orthodox Church in the United Kingdom: RG8

The War Office List and Administrative Directory for the British Army.
1918

The Army List

The Navy List

The British Imperial Calendar and Civil Service List

II. Theses, Published Books and Articles

Alexandra Feodorovna, Empress-Consort of Nicholas II, Emperor of
    Russia. *Letters of the Tsaritsa to the Tsar, 1914–1916. With an intro-*
    duction by Sir Bernard Pares, Duckworth & Co., London, 1923
Alexis, Prince of Bourbon-Condé. *Moi, Alexis, arrière-petit-fils du*
    Tsar, Paris, 1979

Bevan, V. *The Development of British Immigration Law*, Croom Helm, London, 1986

Bolitho, H. *The Galloping Third: The Story of the 3rd the King's Own Hussars*, John Murray, London, 1963

Botkin, G. *The Real Romanovs*, Putnam, London, 1932

Brook-Shepherd, G. *The Last Habsburg*, Weidenfeld & Nicolson, London, 1968

Buchanan, The Rt. Hon. Sir George. *My Mission to Russia and Other Diplomatic Memories*, 2 vols, Cassell & Co. Ltd, London, 1923

—— *Nicholas II et la Révolution Bolcheviste*, in *La Revue de Paris*, 15 March 1923

Buchanan, M. *The Dissolution of an Empire*, John Murray, London, 1932

Bulygin, Captain P. *The Murder of the Romanovs*, Hutchinson, London, 1935

Burke's Peerage. *Burke's Peerage, Baronetage and Knightage*, Burke's Peerage, London, various dates

—— *Burke's Royal Families of the World*, Vol. I, *Europe and Latin America*, Burke's Peerage, London, 1977

Burnside, Lt-Col. F.R. *A Short History of 3rd the King's Own Hussars*, Gale & Polden Ltd, Aldershot, 1947

Bykov, P. M. *The Last Days of Tsardom* (translated with an Historical Preface by Andrew Rothstein), Martin Lawrence Ltd, London, 1934

Cocker, M. *Richard Meinertzhagen Soldier, Scientist and Spy*, Secker & Warburg, London, 1989

Cowles, V. *The Last Tsar and Tsarina*, Weidenfeld & Nicolson, London, 1977

Dehn, L. *The Real Tsaritsa*, Little, Brown & Co., Boston, Mass., 1922

Dobson, C. and Miller, J. *The Day We Almost Bombed Moscow: The Allied War in Russia, 1918–1920*, Hodder & Stoughton, London, 1986

Dukes, P. *A History of Russia, Medieval, Modern, Contemporary*, 2nd edn, Macmillan, London, 1990

Fellowes, Air Commodore P. F. M. *et al. First Over Everest, The Houston–Mount Everest Expedition*, John Lane The Bodley Head, London, 1935

Ferro, M. *Nicholas II*, Viking, London, 1991

Freund, G. *Unholy Alliance: Russian–German Relations from the Treaty of Brest-Litovsk to the Treaty of Berlin*, Chatto & Windus, London, 1957

Furse, Sir Ralph. *Aucuparius, Recollections of a Recruiting Officer*, Oxford University Press, London, 1962

Gilliard, P. *Le Tragique Destin de Nicolas II et de sa famille*, Payot & Cie., Paris, 1921

Gorky, M. *et al. The History of the Civil War in the USSR*, 2 vols, Foreign Languages Publishing House, Moscow/Lawrence and Wishart Ltd, London, 1947

Grey, P. *The Grand Duke's Woman: The Story of the Morganatic Marriage of the Brother of Tsar Nicholas II*, Macdonald & Jane's, London, 1976

Hanbury-Williams, Maj-General Sir John, KCB, KCVO, CMG. *The Emperor Nicholas II as I Knew Him*, Arthur L. Humphreys, London, 1922

Hoffmann, M. *War Diaries and Other Papers* (translated by Eric Sutton), Martin Secker, London, 1929

Hopley, D. *John Ward and the Russian Civil War*, University of Keele BA Hons dissertation, 1986

Javierre, J. M. *Merry Del Val* (2nd edn), Barcelona, Spain, 1965

Jones, H. A. and Raleigh, W. *Official History of the War: The War in the Air*, 6 vols, The Clarendon Press, Oxford, 1922–37

Kerensky, A. *La Vérité sur le Massacre des Romanov*, Payot, Paris, 1936

Lasies, J. *La Tragédie Sibérienne,* in *L'Edition Française Illustrée*, Paris, 1920

Lenin, V. I. *Selected Works*, Vols 1–3, Progress Publishers, Moscow, 1977

Lloyd George, D. *War Memoirs*, 2 vols, Odhams Press Ltd, London, 1938

Lord, J. *Duty, Honour, Empire: Life and Times of Colonel Richard Meinertzhagen*, Hutchinson, London, 1971

Lovell, J. B. *Anastasia: The Lost Princess*, Hutchinson, London, 1991

Luckett, R. *The White Generals*, Longman, London, 1971

Ludendorff, General-Lieutenant E. *My War Memories, 1914–1918*, Hutchinson, London, 1919

Mack, J. E. *A Prince of Our Disorder*, Weidenfeld & Nicolson, London, 1976

Mawdsley, E. *The Russian Civil War*, Allen & Unwin Inc., Winchester, Mass., 1987

Mel'gunov, S. P. *Sud'ba Imperatora Nikolaya II poslye otrechniya*, La Renaissance, Paris, 1951

Mikhail Mikhailovitch, Grand Duke. *Never Say Die*, Collier & Co., London, 1908

Newbolt, H. *Official History of the War: Naval Operations*, Vol. V, Longman, Green & Co., London, 1931

Nicholas II. *The Letters of the Tsar to the Tsaritsa, 1914–1917* (translated from the official edition of Romanov correspondence, (edited by M. N. Pokrovsky), John Lane, London, 1929

Null, G. *The Conspirator who Saved the Romanovs*, Prentice-Hall Inc., New Jersey, 1971

O'Conor, J. F. *The Sokolov Inquiry*, Souvenir Press, London, 1972

Pares, B. *The Fall of the Russian Monarchy*, Cassell, London, 1988

Pipes, R. *The Russian Revolution*, Collins Harvill, London, 1990

Poole, Major J. S., DSO, OBE, MC. *Undiscovered Ends*, Cassell & Co., London, 1957

Preston, T. *Before The Curtain*, John Murray, London, 1950

Radzinsky, E. *The Last Tsar: The Life and Death of Nicholas II*, Hodder & Stoughton, London, 1992

Riezler, K. *Tagebücher – Aufsätze – Dokumente. Eingeleiter und herausgegeben von Karl Dietrich Erdmann*, Vandenhoek & Rupprecht, Göttingen, 1972

Richards, G. *The Hunt for the Czar*, Sphere Books, London, 1972

—— *The Rescue of the Romanovs*, The Devin–Adair Co., Old Greenwich, Conn., 1975

Roche, T. W. E. *The Key in the Lock. Immigration Control in England from 1066 to the Present Day*, John Murray, London, 1969

Rose, K. *King George V*, Weidenfeld & Nicolson, London, 1983

Ross, N. G. *Gibel Tsarskoye sem'i*, Possev Verlag, Frankfurt-am-Main, 1987

Sokolov, N. A. *Enquête Judiciaire sur l'Assassinat de la Famille Impériale Russe, avec les Preuves, les Interrogatoires et les Dépositions, des Témoins et des Accusés*, Payot, Paris, 1926

Stewart, D. *T. E. Lawrence*, Hamish Hamilton, London, 1977

Stoeckl, A. de (ed. G. Kinnaird). *Not All Vanity*, John Murray, London, 1950

Summers, A. and Mangold, T. *The File on the Tsar*, Victor Gollancz Ltd, London, 1976 and Gollancz Paperbacks, 1987

Sumner, B. H. *A Short History of Russia*, Reynal & Hitchcock, New York, 1943

Teague-Jones, R. (alias Ronald Sinclair, OBE, MC). *The Spy Who Disappeared: Diary of a Secret Mission to Russian Central Asia in 1918*, Victor Gollancz Ltd, London, 1990

Tisdall, E. E. P. *The Dowager Empress*, Stanley Paul, London, 1957

Trew, S. C. *The Czechoslovak Army Corps ('The Czech Legion') in Russia 1914–1920*, University of Keele BA Hons Dissertation, 1986

Trewin, J. C. *Tutor to the Tsarevich. An Intimate Portrait of the Russian Imperial Family Compiled from the Papers of Charles Sidney Gibbes now in the Possession of George Gibbes*, Macmillan, London, 1975

Trotsky, L. *The History of the Russian Revolution*, 3 vols, Victor Gollancz Ltd, London, 1932–3

Vassili, Count Paul *Behind the Veil at the Russian Court*, Cassell & Co. Ltd, London, 1913

Vorres, I. *The Last Grand Duchess*, Hutchinson, London, 1964

Wilton, R. *The Last Days of the Romanovs*, Thornton Butterworth Ltd, London, 1920

Woodhall, E. T. *Guardians of the Great*, Blandford Press Ltd, London, 1934

Yardley, M. *Backing into the Limelight*, Harrap, London, 1985

Zeman, Z. A. B. (ed.). *Germany and the Revolution in Russia, 1915–1918 – Documents from the Archives of the German Foreign Ministry*, Oxford University Press, London, 1958

Zeman, Z. A. B. & Scharlau, W. B. *The Merchant of Revolution: The Life of Alexander Israel Helphand (Parvus) 1867–1924*, Oxford University Press, London, 1965

INDEX